THE JESUS RULE

THE JESUS RULE

WILLIAM WHALLON

BENNETT & KITCHEL

published by Bennett & Kitchel
P.O. Box 4422
East Lansing, Michigan 48826

Library of Congress Control Number: 2002111302

Preface

Between ethics and miracles, the church made the wrong choice. Jesus is held by many to have been a healer who was born of a virgin and arose from the grave. The thought in this book is that he was a teacher, and that the stories of the resurrection, the virgin birth, and the healing were created by his followers. That is, Jesus is here regarded not as a savior but as a spokesman for goodness.

There are two chief issues dividing Christianity from Judaism: whether to love your enemy as yourself, and whether the messiah has come. The first of these, the Jesus rule, is here considered the more important. The other issue is minor; faith is a dubious passport to a kingdom. Is it then being said that you can be a Christian without Christ? Yes, *you ought to be generous even to those that hate you, but you need not believe either in God the Son or in God the Father.* There are crucial qualifications, though: *as it is a mistake to be generous no matter what, so is it one to believe in nothing beyond yourself.*

The problem may be recast for the sake of the moment. Not long ago the "World Islamic Front," the organization of Osama bin Laden, issued a religious ruling, or fatwa, for a "Jihad Against Jews and Crusaders." In that phrase there are four gatherings, three of them explicit, one implicit. The first is Islam, another is Judaism, a third is the militant Christianity of a thousand years ago, and the fourth is present-day America with Britain and others. There is much to admire in all four, but I would speak against them, to the degree they are warlike. I accept instead what Jesus taught. There is a danger though that his sayings will be regarded as tightly binding; in truth they are loosely so; to his mind charity should go only so far. We ought to have kind intentions even towards our adversaries, looking at things from their point of view, but we ought not to yield beyond measure. The Jesus rule is the answer, but it must be qualified. Our duty is to think matters through.

To some followers the faith is otherworldly; to them love for the enemy is not relevant. This book argues to the contrary that Jesus did not die for our sins, or to pay the debt of Adam, or to complete the destiny of his people; he died from a way of living on earth—an example to nations as well as persons. But now there is the menace of an opposite absolutism. Complete earthiness, or utter practicality, is also wrong. Those who need mysticism for their well being ought to have it. Not all of us are lumps of clay; otherworldliness is an element we have room for; we can be inspired and made better. Some of us are nourished by communing with Jesus in a meal on his day of the week. But the daily bread for everyone should be his *rule*.

My aim is first (I) at commenting on Jesus' interpretation of the ten commandments by his sense of right and wrong, next (II) at applying his rule to certain issues of our day, then (III) at seeing whether Jesus is with his followers in ritual, and finally (IV) at mapping some highways and byways to God.

Does the Bible have a sanctity that exempts it from analysis? No, the commandments and the rest of the Old Testament, as well as the sayings of Jesus and the rest of the New, are here regarded as the work of man, though of man often inspired (as in "For now we see through a glass, darkly; but then face to face"). Not every verse of scripture is equally important with every other: some verses should be pondered ("whosoever will save his life shall lose it"); some should be rejected ("let your women keep silence in the churches"). At times biblical science is to be doubted ("And God made two great lights; the greater light to rule the day, and the lesser light to rule the night"; "A wise man's heart is at his right hand; but a fool's heart at his left"). And if the sense is erotic we need not think it must be an allegory ("I will get me to the mountain of myrrh, and to the hill of frankincense").

Some of the commandments are brief; it may be that all were brief once. Some are enveloped in commentary; at times we say of them, "too much." At other times we say of scripture, "not enough"; the whole of the matter has not been given to us; "there are also many other things which Jesus did" (John 21.25). His own commandment, "love one another" (John 13.34, 15.12, 1 John 3.23, 2 John 5), together with "love God," would replace all the others; the problem is how far we ought to follow in a world of hard knocks. Whether the supernatural in Christianity ranks above its social values is also of immediacy today; the argument here would be that what counts is behavior; the tree is known by his fruit. A final issue is whether living after the example of Jesus will lead to God, and a word towards an answer is that we are becoming godlike by degrees.

Sacred or secular lore is not here regarded as authoritative or even as authentic. Did Judas hang himself (Matthew 27.5) or did he burst asunder, so that all his bowels gushed out (Acts 1.18)? Such discrepancies are a reason not to cite scripture as conclusive; another reason is that Satan can match us at that game (Matthew 4.6, Luke 4.10). I disagree with those who believe that the genuine can be cleanly separated from the spurious. And I do not assume that a speaker will speak for his culture. The opposite seems more likely, since a visionary or a preacher, or a storyteller such as Homer, wants to say things that have not been said before. You cannot tell what the audience of the *Odyssey* had been thinking about the underworld; part of what the poet says must be just what they had *not* thought. When Jesus calls his own commandment a new one, we should regard it not as an additional one, but as a change on the grand scale.

This arguing from what is contrary can be carried further. The sermon on the mount (or the plain) and the parable of the Good Samaritan, *because* they were against what everyone else would have said, are the elements most to be trusted as really and truly of Jesus. The wonders about him, such as his being taken up into heaven as Elijah was, would have been expected and are for that reason not so clearly real and true. The sermon on the mount and the Good Samaritan parable are the cornerstone and the capstone. Did St. Paul say the same? did Luther or Calvin? No, but there was much of Jesus in Martin Luther King, Jr., and in Mohandas K. Gandhi.

Are the Old and New Testaments, either or both, the word of God? Are the heavens and the earth the work of his hands? Only in a sense so remote as to be of no use. There are dreadful things told with approval in the Bible and there are dreadful things for no reason in the world. To call them God's will is blasphemous. What *is* of use, and of honor to God, can be found in the famous sermon and the most famous of the parables. It is not merely—I would say not even mainly—that we ought to be righteous and dutiful; it is that we should follow the Jesus rule for our survival on earth. Do not think you are earning wages to be paid in heaven, but do the right thing—the generous thing (within bounds)—in the here and now. The afterlife is as far beyond us as the beforelife; how you manage this life is the thing to consider. Walk in the steps of the pathfinder, keeping his rule, and hear the words (if you are minded to) "in remembrance of me."

Jacob was named Israel, from the word for wrestle, after he had wrestled with an angel, and his twelve sons became the forebears of twelve tribes (Genesis 49). At the death of Solomon (nearly a thousand years before Jesus), ten of the tribes—those of Reuben, Simeon, Levi, Zebulun, Issachar, Dan, Gad, Asher, Naphtali, and Joseph—had settled in a middle territory or else to the north. (The tribe of Levi did not have land of their own; as a priestly caste they were supported by the tithes of the others; if they are not counted among the ten, the tribes of Ephraim and Manasseh, the sons of Joseph, may be regarded as two rather than one; see 1 Kings 11.31–36.) The region of the ten tribes, in a narrow sense not used here, was then known as Israel, and after their complete or partial removal by the Assyrians under Sargon, two hundred years later, those who had lived in the region became the ten lost tribes of Israel. The most nearly identifiable remnant of the lost tribes in the time of Jesus was the religious community of the Samaritans, who claimed descent from Ephraim, but whose blood had come to have, seemingly, an infusion from the heathen peoples that the Assyrians had brought into the area, to fill it up again after they had emptied it out. The other two tribes, those of Judah and Benjamin (1 Kings 12.21), had settled in the south; many among them were deported, a hundred years after the Assyrians, by the Babylonians under Nebuchadnezzar; not long afterwards Cyrus the Persian allowed them to return if they wanted to. (Jesus was thought descended from Judah; St. Paul claimed descent from Benjamin.) From the name Judah is derived, again in a narrow sense not used here, the word Jew. That is, in this book *Israel* (for the land) and *Jew* (for the people) will denote the Hebrew nation as a whole. The two terms have affinity with each other, but how great that affinity may be is disputed. Did the Jews have a right to Israel, and do they have one now? Those matters are not here commented upon. Who among us has a clear right to anything? There is also the question of faith and culture. The wishes are respected of those who, like St. John of the Cross or St. Theresa of Avila, do not think of themselves as Jews even though by birth they have a warrant to do so, and similarly for the wishes of those who convert to Judaism, like Ruth the great-grandmother of David, or the Khazars of central Asia, "the thirteenth tribe."[1]

The *Oxford Dictionary of the Christian Church* (a work I turn to every day, except perhaps on the sabbath) says "Christ" when speaking of Jesus; the practice here will be to say "Jesus" for the man who lived on earth. The terms BC and AD will have a conventional meaning and no religious color. Jesus did not use the name of God, but said "the Lord" instead, and I shall do the same, after the practice of the King James version, though without the small capitals for the last three letters. "Catholic" here excludes Anglicans and means Roman Catholic; "Orthodox" designates sometimes the Eastern Christian church and sometimes Jewish orthodoxy; "eucharist" refers to the communion elements of the Christian ceremony and not to any other meal that thanks or a blessing has been said over.

My book need not be gone through from the beginning onwards. If a chapter or section looks worth reading before its time has come, then it should be read early on. Each section, though, is meant to have continuity. For that reason a good deal of material has been put into endnotes. I hope that a reader with the time will read the notes, but one with less time should keep them for a rainy day. Certain matters, both in the main text and in the notes, may require disagreeably close attention. They are hard going by nature; I try to make them as easy as pi. Some relevant issues are turned away from, for numerous detours cause a destination to be long in coming. Nor has every predecessor been cited; when I say there is reason to assassinate a Hitler or a Stalin, I neglect to mention that Cicero said the same about Julius Caesar. I try to acknowledge my debts but not to name-drop all the commentators upon universal history. Since I have both harsh and friendly words for Christianity, and also for Judaism, I cite texts about them with care; with other documentary matters I am more casual.

The pages on the origin of the eucharist, and on why a meal was called a love-feast, appeared in *New Testament Studies*, and other writing of mine has been used besides. The idiom here is closer to everyday life, except that I say *dorian* for the counterpart of *lesbian*. As a Celt I resent the Anglo-Saxons (and the Romans), but I do have affection for the English language and shall accordingly not be using the "his or her" construction. Against both the practice of *The Economist* and the opinion of the Burchfield *New Fowler's Modern English Usage*, I hold that when there is a choice a verbal noun needs a possessive, as in "the first case of researchers' having successfully harnessed this material" (the New York *Times*). The words *Bible*, *Gentile*, and *the Last Supper* are given capital initial letters, but *biblical*, the *pentateuch*, the *crucifixion*, and the *last judgment* are not. Hebrew is transliterated after the manner of Herbert Danby (in his edition of the *Mishnah*), and Greek long vowels are unmarked.

As I have said elsewhere, I would appreciate having every error, no matter how small or large, called to my attention.

Contents

The Jesus Rule

I. Jesus for and against the old law

The Hebrew means "words."[2] Commonly they are the commandments, the best-known ones in the world. According to sacred writ, the Lord spoke them "out of the midst of the fire, of the cloud, and of the thick darkness, with a great voice; and he added no more. And he wrote them in two tables of stone" (Deuteronomy 5.22, 4.13; *tablets* is the sense). "The tables were written on both their sides; on the one side and on the other" (Exodus 32.15), and the number of the commandments was ten (Deuteronomy 4.13, 10.4; Exodus 34.28). The Lord delivered the tablets to Moses, who broke them in anger when he found that the people had returned to idolatry. The commandments were then written a second time, on "tables of stone like unto the first" (Exodus 34.1). Some of the commandments are taut, others diffuse; as we read them now they are asymmetrical; even how to separate them is a matter of dispute. But in their original form (we may believe) they were harmonious—rhythmical in sense if not also in sound. I will consider the commandments one by one, generally in the language of the King James version, and generally from Exodus, with reference to Deuteronomy. My aim is at seeing what they meant in their time, and to Jesus afterwards, and finally what they should mean to a Christian today. A primary matter is whether there are exceptions.

1. How the commandments came to us   The Old Testament, like the poetry of Homer, appears to have been made from various sources. Some things had been told by one person to another, no doubt with a change at every retelling. Other things

had been written—some at an early time, some at a late one—
and they too were subject to change. It would seem for the Bible
that a marginal comment was often put into the text by the next
copyist. Sometimes the stitches from such transplants or from
other surgery can be seen. The book of Isaiah, to judge by its
allusions, is partly from one era, partly from at least another.
Psalms 107.40, "He poureth contempt upon princes; and causeth
them to wander in the wilderness, where there is no way," recurs
as Job 12.21–24 with a ponderous supplement. A passage from a
tradition that refers to the Lord may be joined to one that refers
to God. It must be allowed, though, that at times, perhaps even
usually, the stitches can*not* be seen. That means, any chapter—
or any verse—is likely to be a composite even without our being
aware of that. Accordingly no element of law can be assumed to
be the unaltered thought of the lawmaker. No surviving narrative
or prophecy or psalm is certain to have come from the narrator or
prophet or psalmist himself. "Moses" and "David" were great
names, as "Homer" was, and a history or a proverb, when its
author was said to be Moses or David, or Homer, was the likelier
to be respected and kept. To recover the commandments in their
earliest form is fraught with problems, most of them fascinating
to work on; and we cannot tell when our task has been completed. In essence the commandments are these:

a. I am the Lord thy God, who brought thee out of Egypt.
b. Thou shalt have no other gods.
c. Thou shalt not make unto thee any image to worship.
d. Thou shalt not take the name of thy God in vain.
e. Keep the sabbath day.
f. Honor thy father and thy mother.
g. Thou shalt not kill.
h. Thou shalt not commit adultery.
i. Thou shalt not steal.
j. Thou shalt not bear false witness.

k. Thou shalt not covet thy neighbor's wife.
l. Thou shalt not covet thy neighbor's (other) possessions.
m. Thou shalt love thy neighbor as thyself.
n. Thou shall set up an altar on mount Gerizim.

Everybody knows there are ten commandments (if that is the right term for them), just as everybody knows there are twelve tribes of Israel, twelve disciples of Jesus, and twelve peers in the *Song of Roland*. The lists vary, though, when the ten (or twelve) are named. How do we make ten commandments of these fourteen? The Jewish notation (of the last thousand years) has the first one as a distinct entity; Christian notations do not. Catholics and Lutherans keep (k) and (l) distinct from each other; other Christians, and Jews, do not. Orthodox Christians and most Protestants (including Anglicans) distinguish between (b) and (c); Catholics, Lutherans, and Jews take (b) and (c) together.[3] The commandment to love your neighbor, listed with the others by Jesus (once) and by St. Paul, is from another directive of the Lord to Moses (Leviticus 19.18), and is not on the two tablets. Only Samaritans recognize the last. The method here will be to refrain from speaking of "the seventh commandment" as if everybody knew which one that was.

Jesus was aware that his ideas of right and wrong were not always the ones commonly accepted. Did he ever actually break any of the commandments? Would he have had others break them? One by one the commandments are to be studied first for the intent behind them (so far as we can see what that was) and secondly for what Jesus would make of them.

2. *The first commandment in Judaism* (a. in the list of 14) "I am the Lord thy God, which have brought thee out of the land of Egypt, out of the house of bondage" (Exodus 20.2, Deuteronomy 5.6). To the Jewish men of letters Philo (*Decalogue* paragraph 51) and Josephus (*Antiquities* 3.91), who lived about when Jesus

did, and to Christians, this verse is a preface rather than one of the ten. Because the Hebrew term for that group is *words* rather than *commandments*, though, the Judaic ennumeration can be argued for, especially if there are fewer than ten ideas in the commandments remaining. The matter spoken of is the passover and exodus: the Lord passed over (without afflicting) the houses that had been marked with the blood of a lamb, so that his chosen people might escape from captivity. It is the most important event in Judaism, referred to not only in the Old Testament, but in the New as well ("for ye were strangers in the land of Egypt," Deuteronomy 10.19; "out of Egypt I called my son," Matthew 2.15; "brought us out of the land of Egypt," Acts 7.40, 13.17). The deliverance was an ethnic happening and exclusive. So Jews have good reason, but other nations do not, to regard the verse as a complete whole. Unlike the remaining commandments, though, it does not enjoin or forbid anything.

Jesus, his mother Mary, his father Joseph, the disciples, John the Baptist, and the apostle Paul were Jews. The only qualification is that Jesus and the disciples, except for Judas (of Judea), came from Galilee. (Of the three main regions of Palestine—"Judea and Galilee and Samaria," Acts 9.31, Luke 17.11—Judea was the southernmost and Galilee the north-ernmost, with Samaria in between.) It was known as "Galilee of the Gentiles," that is, "border of foreigners" (1 Maccabees 5.15; Isaiah 9.1, quoted in Matthew 4.15), meaning that Galilee was a frontier against races of other kinds. Or the phrase may have meant that Galilee itself was thick with settlements of those other kinds. Who were they, these Galileans, in the time of Jesus?

The Jews came into Canaan, a name meaning lowland. To the west was the Mediterranean, and to the southwest, Egypt. Eastwards, beyond the Jordan river, were an arid plateau, a desert, and then the valley of the Euphrates. To the north of

Canaan was Syria, and far to the northeast, Assyria (the names Syria and Assyria being related). Much or all of Syria and the region near by was known as Aram, meaning highland. Canaan was also known as Palestine, named for the Philistines in its southwest corner; Phoenicia, also known as Lebanon, was in its northwest. The names for these broad areas are inexact and inconstant, though; Syria was at times thought to include Palestine. Some of the chief cities, not of course dominant at the same moment, were (going through a narrow ellipse clockwise from 5:25) Jerusalem, Gaza, Tyre, Sidon, and Damascus; Babylon (now ruins fifty miles south of Baghdad) was a good distance to the east.

Except for the Philistines, the peoples of all these places were Semites. Their languages differed less from each other (in the estimate of C. A. Briggs) than the Romance languages do, or the Germanic; but they did differ enough not to be the same. The Canaanites and the Jews spoke Hebrew, but the Egyptians had their own language, and when Joseph in Egypt did not want to be recognized by his brothers "he spake unto them by an interpreter" (Genesis 42.23). The Arameans spoke Aramaic, which became at an early time, throughout a great area, either the primary language or the chief second one, known to those of rank or commerce though not to every ordinary person. When an Assyrian ambassador to Hezekiah, in the eighth century before Jesus, spoke in Hebrew, he was asked to speak instead in Aramaic so that the people sitting on the wall should not understand (2 Kings 18.26). As the language in common, Aramaic might be called the English of its day (and Briggs used that phrase for it a hundred years ago). Even in the time of the Persian empire Aramaic was the common language of Palestine (and Syria and Babylonia),[4] and that yeoman service it continued to perform throughout western Asia until Arabic was established by Islam.

The tribes in or near Galilee that were removed by the

Assyrians, never to return with their old identities, were those of Naphtali, Zebulun, Issachar, and Asher. The foreigners that were emplaced onto their land would seem to have been Arameans from western Babylonia. And, unless the exchange was orderly, there would have been mingling, lawful or not, of the one group with the other, just as there was two hundred years later between the Judeans and "the Canaanites, the Hittites, the Perizzites, the Jebusites, the Ammonites, the Moabites, the Egyptians, and the Amorites" (Ezra 9.1, see also Nehemiah 13.23, Deuteronomy 7.1–3). Under the permissive quiet of Persian rule there were further infusions of foreign blood into the body of Galilee. And then Alexander, in the later fourth century before Jesus, came down like a wolf on the fold. Those of the island city Tyre "the rock" thought their fortress impregnable, but Alexander built a causeway and the end was slavery or painful death. The lands nearby made peace at once. As with everywhere else in the known world, the culture became largely Greek. And again there must have been (must there not?) some combining of the one race with the other, the two now being (1) Semitic of various strains and (2) Aryan of the Hellenes. Alexander would marry for her beauty Roxana, a Persian, and would have many of his army do the like. Would not that broad policy of intermarriage have been the same for Galilee (and the rest of Palestine)? And besides the recorded marriages there must have been any number of other marriages in the eyes of God. "Galilee of the Gentiles" is an old phrase that would continue to speak truly for itself.[5]

At Alexander's death the kingship of Palestine went to the dynasties of his generals and countrymen Ptolemy (which governed from the metropolis Alexandria in Egypt) and Seleucus (from Damascus and Babylon). But when the Seleucids tried to stamp out Judaism, the warlord and high priest John Hyrcanus defended his faith against them. (At one moment Demetrius with a Greek army and some Jewish mercenaries was fighting against Hyrcanus with a Jewish army and some Greek mercenaries, and each force tried to corrupt its landsmen into deserting, Josephus *Antiquities* 13.378.) At the death of Hyrcanus his son Aristobulus took the war into Galilee, now only a century before Jesus or four generations before his preaching.

Hyrcanus and Aristobulus prevailed the more easily because they allowed the people to remain if they would accept circumcision and the other customs of Judaism (Josephus *Antiquities* 13.257 and 318). The men of Galilee were converted through their bodies, and the indignity was better than slavery or death. The Galileans had been inured to war from their infancy (Josephus *Wars* 3.3.2); their history had been in their blood and bones; it was now in their loins as well. Other kinds of conversion are liable to second thoughts, but circumcision is a matter of no return, like a woman's loss of virginity. The change in the body brings about different values and morals. At every working of the kidneys a man was reminded that he had been modified and should no longer seethe a kid in its mother's milk or eat of a creature that divideth the hoof but cheweth not the cud.[6]

When Galilee and the rest of Palestine, not in array against their enemies without, were in disarray from brother against brother within, Jewry was overcome by the general Pompey for Rome. The first Herod, a descendant of the defrauded Esau, was made king, dying the year that Jesus was born. Latin was now the language of the emperor and the army command; Greek was the language of local rule, the coinage, and the Bible; and Aramaic (sometimes called Hebrew) was the language of the commons. The inscription on the cross was in all three (Luke 23.38). Jesus spoke to Pilate in Greek, but to God in Aramaic (Matthew 27.46, Mark 15.34).

(Was Greek the language of the Bible in Galilee at the time of Herod and into the time of Jesus? Most scholars have thought so; Bagnall is doubtful from his understanding of the region in that period; the alternative is Hebrew, not her more sociable sister Aramaic. So was it in Greek or in Hebrew that Jesus read Isaiah in the synagogue of Nazareth, Luke 4.16–22? After the reading, the gospel says, Jesus spoke of himself and Elijah and Elisha as prophets not accepted in their own lands, and "all they in the synagogue, when they heard these things, were filled with wrath, and rose up, and thrust him out of the city, and led him into the brow of the hill whereon their city was built, that they might cast him down headlong. But he, passing through the midst of them, went his way," Luke 4.29–30. Since to my mind this escape is a fable, not a happening, I do not find the reading in the synagogue to be an earthly event either. So the choice between Greek and Hebrew, here, seems to me imaginary as well. It could still be wondered what language Jesus would have read the Bible in if he had read it at all. I myself doubt whether he did read it at all. My impression is that he knew stories and sayings and the idiom of parallelism, but like Mohammed was not a scholar in the text.)

If asked again just who the Galileans were in the time of Jesus, we shall say that they had at knife's edge become Jews in the skin, but were of many races inside, partly Semitic and partly Aryan (Greek but also Roman and Persian, not to mention Hittite). Along the border of Tyre and Sidon, Jesus was asked by a Greek woman, Syrophoenician by nation (Mark 7.26, Matthew 15.22), to heal her child (a story like that of the centurion and his servant, Matthew 10.4–13, Luke 7.2–10; see John 4.46–53). Were Jesus and the woman of Phoenicia different in race, in religion, in language? I gather that he spoke Greek for her sake, that in religion they both believed he could heal at a distance, and that in race they were similar if not the same. As a Galilean, Jesus was (almost beyond doubt) of more kinds than one. In a later calumny—"an accusation often made because often justified," as Morton Smith remarks—his father would be a Roman soldier.

There may be a clue in language to the ethnic character. For Peter was recognized by his speech when he denied knowing Jesus (Matthew 26.73, Mark 14.70). If those of Galilee did not distinguish between the sounds of alef and ayin or between he and het (as scholars gather from faults in the inscriptions: see Bloedhorn, p. 282), the reason could be that the great-grandparents of the Galileans had spoken Greek and had come to Aramaic, as to Judaism, under duress.[7] Galilee and Judea and Samaria were aware of the differences among them, and were unfriendly neighbors. Christianity was a branch from a graft onto the main stem of Judaism, and Jesus the Galilean, though his lineage was traced to David, can be regarded as a Jew who was also a Gentile.

A branch from a graft, Christianity was Judaic all the same. When Mary is told that she is blessed among women for the fruit of her womb, she thanks God because "he hath holpen his servant Israel" (Luke 1.54), and it is foretold of the Baptist that "many of the children of Israel shall he turn to the Lord their God" (Luke 1.16). Jesus regards himself as a Jew; when he is asked to say the first commandment, he begins his answer with the *shma* "hear"—the words more central to Judaism than any others, words that many Jews would say in Hebrew as they were being led to the death chambers of Nazi Germany—"Hear, O Israel, the Lord our God, the Lord is One" (Mark 12.29, Deuteronomy 6.4, my wording, not that of the King James). Jesus also distinguishes between his fellow countrymen the Jews (whom he is speaking to) and the Gentiles (nations, races; Matthew 6.32, Luke 18.32, 21.24, 22.25). When he sends out his disciples it is with the word: "Go not into the way of the Gentiles, and into any city of the Samaritans enter ye not; but go rather to the lost sheep of the house of Israel" (Matthew 10.5–6;

there may even have been the thought among the Jews that the persons—the houses, the utensils—of Gentiles and Samaritans were unclean: Watson, p. 84, citing Acts 10.28 and the *Mishnah*). Jesus promises his twelve disciples (including Judas, it would seem) that in the latter day they will judge the twelve tribes of Israel (Matthew 19.28), and tells the woman of Canaan that he is "not sent but unto the lost sheep of the house of Israel," for "it is not meet to take the children's bread, and to cast it to dogs" (Matthew 15.22–26, see Mark 7.24–27). At these moments, as the evangelist tells the story, the mission of Jesus is to the Jews only. And the matter is heightened by being told, not in Aramaic or Hebrew, but in Greek, as if the storyteller himself were not among the sheep of Israel, but among the dogs outside the fold.

It is only after the resurrection, in the year 30 or thereabouts, that Jesus—as the risen Christ—tells his disciples (so they believe) to go into all nations and baptize and teach (Matthew 29.19–20). Twenty years later there are three groups to distinguish among: (1) unconverted Jews, who follow the law of Moses; (2) converted Jews or Jewish Christians, who associate solely with other Jews (Acts 11.19) and continue to follow the law of Moses (Paul circumcises Timothy whose father was a Greek, Acts 16.3, to keep him from seeming an outsider); and (3) converted Gentiles, upon whom the laws of Moses are not binding. Paul contrasts the unconverted Jews—who are righteous in the old way but do not believe in Jesus—with the (converted) Gentiles, who are righteous by reason of faith (Romans 9.30–31); to his mind it is the fulfillment of a prophecy, "I will call them my people, which were not my people" (9.25, Hosea 1.10). The converted Jews are few, and they are thought to fulfill the verse "a remnant shall be saved" (Romans 9.27, Isaiah 10.22–3, 7.3). After the war of the years 66–71, the followers of Jesus are Gentiles almost every one. The gospels are then written in a Gentile language, and are sometimes hostile towards the Jews for having rejected Jesus and brought about his death.

And now we have come to one of the most momentous of all questions: *Who is to blame for the death of Jesus?* Did the Jews put to death a sabbath-breaker and blasphemer (John 5.18), or did the Romans put to death an insurrectionist? The answer might be thought to lie in the means: stoning among the Jews, crucifixion among the Romans: "thou shalt stone him with stones, that he die; because he hath sought to thrust thee away from the Lord thy God" (Deuteronomy 13.10). No, that is not the answer, for Alexander Jannaeus, a son of Hyrcanus and brother of Aristobulus, had crucified 800 of his countrymen, butchering their wives and children before their eyes (Josephus *Antiquities* 13.380). Some verses argue that for the death of Jesus the Romans bear the guilt: "he shall be delivered unto the Gentiles . . . And they shall scourge him, and put him to death" (Luke 18.32–33). Other verses argue the contrary: "And the chief priests and scribes sought how they might kill him" (Luke 22.2). Why did they have to seek how to do that? It was because they could not do it lawfully (John 18.31). The way they found was to arouse the rabble into charging him with sedition. "And the whole multitude of them arose, and led him unto Pilate . . . saying, We found this fellow perverting the nation, and forbidding to give tribute to Caesar" (Luke 23.1). Pilate washed his hands and said, "I am innocent of the blood of this just person" (Matthew 27.24); but the crowd of Jews cried, "Crucify him, crucify him" (Luke 23.21), and Pilate "gave sentence that it should be as they required" (Luke 23.24).

In the fourth gospel the Jews seem to be not fellow countrymen but a horde from abroad. When Pilate says to Jesus that his own nation has delivered him, he replies, "My kingdom is not of this world: if my kingdom were of this world, then would my servants fight, that I should not be delivered to the Jews" (John 18.35–36). We should never have gathered from such phrasing that the speaker was a Jew himself or that the author was. Was Savonarola burnt in the 15th century by the Florentines, and William Tyndale in the 16th by the English? It would be strange to say so, and it is strange that Jesus spoke of his enemies as Jews, rather than as priests and scribes, or Pharisees and Sadducees, or the felonious commons. Some remarks of mine upon the problem are these. (1) It seems unlikely that from racism a Gentile reviser changed the texts, for example from "the crowd" to "the Jews," since in general the story is from within Jewry, not from without. (2) It is more plausible that to John "the Jews." meant the Judeans, a tribe at odds with the Galileans, not just in how far to follow the old law, but also in blood and dialect ("Jesus walked in Galilee: for he would not walk in Jewry," John 7.1). (3) It is also plausible that the gospel was phrased so as to be acceptable to the Roman rulers, much as the biblical commentaries of Philo were meant to safeguard the books of Moses by making them seem harmless Neoplatonic philosophy, as Goodenough (p. 2) argues brilliantly.

Jesus was a Jew in religion (indelibly through circumcision), but a freethinking one. In race he was Jewish or Syrian or Greek, or a mixture from Galilee of the Gentiles. Against the uncertainty one thing is beyond dispute. Namely that to Gentiles unaware, or unwilling to acknowledge, that Jesus *was* a Jew in some ways if not in all, certain verses—not just in John but elsewhere also—have worked directly against the Christian message. *It is the most grievous instance there has ever been of misleading language.* Many of the most devout worshipers of Jesus will take the guilt to be hereditary ("His blood be on us, and on our children," Matthew 27.25). When the clergy of France, a century ago, found that pilgrimages and other spiritual exercises were of no avail, they brought about a renewal of faith by a campaign of hatred against the Jews (Weber). And it cannot be doubted that the gospels, worded as they are, had a share in the massacre of the Jews by the Germans.

In large part if not in their entireties, the gospels agree with the "out of Egypt" verse (Exodus 20.2, Deuteronomy 5.6), but no Gentile can easily regard it as a commandment at all.

3. The commandments respecting God (b. in the list of 14) "Thou shalt have no other gods before me" (Exodus 20.2). This is the second commandment in Judaism, but the first in Christianity. The meaning to begin with was not that there are no other gods, but that the Lord is the god of the Israelites, as Dagon is of the Philistines, Chemosh of the Moabites, Milcom of the Ammonites, and Ashtoreth of the Sidonians. You will be loyal to your tribe and its rites, and you may say that your ways are the best, but you will allow that others have ways of their own, which may after all be effective for them, or may not. Every nation worshiped its deity within its borders. After Naaman the Syrian, abroad in Israel, had been cured of his leprosy by the Lord and not by his own god, he took some of the earth with him, so that he might make sacrifice to the Lord at home (2 Kings 5.17). Moses was not a monotheist but a worshiper of the god of his fathers.

In the Song of Moses (Deuteronomy 32.8–9) there may be a Power above the Lord. "When the Most High parcelled out the nations, when he dispersed all mankind, he laid down the boundaries of every people, according to the number of the sons of God, but the Lord's share was his own people, Jacob was his allotted portion" (Revised Standard Version).[8] These words are thought to mean that the Lord divided the other nations among the gods, saving the tribe of Jacob for himself. I believe instead that the Lord and the Most High, here, are not the same; the Lord is one of the equals beneath the Sovereign and is being given his fief when the others are given theirs. That is, *elyon* "the Most High" is the title of titles, loftier than "the Lord of Israel" would be, or "Chemosh of the Moabites," or any other regional name.

That the Lord and the other gods competed as equals is a conception to ponder, and to me it appears primordial, for "the sons of God" in the Song of Moses are told of elsewhere. "There were giants in the earth in those days; and also after that, when the sons of God came in unto the daughters of men, and they bare children to them, the same became mighty men which were of old, men of renown" (Genesis 6.4).[9]

In time the sons of God, including Satan, will present themselves before the Lord as if in council (Job 1.6). The God of Jacob is no longer one among equals, but is now the ruler over the others. The idea of "the sons of God" has been rethought. The prophets Isaiah, Hosea, Amos, and Micah, of the 8th century before Jesus, came to believe that the god they worshiped was not just supreme, but was real when the others were fake. The Lord prevails; "he is the God" (1 Kings 18.39); Baal is undone (18.21–39); the gods of the nations are empty idols (Psalms 96.5); there *are* no other gods. The Lord of Israel has become (to the mind of his people) the god of everyone and of all things, beyond space and time: "the Lord our God, the Lord is One." It is monotheism, favoring the Jews.

Some of the differences between the Semitic and the Greek gods are these. (1) It is not entirely false, but not entirely true either, that the Jews worshiped one god while the Aryans worshiped many. Monotheism did not exist from the beginning in Judaism, but came into being and was then absolute; it did exist from the beginning in Hellenism, but did not become absolute. Zeus was the god of the heavens from the Indus to the North Sea. With slight changes in pronunciation *Zeus pater* is *Dyaus pitar* in Sanskrit, *Ju-piter* in Latin, and *Tiw father* (whom we honor on Tuesday) in Germanic. In the golden age of Greece a religious thinker had awe of that god before all the others: "Zeus, if to him it is pleasing so to be spoken of," from the *Agamemnon* of Aeschylus; "Zeus is the sky, the earth, and heaven; truly, Zeus is all things and whatever is beyond them," in a fragment by the same poet; "All good and evil thou hast joined to make one whole, one plan, eternal and complete," from the hymn to Zeus by Cleanthes (see Sandbach). (2) The many gods of the Semites had their own peoples and territories, but not their own domains of power, such as agriculture or metalworking or justice. Among the Greeks—thanks to the poetry of Homer—the gods did have such domains. Ares "War" is fiery; Aphrodite the goddess of love is lovely. Apollo, whose name resembles the word for destroy, brings death to men with his bow and arrows, and in a counterpart to that role he is a healer (the Hippocratic oath begins, "I swear by Apollo the physician"); he is the patron of music besides, his bow becoming bent into a lyre, and finally he is a barrister at law, defending Orestes. (3) The gods of Judea, Sidon, and Moab were rivals deathly hateful to each other, and did not interact except through their armies. The gods of Greece bore against each other nothing harsher than grudges, and interacted like members of a family, often thwarting each other but sometimes doing favors (as in *Iliad* 14.187–221). Every city state had its patron; Athene was given honors in Athens, and Aphrodite in Corinth; but the entire pantheon, owing to the *Iliad* and the *Odyssey*, was to all the nation, all the culture. Athene was worshiped east of the Aegean as well as west (*Iliad* 6.293–305). The gods add flavor and binding, nutmeg and albumen, to the Homeric pudding of human affairs.

By the time of Jesus, the world is no longer a map of minor kingdoms, each with its Dagon or Moloch. It has become an elemental world of good and evil, light and dark. The rivalry (as Jesus sees it) is not between the gods of enemy nations but between right and wrong—between God and Satan (Matthew

4.10). Jesus regards himself as sent to the sheep of Israel, but the "our" in his prayer "Our Father, which art in heaven" does not mean "Father of Abraham, Isaac, and Jacob" so much as "Father of us all thy children upon earth." And it is in the wide sense, with personal attachment, that Jesus says, "Father, forgive them."

The law is one element of ancient Semitic thought. Another is the apocalyptic tradition (of Daniel, Enoch, and Revelation). A traveler in the world of the New Testament ought to be aware that angels and demons and spectres are always at hand (see Charles *Apocrypha* vol. 2, p. 185). "When the unclean spirit is gone out of a man, he walketh through dry places, seeking rest, and findeth none. Then he saith, I will return into my house from whence I came out; and when he is come, he findeth it empty, swept, and garnished. Then goeth he, and taketh with himself seven other spirits more wicked than himself, and they enter in and dwell there: and the last state of that man is worse than the first" (Matthew 12.43–45). In having no other gods before the Lord, Jesus senses the adversaries, as they sense him: "art thou come hither to torment us?" (Matthew 8.29).

After the death of Jesus and his resurrection—as "the Anointed," the messiah, the Christ—the cult of his followers becomes a religion not just to the lost sheep of one people, but to all people everywhere. There is no other god than God, for Christians, and to them Christ is an aspect of God. Jesus was crucified for making himself the Son of God (John 19.7), but as Christ he is thought to be God the Son. The third of the Semitic religions is comparable but contrasting. The affirmation "There is no god but God" allows no other gods at all, ever, nor any sons of God; God is remote. Mohammed is not God but the messenger, a prophet among other prophets, though the greatest beyond compare. The commandment "Thou shalt have no other gods before me" would have for Islam the sense it has for Judaism and Christianity: thou shalt not even consider that there *are* any other gods. The contention between Judaism and Islam on the one hand, and Christianity on the other, concerns whether in any historical way mankind can participate in God.

(c. in the list of 14) "Thou shalt not make unto thee any graven image, or any likeness of any thing that is in heaven above, or that is in the earth beneath, or that is in the water under the earth: Thou shalt not bow down thyself to them, nor serve them: for I the Lord thy God am a jealous God, visiting the iniquity of the fathers upon the children unto the third and fourth generation of them that hate me; And shewing mercy unto thousands of them that love me, and keep my commandments" (Exodus 20.4–6). It will be agreed that much of this is an explanation, whether one was needed or not. Is it the sense that graven images are forbidden but molten ones allowed? No, molten ones will be forbidden as well (Exodus 32.8, 34.17, Deuteronomy 27.15). Is it sinful to sketch a leaf or to mould an animal out of clay? No, the commandment is surely about the making of an image to worship. The meaning of the verse would seem to be either "Thou shalt have no other gods (whom thou dost sense within a likeness)" or "Thou shalt not represent God in art (since God cannot be measured)." That is, "Do not make an image of another god, for no other god should be honored" or else "Do not make an image of God, for God is without dimension." The two senses are to be chosen between. The former of them would continue the earlier commandment about having no other gods. The latter sense would allow a new and independent commandment. To me the passage reads like a brief utterance lengthened and then lengthened again: *the utterance*, "Thou shalt not make unto thee any graven image"; *the first addition*, "or any likeness of any thing that is in heaven above, or that is in the earth beneath, or that is in the water under the earth"; *the second addition*, "Thou shalt not bow down thyself to them, nor

serve them: for I the Lord thy God am a jealous God, visiting the
iniquity of the fathers upon the children unto the third and fourth
generation of them that hate me; And shewing mercy unto
thousands of them that love me, and keep my commandments."

How should we explain the additions (if they are such) so
as to give to the utterance a meaning of its own? The first
addition elaborates the utterance and may be kept or not. With it
or without, the sense would seem to be: "Do not make an image
that thou dost worship as (the Lord) thy God." But the second
addition, with its emphasis upon rivalry, speaks about the preceding commandment, "Thou shalt have no other gods before
me." (All of that was recognized a century and a half ago if not
earlier: see Stamm, p. 85.)

If the original and ancient meaning was "Do not worship
an image of (the Lord) thy God," must that meaning have been
lost before the first and the second additions were made? Evidently no and yes: the ancient meaning need not have been lost
for the first addition, but would seem to have been lost for the
second. And yet there is a special consideration. When an addition was to be made in a listing of laws, it was often not inserted
where it was supposed to go, but was, from inattention or to save
trouble, simply appended (Daube p. 97, on another matter). We
need merely say that a scribe came upon the second addition in a
margin when he could no longer insert it after the "no other
gods" commandment, where it belonged. So he put it in where it
did not belong but where there was room. In this way all the
explanatory material can be accounted for. Putting the second
addition back with the earlier commandment where it is relevant, we have the distinct and meaningful additional commandment "Do not make an image of me thy God."

There may be an indication of the misplacement in the
wording of the earlier commandment as "no other gods before
me," with the sense "before my face." It may have been a

commonplace idiom, but all the same it is physical, not spiritual. The idols of other gods are an eyesore in the sight of the Lord. The matter forbidden in that earlier no-other-gods commandment is not the worship of other gods in the heart, but their worship through representations, which are hateful to the Lord as he looks upon them. The following no-images commandment, instead of saying as much again, says instead that the Lord himself is not to be worshiped in such a fashion. For any image of him would not be adequate to indicate his majesty. That sense is not immediately evident today, but I believe it was so once.

The no-other-gods and no-image commandments are related to each other (so are the covet and steal commandments, and so may be false-witness and name-in-vain). If a golden calf was worshiped under the name of Baal, that was one iniquity; if a calf were worshiped under the name of the Lord, it would be another. And besides the gods of a people, there were those of a household, teraphim. (Michal made use of one to deceive the messengers of Saul into thinking it was David sick in bed, 1 Samuel 19.13.) These minor idols, given food and drink and honored with incense, would seem to have been "points of access" to the gods (in the phrase of the Eerdmans Bible dictionary). It was as much a matter of daily life as adultery.

Scripture itself breaks the no-image commandment, though in words rather than through the sight. For God is described as apt to be jealous, as rejoicing, as repenting, and as having form and members. When the tablets have been broken, they are written a second time, actually or figuratively, by the finger of God (Deuteronomy 9.10), and in other passages God has a hand, an arm, feet, and eyes that see many things from creation onwards. So say the law and the prophets, and much is gained in immediacy. For to talk about an abstraction is difficult. Emotions are not woken up when we say that "God is a Spirit, infinite, eternal, and unchangeable, in his being, wisdom, power, holiness, justice, goodness, and truth" (the Westminster Shorter Catechism). That is why in Judaism from the earliest time the no-image commandment, broadly forbidding any representation, was broken again and again when God was spoken of. The commandment was as hard to keep as the others.

In the story of a rich man in parching heat and a poor man in Abraham's bosom, the rich man asks that the poor man may wet his finger and reach it down, to cool his tongue (Luke 16.22). Since here God is overhead and hell below ground, it follows that to Jesus, if not to everyone by his time, a breaking of the no-image commandment, by ascribing to God a location in space, was allowable in language, only not allowable in art. In the prayer "which art in heaven" God is in the sky.

The eighth century of Christianity was a time of iconoclasm in the Orthodox branch of the church. Many regarded the icons—of Jesus, the Virgin Mary, and the lesser saints—as idols, either against the commandment about other gods, or against the one about images, or both. (Similarly with the Taliban as they demolished the giant representations of Buddha in Afghanistan.) The reasoning that prevailed among Christians was that of John of Damascus, from the Incarnation: namely, God had wished that (part of) his nature should be evident to the senses. The commandment against making images of God, coming after the one against having other gods, is accordingly to be kept differently by Jews and Muslims than by Christians. Jews and Muslims are not to have other gods (worshiped as images or in any other way) and besides that they are not to think that images represent God. Christians are not to have other gods but may venerate images from the sacred story. The church in the West portrays Jesus and others in three dimensions or in two; the church in the East allows two only. Jews combine equilateral triangles into a star ("there shall come a Star out of Jacob," Numbers 24.17). Muslims create intricate geometrical patterns.

There are then two commandments meaning: (1) do not worship Baal, Ashtoreth, Chemosh, or other gods instead of me, the Lord; (2) do not represent me in a golden calf or a serpent or any other form, for I am beyond form and dimension. Both commandments are powerful, and they are distinct, though related. But a supplement to the first of them, added by a scribe to the second one, has joined the two together, always in Judaism after Nahmanides (though not to Philo or Josephus) and in some sects of Christianity (though not in all).

(d. of the 14) "Thou shalt not take the name of the Lord thy God in vain" (Exodus 20.7). This commandment, and the following one, may once have been more ordinary, less religious, than they are now. I believe the sense of this one was at first twofold. (1) It forbade affirming on oath that the false was true. (It is said that among the Romans a man would swear by his gonads; the Latin for witness is *testis*; the matter sworn to is testimony.) (2) The commandment would seem also to have been against not keeping a sacred promise, whether it was to God or in human affairs on the name of God. "If a man vow a vow unto the Lord, or swear an oath to bind his soul with a bond, he shall not break his word, he shall do according to all that proceedeth out of his mouth" (Numbers 30.2, Leviticus 19.12, Deuteronomy 23.21).

Afterwards (a commonsense inference, possibly incorrect), when there were commandments against bearing false witness and against stealing, the sense of "taking the name in vain" could narrow to "uttering the name of God at all." The name is the tetragrammaton *Yhwh* (or *Jhvh*), which by custom I render as "the Lord"; in other languages it is kurios, dominus, der Herr, le Seigneur, or the like. It is taken to mean "I am that I am" (Exodus 3.14)—existence fraught with mystery. The Lord had not made himself known by name to Abraham, Isaac, and Jacob. When he did tell his name it became sacred, a word never said aloud. After vowels were added to the text, the ones used in writing the Name—5500 times in the Old Testament—were those of the everyday term *adonai* "lord" (except that the first vowel was a simple schwa). The character of the name is profound and there is grandeur in its not being spoken or even fully spelled out.

The same is true, to a far lesser degree, with "God." When Judaism came to think there was one god only, and to declare the oneness of God as the core of its faith, it kept on using the old plural *elohim* "gods." In the first verse of the Bible there is a latent "the gods created the heaven and the earth" (the plural "creators" is used in the Hebrew of "Remember now thy Creator in the days of thy youth," Ecclesiastes 12.1). And the assurance by the serpent, "ye shall be as gods, knowing good and evil" (Genesis 3.5), can be recast as "ye shall be as God." I take then the commandment to have meant: at first (1) that you should not be false to whatever you swore, either on the name itself or on any other word for God or the gods, and then (2) that you should not use the sacred name ever, and should not use any of the other words for God unnecessarily.

Which of these two senses did Jesus honor? He honored both of them: (1) you ought to fulfill whatever you have solemnly pledged yourself to, and (2) you ought not to affirm on the name of the Lord, or even on the word God, that you mean what you say. After speaking of killing and adultery Jesus comes to the matter of swearing, and his advice is wholly practical, not mystical. "Again, ye have heard that it hath been said by them of old time, Thou shalt not forswear thyself, but shalt perform unto the Lord thine oaths; but I say unto you, Swear not at all; neither by heaven; for it is God's throne: nor by the earth; for it is his footstool: neither by Jerusalem; for it is the city of the great King. Neither shalt thou swear by thy head, because thou canst not make one hair white or black. But let your communication be, Yea, yea; Nay, nay; for whatsoever is more than these cometh of evil" (Matthew 5.33–37). The words that were "said by them of old time"—which I now quote in italics along with the verses preceding and following—have to do with with crookedness: "Ye shall not steal, neither deal falsely, neither lie one to another. *And ye shall not swear by my name falsely, neither shalt thou profane the name of thy God: I am the Lord.* Thou shalt not defraud thy neighbor, neither rob him, the wages of him that is hired shall not abide with thee all night until the morning" (Leviticus 19.11–13). Here the central verse, in italics, bears on the name commandment directly, and the surrounding ones bear on it indirectly. Stealing and cheating are involved, and so is bearing false witness (though it is lying in general, not just lying to incriminate); but also involved is profanity. Much of this (Leviticus) passage, here cited as commentary (on Exodus 20.7 and Matthew 5.33–37), looks to me like an enlargement by a secondary author; the original edge may have been blunted. We can still gather that the name commandment had to do with earthly matters, not spiritual ones. The sense was, Do not affirm falsehoods on the name of the Lord.

Jesus did not himself speak the sacred Hebrew name of God, *Yhwh.* The word he used was the Greek common noun *kurios* "lord" (Matthew 4.7, 11.25). When he spoke in Aramaic (or Hebrew) he would not have used the sacred name but the common noun *adonai* "lord." There are two striking marginal matters, though. (1) "I and my Father are one" (John 10:30) might contain the "one" from the saying "the Lord our God, the Lord is One"; and (2) "before Abraham was I am" (John 8.58) might suggest "I am that I am." Those are wonderful accidents, or else they were wonderful intentions; there is no fault in them. It is as if Jesus kept the name so deeply within himself that he did not ever use it at all. He also did not heighten his speech with any of the alternatives, but said, "Yea, yea; Nay, nay."

(On the other hand St. Paul came closer to swearing than he needed to in saying, "I call God for a record upon my soul, that to spare you I came not," 2 Corinthians 1.23, or "the things which I write unto you, behold, before God, I lie not," Galatians 1.20, or "God is my record, how greatly I long after you," Philippians 1.8. And many of us nowadays would prefer "heaven forbid" to the King James version, uncalled for by the Greek: "Is there unrigheousness with God? God forbid," Romans 9.14.)

"I and my Father are one" and "before Abraham was I am" may not use the Name in vain but they do speak of God as if with knowledge, and the same is true of "I proceeded forth and came from God" (John 8.42). Those who would judge Jesus were not (by their lights) without a cause against him: he had shown familiarity with God; and the word used in the charge was blasphemy. If "I and my Father are one" and "before Abraham was I am" actually were spoken by Jesus, and not created by the evangelist or the tradition, how are we to regard them? They have an awareness and sense of well being out of accord with the fearsome aspect of God that some of the devout would find in the commandments. In making the aspect friendlier to man, the Son of man is consistent with himself.[10]

4. The four senses of the sabbath (e. of the 14)   "Six days shalt thou labor, and do all thy work: but the seventh day is the sabbath of the Lord thy God: in it thou shalt not do any work, thou, nor thy son, nor thy daughter, nor thy manservant, nor thy maidservant, nor thy cattle, nor thy stranger that is within thy gates; for in six days the Lord made heaven and earth, the sea, and all that in them is, and rested the seventh day: wherefore the Lord blessed the sabbath day, and hallowed it" (Exodus 20.9–11).

There are three certain senses of *sbt* (or *sh-b-t*) "sabbath," and I will argue that there is one more. They are (1) full (moon), (2) seventh, (3) bring to an end, and (4) captivity. The first of

them is the most ancient, the second replaced it forever, the third
is a part of the reason in Exodus, and the fourth (unless I am
mistaken) is a part of Deuteronomy. My aim here is at confirming that in much of the Old Testament the sabbath is the full
moon day rather than the seventh, and at justifying "captivity"
as a conjecture.

In the Assyrian and Babylonian lunar month two phases
were of special importance. The one was *shapattu*, or *shabattu*,
the 15th day; the other was the day of the new moon. (*The
Assyrian Dictionary*, under *shabattu*, quotes the phrase "my
mother shapattu, my father the new moon's day.") Most scholars
in Semitic agree that the origin of *sabbath* lies here. Seemingly,
the Assyrian word is from *shebu*, feminine *shebitu*, and the
Hebrew from *sabea*; their sense is "full, filled, sated, satisfied,
replete." As a time of the month it is the full moon. We may
think of a rite throughout a culture. The feast of the passover was
on the 15th, and so was the feast of the tabernacles, six months
away; they divided the year in two. The new moon and the full
moon similarly divided the month in two.

With a change in pronunciation the sabbath became the 7th
day of a nonlunar week, the word for seventh being *shibah*. (It is
one of the most ancient of all words, and perhaps the hardiest,
being the same throughout both Semitic and Indo-European,
except that a final *t* has been dropped in Hebrew and Germanic.)
We may imagine a time when faith in the full moon had been
lost. The sun, the moon, and the five planets were honored
instead, as in our weekdays. The respect that had been given to
the word for *full* was now given to the sound-alike meaning
seventh. It was not a revolution in thought, but only a reformation. And the interval was now exact, while with the phases of
the moon there had been hours left over.

What is the sense of *sabbath* in the early texts of the Old
Testament? The choice is between the full moon and the seventh.

"Wherefore wilt thou go to him today? it is neither new moon, nor sabbath" (2 Kings 4.23); "incense is an abomination unto me; the new moons and sabbaths" (Isaiah 1.13); "I will also cause all her mirth to cease, her feast days, her new moons, and her sabbaths" (Hosea 2.11); "When will the new moon be gone, that we may sell corn? and the sabbath, that we may set forth wheat" (Amos 8.5); "the eves of the sabbaths, and the sabbaths, and the eves of the new moons, and the new moons" (Judith 8.6). I will argue that *new moon* and *sabbath* were a formula, used first with parallelism (as in the Amos verse), and then used also in series (as in 2 Kings, Isaiah, Hosea, and Judith).

In Homer there is only one style; in the Old Testament there are two: the prose and the poetry. Auerbach compared Homer with the prose, and concluded that they represented two attitudes of mind. He ought to have made the comparison with the poetry. For between Homer and Old Testament poetry there are analogues and similarities.

The hallmark of Hebraic and all other Semitic poetry is a parallelism of clauses. At times the parallelism derives from terms that are opposites, like *full* (of food) and *hungry* (1 Samuel 2.5, Proverbs 27.7), but generally the key terms mean much the same, as *death* and *grave* do, or *mouth* and *lips*. "And the daughter of Zion is left as a cottage in a vineyard, and as a lodge in a garden of cucumbers" (Isaiah 1.8). Here *cottage* and *lodge* are identical twins in sense, *vineyard* and *garden of cucumbers* are cousins. It is a wonderful idiom; its beauty is distinctive. Usually there are two parallel terms, as with *cottage* and *lodge*, or *sabbath* and *new moon*, or *father* and *mother*, or *waters* and *flood*, but there may be three, as with *sin, iniquity*, and *transgression*, and there may even be more, in a tour de force (five words for *lion* in the Hebrew of Job 4.10–11, six for *trap* in Job 18.8). The element connecting the half verses is ordinarily the letter *waw*, meaning "and" or "but," though so vaguely as hardly to matter at all. That is, if we doubt with a given verse whether the second half goes further than the first, we shall usually decide that it does not; *new moon* does differ from *sabbath*, but *lodge* is the same as *cottage*, and "a lodge in a garden of cucumbers" is really a variation upon "a cottage in a vineyard." Remarkably, we in our remote culture may understand the idiom better than an ancient native speaker did. For sometimes an adapter, deaf to synonymy, found a forward movement where there was none. The verse "They part my garments among them, and cast lots upon my vesture" (Psalms 22.18) is worked out as "the soldiers, when they had crucified Jesus, took his garments, and made four parts, to every soldier a part; and also his coat: now the coat was without seam, woven from the top throughout. They said therefore among themselves, Let us not rend it, but cast lots for it" (John 19.23–24).[11]

One member of a pair, *yayin* "wine," may be balanced by the other, *shekar* "strong drink," in a separate clause: "Wine is a mocker, strong drink is raging" (Proverbs 20.1 and often). The two may also be used in a series: "Do not drink wine nor strong drink" (Leviticus 10.9 and often). Which use is the older, the echo in half verses or the sum in a single half verse? The use in the echoing halves is the older; the terms became attached to each other as a single formula, solving the problem faced by the poet, How shall I phrase my idea a second time, as the poetic convention requires? The reason why the words for the two chief phases of the moon came to occur as a pair is represented by "When will the new moon be gone, that we may sell corn? and the sabbath, that we may set forth wheat" (Amos 8.5). It was only afterwards that the new moon and the sabbath might be listed in the same half verse.

If to the contrary the sabbath in this verse meant the 7th, a day of a solar week would complement a lunar phase, and the parallelism would be inferior. In time *sabbath* and *new moon*, with *feast days* as in the Hosea verse, came to mind together (1 Chronicles 23.31, 2 Chronicles 2.4, 8.13, 31.3, Nehemiah 10.33; Colossians 2.16); they may then have referred to days of the week, the month, and the year, as the *Anchor Bible Dictionary* suggests (though "feast day" in Psalms 81.3 might tell against the idea). But to begin with, the full moon answered to the new moon in elegant parallelism.

". . . shall be shut the six working days; but on the sabbath it shall be opened, and in the day of the new moon it shall be opened" (Ezekiel 46.1). Here *sabbath*, combining with (or corresponding to) the new moon, must be the 7th rather than the 15th. The commentators agree, though, that the earlier part— "shall be shut the six working days"—is an addition made after the sense of the word had changed; earlier the full moon and the new had been parallel more clearly. And similarly with "from one new moon to another, and from one sabbath to another" (Isaiah 66.23), which the Revised English Bible gives as "month after month at the new moon, week after week on the sabbath." That rendering is really from the later sense of the word, not the earlier one; it is not a translation but an interpretation; surely it cannot be right. In truth the time is still being reckoned by the lunar half-month, not by a sum of days; the word *month* is not parallel to *week*; what the prophet means is "from one new moon to another, and from one full moon to another."

If the poetry of the Old Testament were relatively recent, we would favor for all texts the later meaning of *sabbath*, namely the *7th*. But the poetry is primordial, as can be shown by argument. It is true that in many pairs, such as *gold* and *silver*, one of the two suggests the other. The same cannot be said, though, of *dragons* and *owls* (Job 30.29, Isaiah 34.13, Micah 1.8). Those two words would not have occurred to everybody as a pair had there been no custom that they belonged together; and yet they are a word pair in different books; one of the words brought the other to mind; there must have been a convention uniting them as a twosome. We may think of a treasury of such formulas given by mouth from one generation to the next, as properties to be shared among all Hebrew, Assyrian, and Ugaritic poets. It was a tradition half as old as the hills.[12]

The Exodus version of the commandments refers to the story of the Creation and the resting of the Lord after all had been made. Here the association is with *shabat*, which did not at first mean "rest" (as Gnana Robinson among others has shown) but "break off, desist from, cease doing, bring to an end." Only afterwards did it come to mean "rest" as well. Consider the verses quoted a moment ago as instances of *new moon* and *sabbath*. Hosea 2.11 indicates that the two days are times of gladness, not of repose or austerity; Amos 8.5 shows only that they are times when commerce is abstained from. In 2 Kings 4.23 the new moon and the sabbath are days when the prophet of Israel may be consulted, and in Isaiah 1.13 they are days of religious observance. The idea of rest is not in any of those verses. *Rest* is not the earliest sense of the word; it is not even the next-earliest; it is a late sense, and the Genesis verses about the Lord's resting are late accordingly, though of course they are as grand as can be. The sounds that meant "break off, desist from, cease doing, bring to an end" took on the sense of "rest (as an aftermath)." The sacredness upon the day of the full moon, *shabbat*, which had come to be upon "seven" *sheba* (with a final *t* as in Assyrian), now came to be upon "rest," *shabat*. (It is true that in the allusion—"rested the seventh day: wherefore the Lord blessed the sabbath day," Exodus 20.11—the "rest" is not *shabat* but *nuwah*, but that is because a word ought not to comment upon itself; in the *Iliad* Zeus is called the cloud-gatherer except that when clouds are mentioned he is the lightning-gatherer instead, 16.298.) A day of gladness and abstaining from commerce, a day to consult the prophet or burn

incense (*shabbat* in Hosea 2.11, Amos 8.5, 2 Kings 4.23, and
Isaiah 1.13), had become a day of pausing from labor. Because of
their near identity in sound, *shabbat* "the full moon day," *sheba*
"seven," and *shabat* "rest" accommodated and confirmed each
other as if by fiat.

What remains is to explain Deuteronomy (5.15): "And
remember that thou wast a servant in the land of Egypt, and that
the Lord thy God brought thee out thence through a mighty hand
and by a stretched out arm: therefore the Lord thy God commanded thee to keep the sabbath day." Why is the Creation not
spoken of? It is as if that story were not known, for if it had
been known, who could tell of anything else? The exodus, a
great event but a small one in comparison with the making of the
world, is spoken of instead. What brought the deliverance and
departure to mind? What does the exodus have in common with
the sabbath? The thoughts of the deuteronomist are remote. It
makes plain sense that in gratitude for your release you ought
to give your servants and animals a regular day for rest or
worship. But does it make sense that from such gratitude you
yourself ought not to labor either? It has been argued that Egypt
was a land where you worked every day, so that escape from
there meant a day of rest you could count on. If that were the
explanation the contrast in the passage would not be bondage
versus freedom, but work every day versus work six days out of
seven. In the Exodus version of the commandment the Creation
(with its seventh day) and the sabbath (on the seventh day) are
in accord with each other. In the Deuteronomy version the
exodus and the sabbath do not have so evident an association. Is
there some rhyme or reason besides? I believe that behind the
passage, though unexpressed, can be heard *shebut* "captivity"
(Deuteronomy 30.3, Job 42.10, Psalms 14.7, Jeremiah 29.14,
Lamentations 2.14, Ezekiel 16.53, Hosea 6.11, Amos 9.14,
Zephaniah 2.7, and often). Just as *shabat* "rest," even in the

course of being explained, is not in (the Hebrew of) "rested the seventh day: wherefore the Lord blessed the sabbath day" (Exodus 20.11), so *shebut* is not a textual part of Deuteronomy 5.12–15, except that it led the author to say what he did. The resemblances in sound tell why the sabbath (*shabbat*), once the day of the full moon (*sebea*), became on day seven (*sheba*) a cessation from labor (*shabat*); there was a remembrance sometimes of the creation, sometimes of the captivity in Egypt (*shebut*).

Jesus did not connect the sabbath with the moon or the captivity. He did not even connect it with the Lord's rest at the end of the Creation. "The sabbath was made for man and not man for the sabbath" (Mark 2.27). That is a surprise; how do you account for it? Anybody today will say that the sabbath honors the Lord's ceasing from labor. Such a reason was evidently unknown to Jesus. So we must not think of him as a scholar in the text (of Genesis). And to him the commandment was not so strict that it should not be broken if need be. Would not anyone on the sabbath help an ox or an ass from a pit (Luke 14.5)? If you are hungry then, pluck corn and eat it, as David ate the shewbread; for "the Son of man is Lord even of the sabbath day" (Matthew 12.8, Mark 2.28, Luke 6.5). (Not to risk your life for sabbath rest should have been a lesson already learned, seeing that those unwilling to defend themselves on that day had been massacred, so that their survivors had come to second thoughts, 1 Maccabees 2.32–41.) Would Jesus have done routine carpentry on the sabbath? It may be that he would not. But to heal on the sabbath—and to tell the man you have healed to take up his bed and walk—that was for him another matter.

5. *Jesus and the Ethical Commandments* (f. of the 14)   "Honor thy father and thy mother" (Exodus 20.12). Psalms 3, which begins, "A Psalm of David, when he fled from Absalom his

son," might have continued: "He lifteth his hand against me, an arm in rebellion. Why doth he multiply sorrow and add to my grief? I taught him the canon of law, the code of the precepts. As a man is to God, so is a son to his father." If the psalmist had said *that*, we should have glimpsed a time when to respect your parents had weight. As things are, the commandment is a minor one. The words "Cursed be he that setteth light by his father or his mother" (Deuteronomy 27.16) are not taken to heart. Jacob does not honor his father but deceives him (Genesis 27). Jonathan does not honor his father but loves David (1 Samuel 18–20). Seemingly the commandment is broken only when you strike your parents or curse them (Exodus 21.15, 21.17).

Scribes and Pharisees have charged Jesus with the failure of his disciples to wash their hands when they eat. Changing the subject for the sake of a vigorous reply, he charges them in return with not honoring, even with cursing, their father and mother (Matthew 15.1–4). And the parents commandment he remembers again in his advice to the rich young ruler (Matthew 19.16–30, Mark 10.17–19, Luke 18.20), omitting several other commandments and adding one or two. Jesus would, though, set light by his own parents, or at least by the parents commandment, for the sake of a higher good. "If any man come to me, and hate not his father, and mother, and wife, and children, and brethren, and sisters, yea, and his own life also, he cannot be my disciple" (Luke 14.26, Matthew 10.37). With similar willful thoughts at the age of twelve, and regarding God as his father, Jesus lingers to dispute with doctors in the temple, "and his mother said unto him, Son, why hast thou thus dealt with us? behold, thy father and I have sought thee sorrowing. And he said unto them, How is it that ye sought me? wist ye not that I must be about my Father's business?" (Luke 2.48–49). There is no striking or cursing here, but the words are harsh (in agreement with "whosoever shall do the will of God, the same is my brother, and my sister, and mother," Mark 3.33). The evangelists Matthew (1.16) and Luke (3.23) trace the lineage of Joseph to Abraham—even to "Seth, which was the son of Adam, which was the son of God"; but it is nowhere said that Jesus honors Joseph as his earthly father. And the blessedness of Mary is unknown to Jesus or of no moment. "Woman!" he says to her (John 2.4, 19.26; he also says "Woman" to Mary Magdalene, but then calls her by name, John 20.15–16). Are we to have faith in these Bible stories? The question here is: Did Jesus hold the commandments to be important? And the answer with regard to the one about parents seems to be: Yes, the commandments are important, but they are not the highest end in view.

(g. of the 14) "Thou shalt not kill" (Exodus 20.13). What kind of killing is forbidden? The following kinds are here arranged from worst to least bad (a disputable matter). (1) To kill as a person from such a motive as greed or anger. (2) To kill as a nation for lands or resources that are yours by divine promise or manifest destiny. (3) To kill as a nation enraged. (4) To kill as a person in defending yourself. (5) To kill as a nation in defending yourself. (6) To kill a felonious tyrant. (7) To kill yourself when life is a burden. (8) To kill someone else who finds life a burden. (9) To kill a child in the womb who would find life a burden. (10) To kill in enforcing the law.

The phrase that Jesus used was: "Thou shalt do no murder" (Matthew 19.18; "Do not kill," Mark 10.19, Luke 18.20; *phoneuo* rather than *kteino* in all three). Here the questions are: What did he regard as murder? and Would he have been strict or lenient? Of the ten kinds of killing in the list, the first is the one that Jesus condemned clearly, and it is the one now at hand.

"Ye have heard that it was said by them of old time, Thou shalt not kill; and whosoever shall kill shall be in danger of the judgment: but I say unto you, That whosoever is angry with his brother without a cause shall be in danger of the judgment; and whosoever shall say to his brother, Raca, shall be in danger of the council; but whosoever shall say, Thou fool, shall be in danger of hell fire" (Matthew 5.21–22). The words "without a cause" have low textual authority and are now usually omitted; it can be seen why some scribe would have inserted them. With those words or without them, the passage is hard to understand. Killing follows upon anger ("in their anger they slew a man," Genesis 49.6); anger is related to scorn (Michal said Raca "vain fellow" to David, and was childless for doing so, 2 Samuel 6.20–23); and scorn is close to contempt (Jesus says, "Ye fools and blind," to the scribes and Pharisees, Matthew 23.17 and 19, and quotes God in a parable as saying, "Thou fool," Luke 12.20). That is: killing, anger, scorn, and contempt. Was the evangelist combining materials that did not belong together? No, his sequence is well made: the order is from heat to cold. "Do not commit a wrong with violent hands" becomes "Do not be malicious in your heart." You deserve to face a judge not only for killing but even for being angry; you deserve an assembly of judges for being scornful; and hell itself is what you deserve for being contemptuous. Not that bad deeds are excused, but ill will is bad too, even worse.

Why is the word *raca* not said in Greek? The cry of despair from the cross, in Aramaic or Hebrew, is a quotation, but nothing is being quoted here. And surely no one will argue that *raca* had become hellenized, so that it sounded as familiar as the rest. So the answer must be: (1) that the passage was being rendered from Aramaic; (2) that different Aramaic words for fool, *raca* being one of them, were used in the two clauses "whosoever shall say to his brother, Raca" and "whosoever shall say, Thou fool"; (3) that to keep the variation the translator needed a pair of words in Greek; (4) that he planned to use *moros* in a moment and could not think of anything else—such as *anoetos*, Luke

24.25, Romans 1.14—for the *raca* clause; and (5) that accordingly he kept the word of his original.

Jesus a-hungered comes to a fig tree, too early in the season, and because it is not bearing he blights it, "Let no fruit grow on thee henceforward for ever" (Matthew 21.19, Mark 11.14). No harm is done, for the thought is Near Eastern, not Far Eastern: the fig tree does not matter as it would in Buddhist or Hindu thought; only mankind matters. But the anger is without a cause, and it is yielded to. Can we find an edifying truth? Do we admire Jesus the more because he is human? No, the story is interesting in the way of Bible stories, which often have a moral for the worse. The revision of "Thou shalt not kill"—as "Thou shalt not even have hard feelings"—remains and may be written down to live by.

(h. of the list) "Thou shalt not commit adultery" (Exodus 20.14). A matter to bear in mind is that adultery must involve a married woman. (That makes sense because it safeguards the home, for a woman can, but a man cannot, bring into a household a child that does not belong there.) If only the man is married, the deed is not adultery but fornication, and it is not so wicked. "For the lips of a strange woman drop as a honeycomb, and her mouth is smoother than oil, but her end is bitter as wormwood, sharp as a two-edged sword" (Proverbs 5.3–4). Sin is not spoken of in that verse; there is no thought of the commandment; it is just a matter of wisdom, like "Pride goeth before destruction." Samson, consecrated as a Nazarite, went into a harlot of Gaza (Judges 16.1) and does not seem to have angered the Lord. "And if a man entice a maid that is not betrothed, and lie with her, he shall surely endow her to be his wife. If her father utterly refuse to give her unto him, he shall pay money according to the dowry of virgins. Thou shalt not suffer a witch to live. Whosoever lieth with a beast shall surely be put to

death" (Exodus 22.16–19). It would seem from this passage that
a woman was property; the seduction did not call for death, as
witchcraft did, but only for damages. It does not seem that there
was any sin to punish. In contrast: "he that committeth adultery
with his neighbor's wife, the adulterer and the adulteress shall
surely be put to death" (Leviticus 20.10). It is not for enticement,
but for adultery, as with incest, sodomy, and bestiality (20.11–
16): their blood shall be upon them.

As a man might without utter guilt lie with an unmarried
woman, so might an unmarried woman without utter guilt be a
whore. The whoredom is not a crime under statute nor is it
contrary to the commandment. It is wicked all the same and is
used as a figure of speech for devotion against the Lord. Samaria
and Jerusalem are whores doting upon lovers "whose flesh is as
the flesh of asses, and whose issue is like the issue of horses"
(Ezekiel 23.20, a passage of Jurassic power, with a refrain at 6,
12, and 23; the flesh surely refers to the sexual member, and the
issue to seminal fluid: astonishing parallelism). In a variation
upon the whoredom, the false devotion might be adultery: "it
came to pass through the lightness of her whoredom, that she
defiled the land, and committed adultery with stocks and stones"
(Jeremiah 3.9, see also Hosea 2.2). In these figures of speech for
unfaithfulness to the Lord the adultery and the whoredom were
equally wicked. But in the realm of humanity the law upon a
woman meant adultery within marriage, not whoredom without.

Was it a sin committed often or seldom in New Testament
times? The generation was not "murderous and sinful," nor
"perjured and sinful," nor robbing nor blasphemous nor whor-
ish and sinful; it was an "adulterous and sinful generation"
(Mark 8.38). Of the bad things that we do rather than merely
daydream about, adultery can more easily escape notice than
many; there is no corpse, no missing cup. The words of Jesus

about adultery are famously "That whosoever looketh on a woman to lust after her hath committed adultery with her already in his heart" (Matthew 5.28). For it is in the looking, by man or by woman, that the sin begins. "Joseph was a goodly person, and well-favored. And it came to pass after these things, that his master's wife cast her eyes upon Joseph" (Genesis 39.6–7); Bathsheba "was very beautiful to look upon" (2 Samuel 11.2). The warning is that the world fills the eye with temptations. The sin may be adultery in the loins, but desire from gazing is wicked too. The good man will be able to say, "I made a covenant with mine eyes" (Job 31.1). As with killing-and-anger, so with adultery-and-lusting: the greater (killing, adultery) and the lesser (anger, lusting) are different rungs on the same downward ladder. To respond like an animal, rather than like a god, may not be an abomination, but it is not righteous either. The teaching of Jesus would seem to have been: to the degree that adultery is human, it may go unpunished, but it ought to be repented of.

"And the scribes and Pharisees brought unto him a woman taken in adultery; and when they had set her in the midst, they say unto him, Master, this woman was taken in adultery, in the very act. Now Moses in the law commanded us, that such should be stoned: but what sayest thou? This they said, tempting him, that they might have to accuse him. But Jesus stooped down and with his finger wrote on the ground, as though he heard them not. So when they continued asking him, he lifted up himself, and said unto them, He that is without sin among you, let him first cast a stone at her. And again he stooped down, and wrote on the ground. And they which heard it, being convicted by their own conscience, went out one by one, beginning at the eldest, even unto the last: and Jesus was left alone, and the woman standing in the midst. When Jesus had lifted up himself, and saw none but the woman, he said unto her, Woman, where are those thine

accusers? hath no man condemned thee? She said, No man,
Lord. And Jesus said unto her, neither do I condemn thee: go,
and sin no more" (John 8.3–11).

A wonderful story!—(1) in its sparsity of detail (was the
husband involved?), (2) in the mystery of the writing on the
ground (was it in meaningful words?), (3) in the dispersing of
the crowd (were they all sinners, or were they merely ashamed to
act one by one, or were there various motives?), and (4) in the
silence of the woman about whether she was sorry (did she
resolve to sin no more?). It is a prose poem, a matter to think
about, not one to understand. Has Jesus forgiven all adulteries
and other high crimes? No, the thrust of the story is not that
adultery may go unpunished, but that the self-righteous should
look to themselves.

As with adultery, so with whoredom. It cannot be shown
but is to be inferred that the sinful woman who washed the feet
of Jesus with her tears (Luke 7.36–50) was Mary Magdalene,
"out of whom went seven devils" (8.2) when he healed her.
Those two passages—the end of chapter 7 and the beginning of
chapter 8—may not be continuous, or they may be, or they may
once have been. They are at any rate harmonious with each
other. Why else might a single woman have been thought a
sinner? for what else might devils have congregated within her?
It is accordingly traditional that this Mary had been a whore. The
two crimes of women, adultery and whoredom, are then regarded similarly. They are great impurities but may be washed
away.

The ideal—treating women and men alike, against older
usage—would seem to be: first, that unless you will be celibate
you should marry (and come together, for not to do so would be
fraud, 1 Corinthians 7.5), and secondly that you should not (if
she has been faithful) put your wife away, or your husband, and
marry another, for that would be adultery (a composite of Mat-

thew 19.9, Mark 10.11–12, and Luke 16.18). The thought is of a kind with the other teachings of Jesus, for if you have one partner rather than many there will be less competition and resentment. It is like biting your lip in forbearance instead of calling your brother a fool.

(i. of the list) "Thou shalt not steal" (Ex 20.15). Stealing may be just as hateful to God as murder, but it is less grave to mankind. Even if the felon is not found out, the effect may be small; and often the felon *is* found out and the stolen cup or sheep can be brought back. Stealing is also less grave than adultery. So the punishment is double or threefold restitution rather than death. A brother to stealing is fraud: "Ye shall not steal, neither deal falsely . . . Thou shalt not defraud thy neighbor, neither rob him: the wages of him that is hired shall not abide with thee all night until the morning" (Leviticus 19.11–13); "whose ox have I taken? or whose ass have I taken? or whom have I defrauded?" (1 Samuel 12.3); "Do not commit adultery, Do not kill, Do not steal, Do not bear false witness, Defraud not" (Mark 10.19). In ordinary usage stealing will include fraud, robbery, thievery, and dishonesty in general. (To take land by force is another matter. Jacob can be said to have stolen from Esau their father's blessing; the Israelites cannot be said to have stolen territory from the Canaanites.)

The commandments against killing and adultery forbade the deed, and Jesus forbade the wish. But with stealing there is a separate commandment, a lengthy one (perhaps even a pair of commandments) forbidding the wish: thou shalt not covet. And yet the old law is redone even with stealing; for there is a new ideal—new in its extremity. The needy had already been cared for; the gleaning of a field or a vineyard had been left to them (Leviticus 19.9–10, 23.22, Deuteronomy 24.19); they had been allowed a portion, though it was a pittance. The giving of alms had been a part of life (Matthew 6.1), but there too the portion was small. Jesus asks for more: "sell all that thou hast, and distribute unto the poor" (Luke 18.22, see 1 Corinthians 13.3). It is an antitode, an absolute opposite, not to coveting—which is merely a matter of thoughts—but to stealing. Distributing your wealth is not thoughts but action. And that is what Jesus tells the young ruler he should do to gain eternal life. "When he heard this, he was very sorrowful: for he was very rich."

Was he to give away his last shekel? When you prepare a feast, go out into the highways and hedges, to invite the needy (Luke 14.23). "Woe unto you that are rich! for ye have received your consolation. Woe unto you that are full! for ye shall hunger" (Luke 6.24–25). "It is easier for a camel to go through the eye of a needle, than for a rich man to enter into the kingdom of God" (Matthew 19.24). Are those sayings to be regarded as condemnations or as mere reproofs? They tell of things beyond us, such as not even desiring a woman or never becoming angry; they are not requirements for the beginner. And if we look elsewhere we shall find reason not to regard them as so severe after all. We are to be generous but not to a degree beyond reason. The people of Jesus' time had the poor with them always, but him they did not have always (Matthew 26.11, Mark 14.7); it was well that he should be anointed with precious spikenard. The prodigal son is to be given not just a feast but a ring on his hand (Luke 15.22). Jesus would have us be kind and sharing against our desires, but would not have us constantly train for spiritual athleticism.

(j.) "Thou shalt not bear false witness" (Exodus 20.16). The best-known instance is the accusation of Joseph by Potiphar's wife (Genesis 39). The chief instance is the accusation of Susanna (in the apocryphal book bearing her name) by the two elders who desired her. That story ends with poetic justice in keeping with the regulation that if any man testify falsely, "then shall ye do unto him, as he had thought to have done" (Deuteronomy

19.19). The elders implicated each other by giving different accounts; so there were in a way two witnesses. They might then be put to death, while Joseph was merely imprisoned. "At the mouth of two witnesses, or three witnesses, shall he that is worthy of death be put to death; but at the mouth of one witness he shall not be put to death" (Deuteronomy 17.6). Jezebel set two men "to bear witness against" Naboth (1 Kings 21.10).

It is an earthly matter, but known in heaven, too. The witness commandment may even have had affinity with the one on the Name. "Ye shall not swear by my name falsely, neither shalt thou profane the name of thy God" (Leviticus 19.12); "into the house of him that sweareth falsely by my name" (Zechariah 5.4). The high priest says to Jesus: "I adjure thee by the living God" (Matthew 26.63).

Bearing false witness requires lying, but there is other lying besides, and in general it is hateful to God. "Behold, ye trust in lying words, that cannot profit. Will ye steal, murder, and commit adultery, and swear falsely, and burn incense unto Baal?" (Jeremiah 7.8). "By swearing, and lying, and killing, and stealing, and committing adultery" (Hosea 4.2). Francis Bacon in his essay "On Truth" quotes Montaigne as saying that to lie is to be brave before God but a coward before man. Lying is not an easy matter to decide upon, all the same. It seems wrong in only a minor way when Sarah lies to the Lord, that she did not laugh (Genesis 18.15), but (to those of us who are not descended from him, though we may honor or worship one who was) it is wrong in a major way when Jacob lies in defrauding Esau (Genesis 27.19). On the other hand: Abraham did well in lying to Pharaoh and Abimelech, for he was protecting Sarah; Jael arguably did well in welcoming Sisera with the words "Turn in my lord, turn in to me; fear not" (Judges 4.18); and the priests suborned soldiers into saying falsely, "His disciples came by night, and stole him away while we slept" (Matthew 28.13).

Did Jesus tighten or loosen the witness commandment? was he tolerant of lies as a weed along the road of life? The devil "is a liar, and the father of it" are his words on the matter (John 8.44), but he did not send Peter away even when he foretold of him, "before the cock crow twice, thou shalt deny me thrice" (Mark 14.30). It was not false witness nor lying when Judas betrayed Jesus with a kiss, but it was more nearly the same than different. Jesus himself was one "who did no sin, neither was guile found in his mouth" (1 Peter 2.22). To be without lies or false witness would be a rarity in our culture today, and it was one in that culture then. Seeing Nathanael coming his way Jesus said of him, "Behold an Israelite indeed, in whom is no guile!" (John 1.47).

(k.) "Thou shalt not covet thy neighbor's house, *thou shalt not covet thy neighbor's wife*, nor his manservant, nor his maidservant, nor his ox, nor his ass, nor any thing that is thy neighbor's" (Exodus 20.17). The English word covet speaks of wanting, more mental than physical; the Greek word *epithumeo*, used in the version of the Old Testament and throughout the New, speaks of desire, as much physical as mental. The commandment treats woman as property, ranking her below a house but above a servant or a beast. As such she is more a vessel than a helpmeet. To covet someone else's wife is halfway towards stealing and also halfway towards adultery. It was not for her abilities that David coveted Bathsheba.

In naming the commandments to the rich young ruler, Jesus lists them as murder, adultery, stealing, false witness, father and mother, and neighbor as thyself (Matthew 19.18–19), or as adultery, killing, stealing, false witness, defrauding, and father and mother (Mark 10.19), or else the same but without defrauding (Luke 18.20); coveting is never among them. In naming the commandments in his letter to the Romans (13.9) Paul lists them as adultery, killing, stealing, false witness, and coveting, omitting father and mother, but adding neighbor as thyself. Since the changes made by Jesus in killing and adultery were towards the wish and away from the deed, and since coveting was already a wish rather than a deed, it was not a matter (evidently) that he always felt a need to mention.

(1.) *"Thou shalt not covet thy neighbor's house,* thou shalt not covet thy neighbor's wife, *nor his manservant, nor his maidservant, nor his ox, nor his ass, nor any thing that is thy neighbor's"* (Exodus 20.17). Whether coveting should be a commandment at all, let alone two, is moot. I believe it must once have been more widely reaching than it is now, for it does not (at first) seem so weighty as the others. A bad will is less evident, and less grave, than a bad act, and property is less than a person. If a woman wishes she could afford to hire her neighbor's babysitter, is that as wicked as committing adultery with her neighbor's husband? No, the coveting is a smaller offense. Surely it cannot be true that the love of money is the root of all evil (1 Timothy 6.10). All the same, greed is to be dreaded, in Judaism and Christianity, if we consider how far it leads. Thirty pieces of silver corrupted Judas. In Buddhism grasping is the wrong above all others. "The love of money gained unjustly is impious, but the love of money gained justly is still shameful, for to be ungenerous is unseemly" (Epicurus, fragment 43). Covetousness is a matter of degree, more than with murder, adultery, stealing, and false witness. *The Book of Common Prayer* (for September 21) has the petition for "grace to forsake all covetous desires, and inordinate love of riches."

With money goes honor, or honor with money. "High on a throne of royal state, which far outshone the wealth of Ormus and of Ind, or where the gorgeous east with richest hand showers on her kings barbaric pearl and gold, Satan exalted sat" (*Paradise Lost* 2.1–5). Among us there is the question of a better place or an inferior one (Luke 14.8–10); among the disciples there was contention "which of them should be accounted the greatest" (Luke 22.24). In asking the people whether Jesus should not be released, Pilate "knew that for envy they had delivered him" (Matthew 27.18). Among the seven deadly sins of the middle ages, avarice is separate from envy and from lust, but in the gospels and in the covet commandment they are related.

(m.) "Thou shall love thy neighbor as thyself." The verse is from another directive of the Lord to Moses (Leviticus 19.18); it is not on the tablets. Jesus once lists it among those others (Matthew 19.19) as if he were remembering it instead of covet. Paul lists the ones he thinks of (including covet, but not father and mother) and adds that "if there be any other commandment, it is briefly comprehended in this saying, namely, Thou shalt love thy neighbor as thyself" (Romans 13.9). Covet and neighbor-as-thyself are alike, perhaps exactly so. If you regard your neighbor as highly as you do yourself, you will not wish that his fine wife or house were yours, but will be glad for his sake that they belong to him.

With both Jesus and Paul: (1) the *words* (as they were called in Hebrew) were commandments, (2) the number ten did not come to mind, (3) the story about the stone tablets did not come to mind either, (4) the honor due to God went without saying, (5) the ethical commandments were known for their meaning rather than by rote learning, and (6) along with them was remembered the rule to love your neighbor.

(n.) "Thou shall set up an altar on mount Gerizim." So reads the final commandment in the notation of the Samaritans, a tribe still following the ritual of sacrifice, but now dying out (see Anderson). It completes the ten as a replacement for the first commandment of Judaism, and has scriptural authority (Deuteronomy 11.29 and 27.2–11), but it has not prevailed, for might makes right (see Moore, v. 1, p. 26). Which alternative did

Jesus favor, the out-of-Egypt commandment or this last one? Both were evidently unknown to him, for he did not recall either of them to the rich young ruler (Matthew 19.18–19, Mark 10.19, Luke 18.20). What we can say is that, if Jesus *had* heard of the Gerizim commandment, he would have spoken against it, for two reasons. His loyalty or ministry was to the Jewish nation: "into any city of the Samaritans enter ye not; but go rather to the lost sheep of the house of Israel" (Matthew 10.5–6). And he did not regard one sanctuary as better than another, for when a woman at a well in Samaria told him that her forebears had worshiped God on the mountain in their land, and added that he no doubt regarded Jerusalem as the right place to worship, the weight of his reply was that God does not reside chiefly in either, for God is a spirit (John 4.20–24).

6. The fourteen trimmed down to ten   The list of ten that I would take from Exodus 20.1–17 and Deuteronomy 5.6–21 is as follows.

ab.   (I am the Lord . . . Egypt.) Thou shalt have no other gods.

c.   Thou shalt not make unto thee any . . . image (of thy God).

d.   Thou shalt not take the name of the Lord thy God in vain.

e.   Remember the sabbath day.

f.   Honor thy father and thy mother.

g.   Thou shalt not kill.

h.   Thou shalt not commit adultery.

i.   Thou shalt not steal.

j.   Thou shalt not bear false witness.

kl.   Thou shalt not covet (whatever belongs to another).

m.   (omitted)

n.   (omitted)

If (a.) "I am the Lord . . . Egypt" is put outside the list, and if (b.) no-other-gods is taken with (c.) no-image, one more commandment is needed. The Jews, though not Philo or Josephus, increased the sum from nine to ten by regarding (a.) "I am the Lord . . . Egypt" as an additional commandment; the Samaritans instead added (n.) Gerizim; Catholics and Lutherans have sub-divided (kl.) covet. All three remedies seem to me unacceptable. Surely the right answer is to keep no-other-gods and no-image as two commandments, saying different things. My list is then essentially or exactly that of Philo and Josephus, and of the non-Lutheran Protestant and Orthodox churches. It makes use of an argument (on another matter) by the Jewish scholar David Daube, and has the approval ("seems to be a satisfactory solu-tion") of S. M. Polan in *The New Catholic Encyclopedia*.

Are there two sets of five, in accord with two as the number of the tablets? Philo thought the first five were towards God and our parents, the other five towards our fellows. One reason to disagree is the saying "the sabbath was made for man, and not man for the sabbath" (Mark 2.27). To Jesus the sabbath com-mandment was among those about mankind on earth. He does not seem to have known that God had finished the creation and rested.

Another reason not to see two sets of five is that, to Jesus, the parents commandment too, like the sabbath commandment, had more to do with earthly life than with worship. For he listed honor-thy-father-and-mother along with (as being of a kind with) not to kill or steal or commit adultery or bear false witness (Matthew 19.18, Mark 10.19, Luke 18.20). Still, it may be that the thinking on the matter was different earlier, before the day of Jesus. We can conceive of an era when honoring your parents, and keeping the sabbath, were aspects of worshiping God. The first five commandments, as Philo and Josephus list them, would at that time have balanced the second five reasonably well. And there may have been such a time. I allow as much but I doubt it.

If it was a mistake of mine not to accept "I am the Lord . . . Egypt" as a separate commandment, and if the sabbath was once a commemoration of the Creation, then there is another way that five commandments might be directed towards God and five towards our fellows. (i.) out of Egypt, (ii.) no other gods, (iii.) no images, (iv.) name in vain, (v.) sabbath, (vi.) parents, (vii.) killing, (viii.) adultery, (ix.) stealing, and (x.) witness. That would omit coveting; but coveting differs from the other ethical commandments in being an intent rather than a deed; coveting is the "near occasion of sin" with regard to stealing and perhaps adultery, though not with regard to killing or false witness; coveting could also have easily been a latecomer when the "out of Egypt" commandment was no longer given its due. That possibility too is worth considering; I myself would not argue on its behalf.

And neither the one arrangement of five against five, nor the other, can be maintained if the tablets are regarded as "written on both their sides" (Exodus 32.15). It would not be a neat division, ten commandments on four sides. So let us agree for the moment that the verse telling of the four sides was another latecomer, added after the commandments had become unreasonably diffuse. Before then, the commandments were spare and there were only two sides with five on each (either two stones written on one side each or one stone written on both sides). It may once have been like that, though there is no evidence it was.

What we *can* say is that Jesus did not think of the commandments as two sets of five any more than most of us do nowadays. Who is it that the ten pertain to? Some of them (other gods, image, name), to God; one (sabbath), to God perhaps in part but not entirely; one (parents), to God remotely; and some (kill, adultery, steal, witness) to our fellows; the last (covet) is an unsatisfactory minor version of a single one or two of the others (steal and adultery).

Let us ask again whether the Bible stories are not myths with truth in them, rather than uncorrupted histories. We think the commandments have put on weight with age when we see their swollen countenance—"he covereth his face with his fatness, and maketh collops of fat on his flanks" (Job 15.27). I would conjecture that *in conception* the list once comprised these ten brief, parallel negatives (the last being a summary, like Deuteronomy 27.26).[13]

1. Thou shalt not have any other god than the Lord.
2. Thou shalt not make unto thee any image of thy God.
3. Thou shalt not take the name of the Lord in vain.
4. Thou shalt not labor on the seventh day.
5. Thou shalt not harm thy parents.
6. Thou shalt not kill thy landsman.
7. Thou shalt not commit adultery.
8. Thou shalt not steal from thy landsman.
9. Thou shalt not bear false witness.
10. Thou shalt not even desire to do any of these things.

7. Is There a Large-Scale Design? Freedman argues in *Bible Review* that the commandments are broken successively in the books from Exodus through Kings. (Genesis is not taken account of because the commandments had not yet been delivered; "sin is not imputed when there is no law," Romans 5.13; Samuel and Kings are regarded as one book each; Ruth is not included seeing that in the Hebrew scriptures it comes later; and, in agreement with Jeremiah 7.9, the order is stealing, killing, adultery.) The passages are: *other gods*, Exodus 32.4 (the molten calf); *image*, Exodus 32.4 (again the molten calf); *the name in vain*, Leviticus 24.11 (a blasphemer); *sabbath*, Numbers 15.32–26 (a man gathering sticks); *father and mother*, Deuteronomy 21.18–21 (a rebellious son); *stealing*, Joshua 7.1 (of the accursed thing); *killing*, Judges 19.29 (of the concubine); *adultery*, 2 Samuel 11.4 (Bathsheba); and *false witness*, 1 Kings 21.13 (against Naboth); if to these is added *coveting*, 1 Kings 21.2 (of

Naboth's vineyard) as suggested in the following volume of *Bible Review* by the journal's editor, a doubling-up at the end will match the one at the beginning.

As a demurrer it could be said that the father-and-mother commandment is not actually broken in Deuteronomy 21.18–21. It is also true that the pattern is obscured (1) by the stealing or robbery by the men of Shechem (Judges 9.25), (2) by the killing of Abner, Ishbosheth, Uriah, Amasa, Elah, the prophets of Baal, and Zachariah (2 Samuel 3.27, 4.6–7, 12.9, 20.9–10, 1 Kings 16.10, 1 Kings 18.40, and 2 Kings 15.10), and (3) by the worship of other gods by Ahab (1 Kings 21.26). And Genesis remains a troubling background—with the thought of stealing in 44.1–12 (the cup found in Benjamin's sack), the killing in 4.8 (Cain and Abel), the adultery (or fornication) in 38.24 (of Tamar), and the multiple crimes in 27.22 (as Jacob deceives Isaac).

The Freedman idea is not tenable as things are, but might be tenable as they once were. It requires that the text was wrought with greater care than is now evident. Is the idea confirmed or opposed by the lists of the commandments in the New Testament? Three of the four lists are in the episode of the rich young ruler (Matthew 19.18–19, Mark 10.19, and Luke 18.20); one is in a pastoral letter (Romans 13.9). Only the ethical commandments are named, and they seem to be recalled casually. "Thou shalt not kill, commit adultery, steal, or bear false witness" are the core. To them Jesus adds "Honor thy father and thy mother," but St. Paul does not. Paul adds "Thou shalt not covet," but Jesus does not, though the idea weighs with him, for he tells the rich young ruler to give his goods to the poor (and in Mark he adds "Defraud not" as if he were remembering Leviticus 19.13). The roll is then completed, by Jesus (Matthew 19.19 only) and by Paul (Galatians 5.14), with "Love thy neighbor as thyself." Where are "Thou shalt have no other gods, nor worship an image, nor take the name of God in vain"? They are to be kept in mind but not necessarily spoken of; Jesus begins his list with the words that only God is good. The law summed up is twofold: remember God; love one another. If there is a pattern of the commandments in the books of law and history, neither Jesus nor Paul would seem to have been aware of it.

The names of Whitman (about a symmetry of episodes in the *Iliad*), Duckworth (about a golden ratio of paragraphs in the *Aeneid*), and Singleton (about the length of cantos in the *Divine Comedy*) come to mind. Their arguments are unworthy of the subjects; if the designs brought forward had been intended, they would have been more impressive, for the poets had a sense of form; by leading us to curiosities the scholars have done more harm than good. The Freedman idea about the breaking of the commandments in sequence is original, but whether it can be confirmed is one question, and whether it ennobles its subject is another.

There is also the occult science known (possibly from the Greek word for geometry) as gematria. The letters of the alphabet in Hebrew and Greek were used as numbers, and those of a name or other word could be added up. The "number of the beast" in Revelation (13.18), 666, is the sum of the Hebrew letters for Nero Caesar; that may be the answer or it may not; the like with Greek has been found in the Epistle of Barnabas; the meaning of 1290 and 1335 at the end of Daniel may also (I would guess) lurk in letters that add up to those figures. And the same for plene or defective spelling, that is, with or without the letters waw and yod (except that the door on that matter has been shut by James Barr). Such special effects usually do not bear scrutiny, but they are worth being alert to. One of the great lines in literature is "Amor condusse noi ad una morte" (*Inferno* 5.106, "Love led us to one death"), where the *amor* recurs in the last two words. Papasamba Hiob has told me that *la ilaha illa la* "there is no god but God" is only one of many powerful effects of sound in the Koran. So it could be that comparable secrets in the commandments are still waiting for someone to come upon them. The more research we do into the scriptures the better, but some studies are worthier than others, and the scholar should follow the advice of Hippocrates: above all, do no harm. I am unwilling that anyone should show me anything bizarre about "Man that is born of woman is of few days, and full of trouble."

8. Other ordinances, rare and common Besides the ten commandments there are heaven-sent ordinances. The most important among them may be the following. (1) "This is my covenant, which ye shall keep, between me and you and thy seed after thee; Every man child among you shall be circumcised" (Genesis 17.11, 17.26–27). (2) "Thou shalt not seethe a kid in his mother's milk" (Exodus 23.19, 34.26, Deuteronomy 14.21). (3) Nor eat of a beast that "cheweth the cud, but divideth not the hoof," such as the camel, nor of one that divideth the hoof but cheweth not the cud, such as the swine (Leviticus 11.4–7, Deuteronomy 14.6–8). (4) "Thou shalt not plow with an ox and an ass" nor "wear a garment of divers sorts, as of woolen and linen together" (Deuteronomy 22.10–11). Reasons can be found, but they may not be the original ones, and they may not be *religious* reasons.

For (1), the ordinance would seem to further health, both for the man and for the woman he enters. The operation may even be needed to repair the condition known as phimosis (one instance has to do with Maria Theresa, see Gray p. 82; for another, see Ackerley p. 104). There may though be a drawback: the physician Sir William Osler, with regard to before and after circumcision, spoke of putting on a stocking when it had been rolled up, in comparison with ramming your foot into it when it had not been. (A figure of speech for "closed" may also be relevant: "uncircumcised hearts," Leviticus 26.41; "their ear is uncircumcised, and they cannot hearken," Jeremiah 6.10; "stiff-necked and uncircumcised in heart and ears," Acts 7.51. And there may be an ethical reason why, contrary to the custom in Egypt, only males need to be circumcised: see Philo *Questions and Answers on Genesis* book 3, section 47.) In Islam circumcision is customary but is not enjoined by the Koran.

For (2), the idea might be of a ghastly symbolic irony in your furthering what you dread most. For (3), there may have been an awareness of trichinosis. For (4), a mixing of kinds may cause disharmony: an ox and an ass do not react alike, and different fabrics shrink differently.

There are other ordinances as well, such as "Thou shalt not remove thy neighbor's landmark" (Deuteronomy 19.14). What did Jesus think of all these supplements to the commandments? He never spoke of them, and his independence of the Mosaic ten, owing to their tyranny over judgment, may mean that to him the customs of Judaism were guidelines often to be erased. That is the subject now to be considered.

9. Whether absolute or conditional   Though Jesus prescribes the commandments to the rich young ruler, his attitude towards them is respectful rather than fearful. The two charges brought against him by his countrymen (John 5.18) were (1) that he blasphemed in claiming to know God on familiar terms, and (2) that he did not keep the sabbath (but healed on that day and encouraged the man he had healed to break the sabbath by taking up his bed). It might also have been charged (3) that Jesus did not honor his parents in Joseph and Mary. In these three matters he was lenient, honoring the commandments lightly; with respect to some others he was strict. Do not swear by the name of the Lord *or even by heaven or earth*; do not kill *or even be angry*; do not commit adultery *even in your heart*; do not steal or covet *or even heap up wealth*. How firmly then did Jesus regard the commandments as binding? It is not so much that he made them less stringent or more, and not merely that he replaced the bad deed with the bad wish. The difference is that a mindless obedience became a thoughtful one. Jesus was aware of the law but was governed by conscience.

The verse "because thou art lukewarm, and neither cold nor hot, I will spue thee out of my mouth" (Revelation 3.16) seems to say that an utter lack of character, or low commitment to any principle, is worse (or at least more contemptible) than being grand in felony, like Satan and the other morning stars. What was to be done with the lukewarm? "The heavens chased them out so as not to be less fair, nor does deep hell receive them, for (if it did) the wicked would have a certain glory over them" (*Inferno* 3.40–42). Is it not better to break the commandments with a smash than to bend them? Those are not the alternatives. The small thing is to follow the commandments without question. The large thing is to have them in mind as you decide what to do about the problem of the moment. Hot-or-cold, with-me-or-against-me action is not always the best; it may be brawling and bluster. The best action, as I understand the mind of Jesus (and as I would say for myself), comes from an awareness of all contingencies, with a readiness for heroism when that is warranted, but with an equal willingness to be thought lukewarm or a coward. As a set of negatives, the commandments of Exodus (and Deuteronomy), to Jesus, are more than borderlines; they are constraints; but they are not a stonewall imprisonment; they are a barbed-wire fence, sometimes to be broken through.

There may be moments when you will be inconsiderate of your parents (Luke 2.48), or angrily curse a living thing (Matthew 21.19 = Mark 11.14), or allow yourself a luxury (Matthew 26.11 = Mark 14.7), or work on the sabbath instead of on another day (Luke 6.9). The law of Moses was absolute in its utterance; it was not to be put aside for a greater good. *The law for Jesus is conditional, depending on how things are.* This I regard as the least well understood essential truth of Christianity. Many people are stricken with remorse when they should not be, for they did what seemed best even though it was against the letter. One person lives by the law further than is warranted; another knows that the law can do harm. The Bible is often turned to by a Christian in time of trouble, but it is not a book of answers. Jesus was not a rigorist but a realist.

Albrecht Alt brought into the usage of biblical scholars the terms *apodictic* and *casuistic* (from the Greek word *apodeik-numi* and the Latin word *casus*). The one is a law of God or by universal agreement, generally a complete prohibition, not depending on anything; the other does depend on things (the facts of the case) and the word *if* is stated or implied. An instance of the one, "Do not plant thistles in your neighbor's garden"; an instance of the other, "When you have made mischief, make threefold amends." Alt characterized the Hebraic commandments (and ordinances) as apodictic; he did not say (for it was not within his subject), but I would say, that Jesus regarded the ethical commandments as casuistic. The more ordinary terms are *absolute* and *conditional* as I have used them. The teaching of Jesus, a matter of profound change, was away from the one and towards the other.

The Sadducees opposed, the Pharisees favored, "the continuous interpretation and re-interpretation of the Law to meet changing circumstances" (Epstein). In that respect Jesus and the Pharisees were in accord, and he has been thought one of their number. He differed with them in not holding the law to be the primary authority. The Pharisees (he said) made long prayer and paid tithe of mint, but would devour widows' houses (Matthew 23.14–23). He favored the prayer and the tithe, but favored the widow even more. To Jesus the commandments were like proverbs: matters of wisdom and a regimen for everyday goodness. To the Pharisees the law was sovereign, to be understood anew from time to time, but never to be overruled. He was independent of the letter; they were servile before it. To him that was their moral undoing.

"Think not that I am come to destroy the law, or the prophets: I am not come to destroy, but to fulfill. For verily I say unto you, Till heaven and earth pass, one jot or one tittle shall in no wise pass from the law, till all be fulfilled. Whosoever therefore shall break one of these least commandments, and shall teach men so, he shall be called the least in the kingdom of heaven: but whosoever shall do and teach them, the same shall be called great in the kingdom of heaven. For I say unto you, That except your righteousness shall exceed the righteousness of the scribes and Pharisees, ye shall in no case enter into the kingdom of heaven" (Matthew 5.17–20). The passage is difficult in its parts; there may be blame upon the evangelist. The phrasing "whosoever shall break one of the least commandments . . . shall be called the least in heaven" seems at first to emphasize "the least . . . the least," as in "to whom little is forgiven, the same loveth little" (Luke 7.47); it would follow (falsely) that "whosoever shall break one of the great commandments shall be called great." And just how Jesus is to fulfill the law may be argued about; the sense (*pleroo*) is "fill to completion"; instead of being cancelled, the law is to be enlarged. Will not Jesus on the contrary diminish (rather than enlarge) the keep-the-sabbath and honor-thy-parents commandments, by at least a jot or a tittle? No, when we look to what is best all told, the sabbath will become a day more worthy of God than it was, and the honor to our parents will be greater. What Jesus would have us aim at is: righteousness from common goodness, not self-righteousness in accordance with directives.

As a set of ten the commandments are imperfect. In the gospels they are mainly a set of two. The first is "Thou shalt love the Lord thy God" (Deuteronomy 6.5); the other is "thou shalt love thy neighbor as thyself" (Leviticus 19.18). The two are fused as "Thou shalt love the Lord thy God . . . and thy neighbor as thyself" (Luke 10.27). What if you cannot love, try as you will? You need merely act as if you loved; even if genuine love does not become a part of your nature, you have done your best.

Between loving God and loving your neighbor, it is the latter, ethical commandment that Jesus changed, wanting his followers to be generous not just to those who might pay them back, but also to those who might bear malice against them. Here lies the essential difference from Judaism in the matter of behavior. Jesus has amended the "love thy neighbor as thyself" rule, and by so doing has created the ethical distinction of Christianity. To love your neighbor as yourself (when your neighbor is an ordinary member of your community whom you deal with every day) is *not enough*. The new rule, together with its limitations, is the subject of the next chapter.

II. The golden rule and the Jesus rule

Jesus was original not only in modifying the commandments but also in giving to his followers a new one, one harder to keep than all the ten put together. It is with the new commandment, "love one another," that the urgent questions arise. Did Jesus himself observe both the spirit and the letter? Can anyone obey the new commandment without withdrawing from the world? Is there a moral certainty about some things, or a moral uncertainty about everything? And is the new commandment useful in making laws for a society that has no single religious commitment?

1. How the gospels came down to us   As with the commandments, so with the gospels. The four accounts are out of harmony with each other, and each is an imperfect assemblage of fragments. Seemingly, (1) some of the materials used for the gospels were written, but (2) some were known only by word of mouth, (3) some matters were just now thought of by the evangelists themselves, and (4) some are the work of later scribes or revisers. The language of the gospels is Greek, but an Aramaic original can sometimes be traced. There are supplements, such as the Gospel of Thomas, the Sayings of Jesus, the Secret Gospel of Mark, and the Gospel of the Hebrews (see Cameron), but they do not affect what is here said about the four gospels that the church accepted. Nothing from the legends of other lands is worth taking account of.

The New Testament, like the Old Testament and Homer, is in part a small library of stories, some of them worldly, some strange. Again like the Old but here unlike Homer, the New

Testament is also a book of wisdom. The stories told by the evangelists are about Jesus, and the wise sayings are credited to him. Have they been well woven together, these stories and sayings of the gospels? They have been pieced together, not inwoven. They are an arrangement, not a composition.

There is a parable about laborers in a vineyard. Some are hired early in the morning and others throughout the day; when they are paid, it is first those who were hired the last, and then those hired the first; the payment is the same for them all, to the disgust of those who had worked the longest. The story is well told, and the moral might be, "Do not reckon up what you deserve, but do your job without envy." That is not the moral drawn. The final word, belonging to Jesus or perhaps to the householder, is twofold: (1) "the last shall be first, and the first last" and (2) "many be called, but few chosen" (Matthew 20.16). Are these conclusions satisfactory? The former of them is relevant to the parable, but teaches the wrong lesson from it; a more accurate lesson would be "the first and the last are treated alike at the end." The other conclusion does not have to do with the parable at all. The two sayings appear to have been ironical proverbs of the time. (The first and the last are also in Matthew 19.28–30 = Mark 10.29–31, Mark 9.35, and Luke 13.30, and the verse about the called and the chosen recurs as Matthew 22.14.) The evangelist has combined materials without thinking them through. What we gather as a general principle is that the gospels, even if somehow the work of God, are at least partly the work of man, and not always of man at his best.

It is the custom that a prisoner should be released (Matthew 27.15), and a choice is offered between Jesus (whose name is a compound of *the Lord* + *salvation*) and Barabbas (*son* + *father*); the chief priests and the elders persuade the multitude that the one to be released should be Barabbas. Again the story is well told, and again there are troubles. One is that a custom of releasing a prisoner is otherwise unknown. Another is that in some manuscripts Barabbas has "Jesus" as an additional name. If the story were about anyone else, we should glimpse a distortion, even a wholecloth fabrication. It seems to me that in an earlier telling, before there was any idea of a choice, the crowd clamored for Jesus (of Nazareth), calling him by his cultic name, "Son of the Father." *Release*, they said in Aramaic, *Barabbas!* That is (or may be) how things were, but the story—as with other folk memory, folktale, folk epic—was retold and rewritten (evidently) and changed beyond recognition. *The Song of Roland*, about an attack upon the rearguard of Charlemagne's army by a battalion of Saracens, is based on an actual happening, and does not even get the enemy right.[14] And from such a composite of history, legend, and creation, the teachings of Jesus are to be gathered. It is against this background that I would offer a sketch of the foreground, namely the way of the world, both how things are and then, if the teachings of Jesus prevail, how they may come to be.

2. *The iron rule: love of yourself*   Things grind against each other; "water-spouts have worn the stones of Troy"; a species displaces its rivals. In 1995 an ecologist walked into an area she knew in Canyonlands National Park, Utah. The natural grassland—"with needle grass, Indian rice grass, saltbush, and the occasional pinyon-juniper tree"—"had become overgrown with 2-foot-high Eurasian cheatgrass." "I was stunned," she says. "Now, we've lost this ecosystem forever." A few years earlier near Belgrade entered unwelcome the western corn rootworm. Into South Africa, from Europe or North America, has come a mite that infects honeybees. What will happen to the native flowers that the bees have been pollinating? (*Science* 17 September 1999, p. 1834). And within a species, when food is scarce, one fellow will be at odds with another. The exception is

that children are a part of the parent. What man of you, when so and so asks for bread, will give him a stone? As Jesus phrases the question, the needy person is not just anybody, but your son. If it were a stranger asking for bread, or even a friend, the matter would be in doubt. In times of famine you might give him the stone. That is the iron rule of competition or self-love. How is it to be softened?

As a curb upon its members, societies have enacted laws. A would-be felon is shackled by fear of what may be done to him. If there were no law, a man from the vermilion clan would kill one from the magenta clan, a magenta would kill in reprisal, and the bloodfeud would last till doomsday. With a system of law, crime is punished by the state and a predator becomes cautious. There is no longer any vengeance between the Montagues and the Capulets. A marauder nation is repressed by a league of nations.

A century ago French archaeologists found the three pieces of a stone pillar (now in the Louvre). On it we read the law code of Hammurabi, the ruler of Babylon around 1800 years before Jesus. The god Marduk had ordered the king to establish justice, and he obeyed with nearly three hundred statutes. What if a priestess opens an ale-house? She is to be burnt. What if a man accuses a priestess or a married woman and does not prove the accusation? He is to be flogged and half his head shaven. What if a woman, for love of another man, causes the death of her husband? Let her be impaled. What if a father, offended by his son, wishes to disinherit him? The son is to be forgiven for the first offense, but disinherited for the second. If a man puts out the eye or breaks the bone of a free man, he is to pay with his own eye or bone; if he so injures a slave, he is to pay half the price of the slave. If by making a deep incision a surgeon saves a man's life, or by opening a carbuncle saves his eye, he shall have ten shekels; if by making the incision he causes death, or by opening the carbuncle ruins the eye, he shall have his forehand cut off. If a builder has built a house that falls down and kills the householder's son, the builder's own son is to be put to death. (Statutes 110, 127, 153, 169, 196, 215, and 230 of *The Babylonian Laws*, edited by Driver.)

Some of the commandments and ordinances delivered to Moses have to do with God, some have to do with man, and for both kinds the penalties may be exact. For blasphemy a man is to be stoned (Leviticus 24.14, 1 Kings 21.10, see John 8.59, Acts 7.59). "Whosoever doeth any work in the sabbath day, he shall surely be put to death" (Exodus 31.15). "Every one that curseth his father or his mother," or commits adultery, shall also be put to death (Leviticus 20.9–10). If a man steals an ox or a sheep, and kills it or sells it, "he shall restore five oxen for an ox, and four sheep for a sheep"; if the animal is alive, the thief "shall restore double" (Exodus 22.1–4). And for crimes against the general welfare the penalty is also exact. If men fight and one injures the other with a stone or his fist, and if by and by the injured man "rise again, and walk abroad upon his staff, then shall he that smote him be quit: only he shall pay for the loss of his time, and shall cause him to be thoroughly healed" (Exodus 21.18).

The Hammurabi code and the Hebraic laws—ancient restraints upon primordial tendencies—are alike but different. They may or may not have had a common source. The similarity between them consists in the equal (or greater) compensation paid by a person who wrongs another. The distinction between them is the weight of the religious element. Under both, if every kind of wickedness is provided for, and if every legal refinement can be kept in mind, no one needs to have any natural decency at all. But if there are things not provided for, or if the nuances are numerous, you may want a basic principle. It is known as the golden rule.

3. The golden rule: love your neighbor   The basis for law in
many cultures, and the basis of good character, is fairness. It is a
matter of ethics, dealing with another person; but in Judaism and
Christianity there is the thought that God too will reward you
evenhandedly. Consider these texts:

1. "life for life, eye for eye, tooth for tooth" (Exodus 21.
   23–24)
2. "if the witness be a false witness, and hath testified falsely
   against his brother, then shall ye do unto him, as he had
   thought to have done unto his brother" (Deuteronomy 19.
   18–19)
3. "thou shalt love thy neighbor as thyself" (Leviticus 19.18,
   Matthew 19.19, 22.39, Mark 12.31, Luke 10.27, Romans
   13.9, Galatians 5.14, James 2.8; see also Leviticus 19.34)
4. "whatsoever ye would that men should do to you, do ye
   even so to them" (Matthew 7.12), "as ye would that men
   should do to you, do ye also to them likewise" (Luke 6.31)
5. "Do that to no man which thou hatest" (Tobit 4.15)
6. "He that hath pity upon the poor lendeth unto the Lord, and
   that which he hath given will he pay him again" (Proverbs
   19.17)
7. "thy Father which seeth in secret himself shall reward thee
   openly" (Matthew 6.4, see also 6.18)
8. "Forgive us our debts as we forgive our debtors" (Matthew
   6.12)
9. "with the same measure that ye mete withal it shall be
   measured to you again" (Luke 6.38)
10. "sell all that thou hast, and distribute unto the poor, and thou
    shalt have treasure in heaven" (Luke 18.22)

The first five enjoin like-for-like justice, called talion justice, or
retaliation. The last five may foresee evenness of recompense
from heaven. And mercy is not unbounded: "When men strive
together one with another, and the wife of the one draweth near

for to deliver her husband out of the hand of him that smiteth him, and putteth forth her hand, and taketh him by the secrets: then thou shalt cut off her hand, thine eye shall not pity her" (Deuteronomy 25.11–12).

The principle belongs to many cultures, though not to all. Essentially it is "do as you hope to be done to," variously phrased. The double negative form as in Tobit (the fifth in the list) is also the one in Confucius: "What I do not wish men to do to me, I also wish not to do to men" (*Analects* 5.11, 15.23). The general formula is known as *sensus communis* "common sense" and *jus naturalis* "natural law," but those terms are liable to misunderstanding; the formula is also known as reciprocity; but the right words for Western and Eastern thought are "the golden rule."

Not boundless, but basic generosity is the idea. My scout-master would sometimes ask his troop to say what good deed they had done that day (for there is the idea that a scout ought to do a good deed every day, just as heart patients are to take an aspirin every day; a better idea would be to do a good deed whenever the chance came along). The scoutmaster may have meant well, but his question, besides being unfriendly, brought us to lies, against the first part of the scout law. We did not *want* to lie, but under pressure we did. He was not following the golden rule, but it is hard to fault him, for he was merely thoughtless. To teach him a lesson, as Jesus when provoked might have done, we could have asked the scoutmaster what good deed *he* had done that day. Or—by the golden rule—we could have (1) said that our good deed was to be revealed to him in private, and then, in private, (2) told him that our good deed came in not causing him shame by asking him in public what good deed he had done.

If the golden rule is respected in heaven, why should Jacob, who did not honor his father but deceived him, and who by fraud stole from his brother, have been loved of the Lord? St. Paul, though he obscures the matter by speaking about mercy and compassion, allows that God, if not unrighteous, is at least willful and arbitrary (Romans 9.14). Since Jacob lived before the commandments had been given down, the Lord may have excused him on the principle that "sin is not imputed when there is no law" (Romans 5.13, phrased in the Nuremberg trials as *nullum crimen sine lege*). No, that cannot be why the Lord favored Jacob. For David, long after the commandments had been made known, committed adultery with Bathsheba and killed Uriah her husband by placing him in peril, and yet the Lord favored David too. "Wherefore do the wicked live, become old, yea, are mighty in power?" (Job 21.7). It could be that Jacob and David were forgiven; but why were they *rewarded*? How did they deserve the fortune that came to them? Is the answer that in their wickedness they did what the Lord intended? If all has been predestined, if to be upright is unavailing, if God is arbitrary, why follow his edicts? Jacob had the same culpable awareness as David did; both of them knew, and to a degree all people have known, of goodness; it was "written in their hearts" (Romans 2.15) before it was lettered in stone. How the histories of Jacob and David can be thought edifying is a mystery. We can only say that God knows of a worth not evident to us.

In the Homeric poems it is the mortals, not the gods, who are the nobler in ethics. Achilles burns the body of Andromache's father, giving glory to a foeman he had slain (*Iliad* 6.418): a fine thing to do. Athene tells lies to persuade Pandarus to break the truce (4.89–104) and Apollo loosens the breastplate of Patroclus (16.804): rotten things to do, even if necessary. As the audience and readers, we know what is fair or unfair; that the gods are exemplars never occurs to us; they are clearly no better than we are. Here lies a distinction between the Homeric tradition and the Hebraic one. In Homer there is no thought that heaven rewards the good; in the proverbs of scripture we are assured against appearances that it does. As everyone has always known, the Homeric view is the correct one; the Old Testament lessons, if there are any, cannot be understood.

The lives of the great biblical figures are one thing; the commandments are another; there is no reconciliation between them; a legalist like Paul will never convince a jury; discussion is futile. Whether God is righteous cannot be answered. The problem is not to be denied, but it is not to be undertaken. What we can say is that the Old Testament stories, like those of Homer, are interesting, and that they do not have a moral. Their being wholly independent of ethics is one of the great things about them as narratives. The golden rule is another matter; it is not for measuring Jacob and David by, but for other people to live by. The scriptural assurance that the good are rewarded by heaven, and the wicked punished, does not apply to the great, so far as we can see; it may apply to the ordinary, ourselves.

4. The Jesus rule: love of your enemy The law of mankind depends on appropriate reaction. If you do wrong, or have been wronged, what you may expect is amends, out-going or in-coming. So as to be fair, love your neighbor as yourself, and do as you would like to be done to. That is the golden rule, the sum of the ethical commandments. Did Jesus modify it in any mean-ingful way?

"Agree with thine adversary quickly" (Matthew 5.25), in the sermon on the mount, is a useful home truth: the "adver-sary" *antidikos* is your rival before a judge; the sense is "keep away from trouble." What then follows is also useful, though moral as well: do not exact an eye for an eye, but turn the other cheek, and go the second mile. And what comes after that, though still useful, is moral to the highest degree, and the grandest matter taught by Jesus: (5.43) Ye have heard that it hath been said, Thou shalt love thy neighbor, and hate thine enemy. (44) But I say unto you, Love your enemies, bless them that curse you, do good to them that hate you, and pray for them which despitefully use you, and persecute you; (45) that ye may be the children of your Father which is in heaven: for he maketh his sun to rise on the evil and on the good, and sendeth rain on the just and on the unjust. (7.12) Therefore all things whatsoever ye would that men should do to you, do ye even so to them: for this is the law and the prophets. (5.46) For if ye love them which love you, what reward have ye? do not even the publicans the same? (47) And if ye salute your brethren only, what do ye more than others? do not even the publicans so? (48) Be ye therefore perfect, even as your Father which is in heaven is perfect.

A verse that had wandered away (7.12, the golden rule) has been brought back.[15] The sense is: "(5.44) love even your enemies, (45) that you may be like God, who is kind to everyone, with his sunshine and rain; (7.12) in the same way be kind to everyone, for that is the sum of the teachings; (46) if you are kind only to those who are kind in return, who will admire you for that, seeing that the wicked do as much among themselves?" So reads the sermon on the mount, and so does the one on the plain, in Luke 6: (27) . . . Love your enemies . . . (28) bless them that curse you . . . (29) unto him that smiteth thee on the one cheek offer also the other . . . (30) . . . of him that taketh away thy goods ask them not again. (31) And as ye would that men should do to you, do ye also to them likewise. (32) For if ye love them which love you, what thank have ye? for sinners also love those that love them. (33) And if ye do good to them which do good to you, what thank have ye? for sinners also do even the same. (34) And if ye lend . . . what thank have ye? . . . (35) But love ye your enemies, and do good, and lend, hoping for nothing again; and your reward shall be great, and ye shall be the children of the

Highest: for he is kind unto the unthankful and to the evil. (36)
Be ye therefore merciful, as your Father also is merciful.[16]

With some words not expressed, the sense is again: "And
live by the golden rule with regard to *everyone*; for if you love
only those that love you, what thanks should you have for that?"
To Jesus, the golden rule, as understood or as followed in his
day—friend towards friend—is not enough. By making the rule
apply towards our enemies, both in the sermon on the mount and
in the one on the plain, he is changing a routine matter into one
of worth.

The rule "love your enemies" does not belong utterly,
uniquely to Jesus. The Stoic or Cynic philosopher Epictetus,
from slightly later in the first century, taught that when you are
being whipped you should love the floggers as a father or a
brother would. And such forbearance had been taught in Egypt
and Babylon and China (see Thiessen). Those other teachers
were theorists, though, not activists. They were inner-directed,
in search of personal well being. Jesus was outer-directed,
minded towards others. When he said (in effect) that we should
share the burden even of those intent upon our ruin, it was not a
private matter only but a public one as well.

What we might not see is the ethnic cast of the golden rule
in Judaism. "Thou shalt not avenge, nor bear any grudge against
the children of thy people, but thou shalt love thy neighbor as
thyself" (Leviticus 19.18). The Jews regarded themselves as the
chosen ones, living in a promised land; the Canaanites and all
others were outsiders, oppressors or fair game. In the saying
(quoted in Matthew 5.43, but not from the Old Testament)
"Thou shalt love thy neighbor, and hate thine enemy," *neighbor*
implies "fellow tribesman," and *enemy* means foreigner. War
was the normal course of events: in the cities afar off the men
should be killed and the women and children taken as spoils, but

in the cities near by not a breathing thing should be spared
(Deuteronomy 20.10–17). The counter-saying by Jesus "Love
your enemies, bless them that curse you" (Matthew 5.44) tells
us not merely to be friends with those we compete against in
everyday commerce, but to be fair even to those who worship in
some other way than we do, or whose blood may be different
from ours. As the Lord at first was thought the god of the Jews
only, so Jesus at times regarded himself as sent unto the lost
sheep of Israel only (Matthew 15.24–26, Mark 7.27). In "Love
your enemies" (Matthew 5, Luke 6) he is well-minded towards
all nations.

5. Whether the Jesus rule was of Hillel   Along with the *written* law—that is, the five books of Moses, or pentateuch—the
Pharisees (but not the Sadducees) believed in a *traditional* law.
Much of it was put into writing, a century or so after Jesus, in
the collections the *Mishnah* and the *Tosephta*. The two are
similar, but between them the *Mishnah*, compiled by Rabbi
Judah the Patriarch, is the one that prevailed. It consists of exact
regulations upon agriculture, festivals, marriage, injuries, ritual,
and purifications (it is here cited from the translation by Herbert
Danby).[17] After a few centuries more there came into writing two
voluminous commentaries on the *Mishnah*—the Babylonian
and the Jerusalem versions of the *Gemara* (the one here cited
is the Babylonian, in the Soncino edition).[18] The *Mishnah* and
the *Gemara* together are the *Talmud*,[19] and I have heard that
"the Bible is as water, the *Mishnah* as wine, and the *Gemara* as
spiced wine." The Talmud is to traditional Judaism as the New
Testament is to Christianity. The Old Testament was the parent
of both, but some of its traits went to the one daughter, and some
to the other.

The tractate "Aboth" from the *Mishnah*, begins by tracing
how the Law (the books of Moses + the traditional law) came to

be handed down from one generation to another. "Moses received the Law from Sinai and committed it to Joshua, and Joshua to the elders, and the elders to the Prophets, and the Prophets committed it to the men of the Great Synagogue"; by and by (the "Aboth" continues) the Law came to Hillel and Shammai, and then to Gamaliel. We have now reached New Testament times, for Gamaliel, who was a son or a grandson of Hillel's, became the teacher of St. Paul (Acts 40.22–23).

It is often told how Hillel, when most of us would have been provoked, replied with the double-negative form of the golden rule, as in Tobit and Confucius: Do not do to others what you would not have done to you (*Gemara* "Shabbat" 31a, p. 140). It is an admonition that *The Jewish Encyclopedia*, on Hillel, regards (in another double negative) as having been "not without its effect on the founder of Christianity." That is a matter worth confirming or denying. The culture was certainly one of making decisions by ancient wisdom. With a similar proverb Gamaliel rescued Peter and the other disciples by saying that if the break-away movement were of men it would fail, but if of God it would prevail no matter what (Acts 5.34–40). Could Hillel or Shammai or Gamaliel have been among the doctors that Jesus, as a boy, disputed with in the temple (Luke 2.48)? There is no telling about that. The question is, Did Hillel or the others (or anyone else) teach the golden rule to Jesus, as *The Jewish Encyclopedia* implies? One reason for saying no is that the idea of fairness was a commonplace in the Hebraic tradition: eye for eye (Exodus 21.24), love thy neighbor as thyself (Leviticus 19.18), He that hath pity upon the poor lendeth unto the Lord, and that which he hath given will he pay him again (Proverbs 19.17). Another reason to say no is that for Jesus the golden rule was not enough. It was not enough so long as it had to do only with your friends. The question to ask is whether Hillel or anyone else had regarded the golden rule as saying, "Love even your enemies."

An answer will be looked for in the *Mishnah* and the *Gemara*—
the summary of the Judaism from the few centuries following.
Either Hillel will appear to have taught the Jesus rule, or there
will be no clue that he did so.

There is no trace of concord, in the *Mishnah*, between the
Jews and the other nations. Just the opposite, for it is specified
that "If the ox of an Israelite gored the ox of a Gentile, the owner
is not culpable. But if the ox of a Gentile gored the ox of an
Israelite, whether it had been accounted harmless or an attested
danger, the owner must pay full damages" ("Baba Kamma"
4.3, p. 337). Our opinion on the matter is affected by which
group we belong to, the Israelites or the Gentiles—whence a
modern proverb about reparations, "That depends on whose ox
is being gored." And similarly: "A bill of divorce given under
compulsion is valid if it is ordered by an Israelitish court, but if
by a Gentile court it is invalid" ("Gittin" 9.8, p. 320); "If he
found lost property in the city and most of the people were
Gentiles, he need not proclaim it; if most of them were Israelites
he must proclaim it" ("Makshirin" 2.8, p. 760). I would accordingly gather that neither Hillel nor anyone else preceded Jesus
in applying the golden rule to the nations beyond.[20] The reform
sect of Jesus' followers and the mainline movement of Judaism
were at odds from the start and continued to diverge.

Not in the *Mishnah*, but in the *Gemara*, we find the
Noachian code, seven precepts that the Jews regarded as binding, not just upon themselves, but also upon everyone else. The
idea was, first, that God had issued (perhaps explicitly, perhaps
implicitly) rules for the whole of mankind descended from the
three sons of Noah, and, secondly, that to Moses on Sinai were
delivered the special rules for the chosen people, the tribe of
Shem. The rules for the peoples not chosen, the tribes of the
other two sons, Japheth and Ham, are these: (1) establish law
courts, (2–3) do not blaspheme or worship an idol, (4–6) do not

commit adultery, murder, or steal, and (7) do not taste the blood of a living creature (after Genesis 9.4). (The seven are listed in "Sanhedrin" 56a, p. 381, and are often referred to, but there is some variation—instead of the mandate to establish courts there is sometimes a prohibition against sorcery or against mating different species or grafting one tree onto another.) The first one of the seven, about the courts, enforces the others, especially upon the Gentiles. Is the code relevant to Jesus and Christianity? Jesus did not know of it, for when he speaks of the commandments, in advising the rich young ruler how to earn eternal life, it is not the Noachian seven he refers to, but the Mosaic ten (including false witness, not in the seven). And, if he *had* known of the code, he would have opposed it, partly because of its hostility to other nations, partly because he preferred conscience to legalities.

The *Gemara* also contains mention of the 613 things mandated or forbidden to a Jew. The number is not a sacred but a fanciful one; at its first mention ("Makkoth" 23b, p.169) it is said to equal the 365 days in the year (for the obligations) + the 248 bones in the body (for the things condemned); the first two of the 613 (the passage continues) were spoken by God; the 611 sum of the others is the total of the numerical values of the letters in the word *torah*. There was of course disputation, not about the number, but about the individual items. *The Jewish Encyclopedia* "Commandments" lists the 613 as Maimonides did, and it is now too late to quarrel. Mandate 187 is to destroy the seven Canaanite nations (see Deuteronomy 20.17), and 235 is to make the non-Hebrew slave serve forever (Leviticus 25.46). There is no trace of any teaching that resembles the Jesus rule to love your enemies. What the 613 teach is the contrary. And even matters that would seem remote from quarrels (such as the prohibition against tying a knot on the sabbath, or untying one, are apt to be imbued with harsh ethnic flavor, since a Jew may ask or hire a Gentile—known as a "sabbath Gentile"—to do things that he is wary of doing for himself. Joseph Lieberman is scrupulous about turning on the light on the sabbath, and there was a time when Albert Gore would do it for him (see *The Economist* 12 August 2000, p. 30). To bypass the law like that might not be righteous, though: "If a Gentile lighted a lamp an Israelite may make use of the light, but if he lighted it for the sake of the Israelite it is forbidden" (*Mishnah* "Shabbath" 16.8, p. 115). *The Jewish Encyclopedia* suggests the use of a golem.[21]

Not everyone, perhaps not anyone, can follow the golden rule without fail. In Judaism one limitation towards leniency is made explicitly, as in other traditions it may be made implicitly. Namely that you need consider only your landsmen. Do unto others (in your tribe) as you would like to be done to; love your neighbor (a member of your tribe) as yourself. The highest form of charity, to Maimonides, followed by Nahmanides, is "that of aiding an Israelite who has become impoverished" (see Ramban, p. 227). It is the golden rule within ethnic boundaries. In the teachings of Jesus the rule is changed so as to go beyond those boundaries. The golden rule to Jesus is a good thing; it is just not the best thing. It comes between the iron and the Jesus rule.

The term "Judeo-Christian" should not be applied to ethics. It is meaningless if not self-contradictory. What Jesus teaches in the sermon on the mount (or the plain) is to have fellow-feeling for your enemy. It is an ideal even further beyond us than the golden rule. As he had bidden others to do (Luke 6.29), he does pray for his enemies (seemingly in particular the foreigners by whose hand he was crucified), "Father, forgive them" (Luke 23.34), and Stephen, following his master, does the same (though with him it is his own people who are the enemies, Acts 7.60). Few other Christians—very few of those now on earth—have ever done the like. It is a failure in them, not a fault in their religion. That an Israeli of today, or of any other day, should pray for a Samaritan, or an Arab, is hardly compatible with any form of Judaism. That Catholics and Protestants should pray for each other (not for their conversion, but for their well being) would seem to be an element of the religion they hold in common, and likewise for Shia and Sunni Moslems. And is it not better for a Jew to act by Judaic teachings than for a Christian to honor but neglect the teaching of Jesus? Yes and no: it is better to keep a possible law than to break an impossible one, but an unattainable ideal is worth aiming at. Though loving is not a voluntary action, you can *wish* you loved your neighbor, even your enemy, and in time the wish may be granted. Whatever the thought in your heart, there is a model on how to behave, in the finest of the parables.

6. The parable of the Good Samaritan   In Mark (12.18–27), after talk between Jesus and the Sadducees about marriage in the afterlife, a scribe (*grammateus*, an expert in the law) asks him which of the commandments is the greatest. He answers, "thou shalt love the Lord thy God" and "shalt love thy neighbor as thyself" (verses 28–31). The scribe repeats the answer, Jesus commends him, and the subject changes to the messiah as the son of David. The ten commandments have been combined into two, the first being from Deuteronomy (6.4), the second from Leviticus (19.18). In Matthew (22.34–36), it is not a scribe but a Pharisee lawyer who asks which commandment is the great one. Jesus answers as in Mark, adding "On these two commandments hang all the law and the prophets"; and then the subject changes as in Mark. In Luke (10.25–28), a lawyer asks how to inherit eternal life, Jesus asks him in return what is written in the law, and the lawyer replies as Jesus had done in Matthew and Mark: love the Lord thy God, and thy neighbor as thyself. The answer is accepted, and then the lawyer asks, "And who is my neighbor?" (10.29). Matthew and Mark have (it would seem) been modified by Luke so as to prepare for the parable of the Good Samaritan. In the timeless story, here summed up, there are three matters that we today might fail to weigh properly: (1) Jesus is speaking not just to someone but to a lawyer (*nomikos*, "doctor of the Jewish law," as the Liddell and Scott dictionary defines the word for the New Testament); (2) the neighbor in the story is from a people with cause to bear ever-lasting hard feelings; and (3) those that Jesus is speaking to are acutely aware that to touch a dead body is forbidden.

A man traveling from Jerusalem to Jericho fell among thieves, who stripped him and left him half dead. A priest (Greek *hiereus*, Hebrew *kohen*) came that way, but passed by on the other side. And the same for a subpriest (Greek *leueites*, Hebrew *lewi*). But a Samaritan tended the man in need, and brought him to an inn, and gave the innkeeper money to care for him. Who was the neighbor? Jesus asks. It was the Samaritan, the lawyer agrees.

Those who hear the parable regard the Samaritans—their neighbors between Galilee and Judea—with contempt. "There be two manner of nations which my heart abhorreth, and the third is no nation: they that sit upon the mountain of Samaria, and they that dwell among the Philistines, and that foolish people that dwell in Shechem" (Ecclesiasticus 50:25). Jesus tells his disciples, "Go not into the way of the Gentiles, and into any city of the Samaritans enter ye not" (Matthew 10:5). Samaritans refuse Jesus because they see that he is bound for Jerusalem (Luke 9:53). A woman at a well says to Jesus, "How is it that thou, being a Jew, askest drink of me, which am a woman of Samaria? for the Jews have no dealings with the Samaritans" (John 4:9). Jesus is trading words with some of the Jews who do not believe in him, and, after he has said that the devil is their father, they say that he is the one with a devil and is a Samaritan besides (John 4:48). The Jews despise the

Samaritans, but the Samaritans have reason to curse the Jews, seeing that, just four generations earlier, the high priest John Hyrcanus of Judea, when he had captured Samaria, "effaced it entirely and left it to be swept away by the mountain torrents, for he dug beneath it until it fell into the beds of the torrents, and so removed all signs of its ever having been a city" (Josephus *Jewish Antiquities* 13.281, Loeb translation). Jesus has been challenged by the lawyer to define "neighbor"; his answer is not "the fellow next door," or "anyone at all, even one who has cause to hate you, as the Samaritans have"; it is really—from the viewpoint of the Samaritan—"anyone at all, even one you have cause to hate bitterly, such as the Jews."

If the wayfarers had been a Judean, a Benjamite, and a Reubenite, consider how much would have been lost. For those three are of a kind in a way that the kohen, the lewi, and the Samaritan are not. It is more as if, when a man has been stricken in Dublin, a Dominican and a Franciscan turn away, and then a Freemason cares for him; or as if in Smalltown U.S.A. a Presbyterian elder and a deacon turn away, but then the town drunk cares for him. That is, the *last* person you would expect is the one who has the generous heart. The contrast is not between knowing and doing, if to know the good is to do the good. The contrast is between (1) those who thought only of themselves and (2) the one who thought of another. And the story is the more powerful from the surprise. The Jews hearing Jesus could never on earth have looked for kindness from a *Samaritan*.

The moral of the Good Samaritan matter—as in the sermon on the plain (Luke 6.31–33) or the mount—is that the golden rule (as commonly understood) should not be an end striven towards, but one taken for granted and gone beyond. "Love your enemies . . . and pray for them which despitefully use you" (6.27–28). The parable says as much in another way; the lawyer agrees to it; and (because he speaks for the law) the matter can be

taken as established. There is now a new understanding of the
words "love thy neighbor as thyself." And Jesus does understand the words in that way; he loves his enemies—not just the
Jews who had clamored against him but also the Romans who
were executing him—and prays for them, "Father, forgive
them" (Luke 23.34). It is the greatest advancement in ethical
philosophy that there has ever been. In Judaism you are to love
your neighbor next door and bear enmity to the enemy to your
people. In Christianity—the Good Samaritan, the sermon on the
plain or the mount, and the words from the cross—you are to
love even your enemy as yourself. That is the first and foremost
lesson of the parable.

Among the laws of Judaism other than the ten commandments there is one against touching a dead body (Leviticus 5.3,
Numbers 5.2, 19.11). It is binding on any Jew or Samaritan but
especially binding on a priest. "Speak unto the priests the sons
of Aaron, and say unto them, There shall none be defiled for the
dead among his people" (Leviticus 21.1–4, Ezekiel 44.25). So
is there any blame upon the priest and the subpriest, the kohen
and the lewi, who passed by on the other side? They did what
their sense of right and wrong told them to; they were not wicked
but scrupulous; the man left for dead would have been a defile-
ment. The fault of callousness that might be imputed to the
kohen and the lewi should be laid instead on the regulation.
Once again the sense would have been different if the passers-by
had been different. What if they had been a Judean and a
Benjamite? The kohen and the lewi had less choice than a
Judean and a Benjamite, or a Sadducee and a Pharisee, would
have had. As things are, more surely than otherwise, the blame is
not upon those who turned away, but upon the law they obeyed.
The lawyer—in agreeing that the Samaritan was the one who
loved his neighbor as himself—gave assent that at times the
rules should not be followed mindlessly. That is the second

lesson of the parable, and it too has been accepted into law by one who has the right to do so.

The Jews once believed that every nation had its god, who was effective in his own territory and over his own people. They themselves with their god, the Lord, Yhwh, would wage war against the Moabites and *their* god, or against the Sidonians and theirs. By and by, however, the Jews came to think, or realize, that the Lord was the *only* god, and that his power was upon everyone everywhere, though the nation that had worshiped him from the beginning would always be his favorite. The entirety of that conception is within the cry "Hear, O Israel, the Lord our God, the Lord is One." The religion of Abraham, Isaac, and Jacob had become universal, but had not become evenhanded.

Jesus believed he had been sent as a reformer to the Jews alone, and that it was "not meet to take the children's bread, and to cast it to dogs" (Matthew 15.26). The Samaritans he may have regarded as nearly the *last* people you could expect to do the generous thing—the *very* last who would be good to a Jew. What he taught, then, was that you should be kind not just to a neighbor, but even to an enemy. That is the Jesus rule, the great commandment in ethics. And even a *Samaritan*—even one from a despised tribe, who has reason to hate your inwards—*may show you* how to follow the rule. The religion of Israel is here becoming evenhanded as well as universal. The teaching of Jesus has been thought (by Calvin and perhaps everyone) to be extended to the Gentiles only at the resurrection. It is really extended to them in this narrative. The Lord is now upon everyone equally.

7. Anti-Semitism and anti-Gentilism   The word anti-Semitism has come to mean animosity not against all the Semites but against the Jews only; anti-Gentilism is the animosity of the Jews against the other nations, some of them cousins of theirs, some foreign altogether. The two words, the two attitudes, are acid and alkali. The aim in this section is at a fair mention of both, through Old Testament times. Was it the iron, or the golden rule, that applied between Jew and Gentile? And what was the thought of those who, from the mount or the plain, heard about the good Samaritan?

After the Flood, Noah and his three sons—Shem, Ham the father of Canaan, and Japheth—went out from the ark. By and by it happened that Noah, drunk from the vineyard he had planted, became uncovered, so that Ham saw his nakedness. Shem and Japheth then walked backwards towards their father, so as not to look on him, and covered him with a garment. When he awoke he knew what had happened, and cursed Ham through Canaan. "Blessed be the Lord God of Shem; and Canaan shall be his servant. God shall enlarge Japheth, and he shall dwell in the tents of Shem; and Canaan shall be his servant" (Genesis 9.26–27). The narrative is a memorable one. It also has the authority of the admonition against uncovering the nakedness of your relatives (Leviticus 18.6–16; but I think the prohibition was against carnal knowledge in the skin rather than with the eyes). And there was an intent: to explain why the Lord gave to the Israelites the land of the Canaanites (Genesis 12.7, Psalms 105.11, 135.11, 1 Kings 9.20–21). It is a wonderful story, but not to everyone.

There follows a table of the nations descended from the three sons—a genealogy based (I believe) on: race, language, area, etymology, and enmity. The table is unreliable, disorderly, and incomplete. Among the matters worth mentioning are these: (1) the phrase "God shall enlarge Japheth" explains the name Japheth "widen, extend," just as the drunken sleep comments on the name Noah "rest." The sons and grandsons of Japheth are in truth extended, and they are of a kind with each other, being seemingly (or fancifully) the Cimmerians or Cymry, the Scythians, the Paphlagonians, the Phrygians, the Medes, the Ionians, the Cyprians, the Iberians, the Rhodians, the Cappadocians, and the Thracians. The word Gentiles is used for them (Genesis 10.5) as if for them alone, but that is happenstance, since everyone not a Jew (or a Samaritan or Galilean) is a Gentile. The line of Japheth might better be called the Aryans. Their contact with the Jews, when the passage is being written, in the eighth century before Jesus or not long afterwards, is remote rather than immediate; they are not really the enemy. (2) The name Ham means hot, and his line appears to include those who live in the hot lands of Ethiopia, Egypt, and Libya. The name Canaan means lowland and tells accordingly of those who live on the lowland west of the Jordan, rather than in the mountains to the east. It may also mean lowly and may in that way speak of the Canaanites as a people subjected. Among them are the inhabitants of Sidon, Babylon, Nineveh, Sodom, and Gomorrah (Genesis 10.10–19)— city states in contact with the Jews and hateful. (3) The Shem lineage is a fragment, seeing that, though the sons of Joktan are listed, those of his brother Peleg—including Abram (Abraham the father of Isaac and Ishmael)—are not. This last entry includes the Assyrians (10.22, but 10.11), but I believe that in the main it refers, or in its primary form referred, to the Jews only.

It may then be said in summary that the table of nations tells of the Jews and of two groups of foreigners. The word Gentile applies to both groups. The one is the farflung unintelligible tribe of Japheth. The other consists of the nearby tribes that the Jews knew to be closely related to themselves. These were the enemy: the oppressors or the destined to be oppressed. "O daughter of Babylon, who art to be destroyed; happy shall he be, that rewardeth thee as thou hast served us. Happy shall he be, that taketh and dasheth thy little ones against the stones" (Psalms 137.8–9). Research continues into the source of anti-Semitism; the ultimate source lies in pro-Semitism or anti-Gentilism. *The*

Economist (2 December 2000, p. 84) finds the stumbling block between Israel and the Palestinians today to be "that traditional Judaism espouses an exclusive morality that does not treat Jews and non-Jews alike." The Jew of Old Testament times and the Gentile bore a mutual enmity; the Jews followed the golden rule among themselves and the iron rule towards those who be-leaguered them; the Gentiles did the same; and if we find fault with these we must do so with those; the blame for anti-Semitism is partly upon the Jew, as that for anti-Gentilism is partly upon the non-Jew.[22] Jesus' teaching and also his behavior may be taken to heart. Was he not a pro-Semite, an anti-Gentile? Yes, at times his words are harsh: "It is not meet to take the children's bread and to cast it to dogs" (Matthew 15.26). And by the gospel account it was only after the resurrection that he directed that his message should be taken to all mankind. But his treatment of the Gentiles is fair, and the finest person he tells about is a Samaritan.

It will be asked whether Jewish writing on Jesus himself in the centuries following was moderate or immoderate. Some of the chief facts are: (1) nothing is said of Jesus in the *Mishnah* and little in the *Gemara*; (2) that little is disrespectful but not pas-sionate; (3) far more is said about Bar Cochba of a century later, who was by many accepted as the messiah, but who in the end did his people great harm; (4) not only are Jesus and his mother Miriam spoken of, in the *Gemara*, but also Magdala and prob-ably Nazareth; (5) Jesus is ordinarily called either ben Pandira or ben Stada, the Pandira and Stada being explained variously; (6) Jesus is said to have been put to death (without any involve-ment by the Romans) on the eve of the passover; (7) the method was by stoning or else by hanging (from a cross: see Acts 5.30, 10.39); (8) it is said that Jesus was a bastard; (9) his crime is said to have been sorcery; and (10) like all such he is said to deserve everlasting boiling in filth. In sum, the writing about Jesus is

moderate. It also seems the stuff of legend, heightened or reduced. I would accordingly regard *pandira* and *stada* as Greek
words misunderstood, the one *parthenos* "virgin," the other
anastasis "resurrection." The *ben Pandira* "son of the virgin"
agrees with (8) the bastardy. The *ben Stada* has borrowed a *b* to
supplement the *n* of *ana-stasis*, as if *ben* were warranted by *ben
Pandira*, and the resurrection agrees with (9) the magic.[23]

What matters here is that the *Gemara* does not, with regard
to Jesus, bear animosity against another race. It looks upon him,
from a distance and without perspective, not as a member of an
enemy nation, but as a Jew who had led his followers astray.
There is hardly any reason why a Gentile devoted to Jesus
should harbor ill feeling towards the thought of the early rabbis.
The grounds for hostility are in the Old Testament. The parable
of the Good Samaritan, telling against tribal animosity, was
timely in its day.

8. Jesus as man made no promises   The first teaching that
Jesus gave from the mount (Matthew 5) or the plain (Luke 6)
was the beatitudes: "Blessed are the poor in spirit: for theirs is
the kingdom of heaven. Blessed are they that mourn: for they
shall be comforted. Blessed are the meek: for they shall inherit
the earth. Blessed are they which do hunger and thirst after
righteousness: for they shall be filled. Blessed are the merciful:
for they shall obtain mercy. Blessed are the pure in heart: for
they shall see God . . . ." By the text these words were said in
Greek; they may actually have been said in Aramaic. In form
and by heritage they are Hebraic, after the manner of the psal-
mists and the prophets. " . . . to comfort all that mourn" (Isaiah
61.2), "meek shall inherit the earth" (Psalms 37.11), "They shall
not hunger nor thirst" (Isaiah 49.10), "Blessed is he that consid-
ereth the poor" (Psalms 41.1), "He that hath clean hands, and a
pure heart" (Psalms 24.4). The beatitudes are traditional utter-

ances. The mighty lines that Jesus speaks from the mount are the words of an orator in a grand lineage from the stone age onwards.

It is not only a matter of language but also one of thought. For it had been said in many ways that the good would be given their due: "his leaf also shall not wither; and whatsoever he doeth shall prosper" (Psalms 1.3); "their inheritance shall be for ever" (Psalms 37.18); "The righteous shall flourish like the palm tree" (Psalms 92.12); "He that covereth his sins shall not prosper" (Proverbs 28.15); "Cast thy bread upon the waters: for thou shalt find it after many days" (Ecclesiastes 11.1).

One problem is whether such warming words from the psalms or the wisdom literature should be taken as truths. No, they are not guarantees of short-term success. They are joyful anticipations of what may befall by and by. They cause us to look forward cheerfully to justice in the long run. Some of them are deathlessly eloquent renderings of such wishful thoughts as: Sooner or later I will get what I deserve! or: Someday you will pay for that! Another problem is whether the verses apply mainly to this life or to the next. They apply in large part to the one we are in the midst of, but might apply to the one we may be going towards.

It is the same with the beatitudes (especially as in the first evangelist). They speak of a happiness not far away, and give us hope of a happiness afterwards. The words should not be construed like a legal document; they are a work of art; their beauty is a part of them. But they do tell of a reward on earth and perhaps of one later as well ("shall be for ever"). And likewise with the later part of the sermon (especially as in the third evangelist), following the admonition to love your enemy. There will be favor to the person who does that. The favor is not sworn to in solemn affirmation, but is offered as a prospect, both for the here-and-now and for the there-and-then. A recompense is in store for those who can keep the golden rule as the Jesus rule. They will be the children of the Highest (Luke 6.35) on earth or in heaven or both. Do not judge and you will not be judged; forgive for the sake of being forgiven. Be charitable and the charity will be repaid: "Give, and it shall be given unto you; good measure, pressed down, and shaken together, and running over, shall men give into your bosom. For with the same measure that ye mete withal it shall be measured to you again" (Luke 6.38).

Is it true? It has truth. The world will be better if we love our enemies. We may trust in that idea even if we do not look for the benefit to come at once or to ourselves. It is a profound reading of human nature by common sense, this idea of what will follow if we are kind against our instinct. It is not a matter of holiness—of obeying a statute for its own sake. On the contrary the teaching to be charitable is practical and everyday. The words are not those of a god but of a worldly wise man. What should we say, though, if the good we cast on the water does not return? Was the promise of repayment an empty one? If we think there was a binding contract, we took the words in the wrong way. We will have the same recompense as the Good Samaritan had. There is no reason to think that prosperity came to him for his goodness; there *is* reason to think he was forever afterwards prosperous in his heart. And as for the present life so for a future one; the idea of a just payment may be harbored and fostered. Jesus teaches a gospel to be kept in mind as we labor and eat our daily bread.

9. Turn the other cheek sometimes David and Jonathan "kissed one another, and wept one with another, until David exceeded" (1 Samuel 20.41, see 2 Samuel 1.26). And "there was leaning on Jesus' bosom one of his disciples, whom Jesus loved" (John 13.23, see 21.20; we wish it had been Mary Magdalene). Such intense love as that is not enjoined. What the gospels teach on the whole, and what St. Paul at times would advise, is just that competition should yield to diffuse generosity towards one and all. It is an absolute matter, and yet it is conditional also, for there are limits.

"Ye have heard that it hath been said, An eye for an eye, and a tooth for a tooth; but I say unto you, That ye resist not evil: but whosoever shall smite thee on thy right cheek, turn to him the other also" (Matthew 5.38–39). Still, turning the other cheek does not mean accepting martyrdom; to go a second mile does not mean trudging day after day; when you must give up your coat, give up your sweater as well, but keep your shoes if you can. Should the rich young ruler bestow *all* his goods to feed the poor? That was an idea, not a directive. How can we be sure? Why is it certain that the young ruler was being only told to share, not to impoverish himself for the kingdom of heaven? The answer is from the entirety of Jesus' teaching and from his life.

He prayed for his enemies as he had bidden others to do. But were his deeds *always* in agreement with his words? He said not to resist evil, but it was with muscle and bravado, not with lovingkindness, that he overthrew the tables of the money-changers when they had made the house of prayer into a den of thieves (Matthew 21.12–13, Mark 11.15–17, Luke 19.45–46). It might be that he meant you should allow pummeling upon your-self but not permit dishonor to God. No, that would be a devious meaning, not his characteristic straight talk. A better harmo-nizing of turn-the-other-cheek with expel-the-moneychangers would be: "Endure as much as you can, and more than others would, but do not hold back, even from mayhem, when the end requires it." And besides the moneychangers we remember (1) that in spite of telling the ruler to give his wealth to the poor, Jesus allowed the spikenard to be lavished on himself (Matthew 26.7–11, Mark 14.3–7), (2) that in spite of saying that anger was next door to killing, he was unreasonably angry against the fig tree (Matthew 21.19, Mark 11.14), and (3) that in spite of reproving those who did not honor their parents, he did not honor those whom he regarded as his own parents, but even (twice) called his mother *Woman* (John 2.4, 19.26), and said you had to hate your parents before you could follow him (Luke 14.26). So is his own commandment unbounded and immutable? No, it is negotiable. Jesus would not have us be more scrupulously obedient to his law than can be found in human nature. We are to follow the new commandment, to love one another, as we follow the old ones. There are times when we ought *not* to love our neighbor as ourselves. We should be as generous as our heart allows, and then even more than that, but we should not be generous when the need is for a strong arm, and we need not be austere to the brink of starvation.

If a precept is at odds with good judgment, which one should be prevail? To follow a precept is a fundamentalist—Judaic, Christian, Islamic—reliance on custom and authority. To use your own judgment shows independence and willfulness. Did Moses and Jesus and Mohammed impose the law rigidly? Jesus did not; to him the world was more than a foreground; it had a background also, with one thing hidden behind another. It is not fundamentalism, but reformation, that he spoke of, whether from the mount (Matthew, chapters 5–7) or from the plain (Luke 6.17–48). Those who had been following a path were told to find their own way. Mindless obedience was no longer to be given to a hallowed principle, for there was a consideration more telling than obedience. Namely *heed the circumstances*.

Those who heard Jesus were astonished, "for he taught them as one having authority, and not as the scribes" (Matthew 7.29). Were those listeners comparing him with copyists? No, the scribes were learned men who discussed the law—the five books of Moses—and reached decisions by deciding how most justly the words were to be construed. A thousand years later— to Maimonides, Thomas Aquinas, and Dante—Aristotle would be cited as the absolute authority on whatever he had written about (which is: everything except the Hebraic law). In the time of Jesus, on the matter What is pleasing to God? the sages were the authority, and they were cited for the weight of their names. "Rabbi so and so said such and such" was how the scribes argued. The method of Jesus was a contrary one, and the crowd "were astonished," for he himself was the authority; the sages were not to be remembered; even scripture itself was not binding when it was plainly wrong.

The narrative about the Good Samaritan could be thought to teach the golden rule. No, that rule had been accepted long before, and Jesus regarded it as not enough. The moral of the story, or one of the morals, is the Jesus rule: love not only your fellow man but even your enemy. The Samaritan was kind to a member of a tribe that held his own in contempt. And, since to touch a dead body was forbidden, a second moral is that at times the law should not be kept. Like the priest and the subpriest, the Samaritan would have passed by on the other side, doing the righteous thing, except that he thought the man in the road might need help, a weightier consideration than an ordinance. Not just the first moral, but the second as well, is confirmed by the lawyer in the framework and confirmed again by Jesus in his other teachings and way of life. A healer may heal on the sabbath, and a man healed may take up his bed and walk (John 5:18, 5:11); a farmer ought to pull an ox or an ass out of a pit on the sabbath (Luke 14.5, see 13:15); when you must be about the business of your Father in heaven, you need not be thoughtful of your father and mother on earth (Luke 2.49). The commandments and ordinances are worth keeping, but there are exceptions. You should not turn the other cheek if there is some reason not to.

I once asked Peter Johnson whether he was a Christian, and his reply was, "I try to be." That seemed to me inadequate, for (in accordance with Romans 9.31–32, rather than James 2.17–24) I was thinking of faith, not of works. I now would say that to follow Jesus requires constant trying—constant effort to act by his words, and by his example of doing the right thing, to the right degree, no matter what the law might say. If you want to do a favor to Jesus, do one to the dregs of society (Matthew 25.40), and be kind even to those who will pay you in vipers; but no more than that. There is such a thing as tough love; suffer only so much and then reply. The Jesus rule is not always gentle; it includes that tough love.

The follower of Jesus will, like a judge or a jury hearing arguments of lawyers, weigh many factors. In the *Oresteia* the furies and Apollo compete for Orestes, who had killed his mother as a religious duty, and the action may be regarded as taking place in his mind. A Christian must similarly debate within himself. To do the right thing ethically, as a Christian, you must sometimes think hard. The specially Christian matter is fellowship with your foeman as well as with your comrade, but the circumstances matter, and by the example of the master you should go only so far.

The fascinating thing about Jesus, as a teacher and not as a savior, is the utterly unlooked-for character of what he says and does. His kingdom may be of another world, but in this world too he is at home. You cannot serve both God and Mammon, but all the same you should "make to yourselves friends of the mammon of unrighteousness" (Luke 16.9) and "Render to Caesar the things that are Caesar's" (Mark 12.17, Matthew 22.21, Luke 20.25). Jesus regarded the absolutes given to Moses (keep the sabbath, honor your parents) as conditionals. *And the same for his own commandment*, to love one another. When the present moment urged him to the contrary (moneychangers, fig tree, spikenard), he acted from the moment. By his example Christians have not only the liberty, but the duty, to do what seems right *all things considered*. It is not Christian to follow either Moses (and the ten commandments), or Jesus (and his new commandment), in unthinking servitude to the letter alone. The Christian thing is, first, to love not just your fellows but, so far as you can, your enemies as well, and secondly to be aware of what is needed right now. The Good Samaritan did the entirety of this Christian thing; the stricken wayfarer was seemingly a traditional enemy, and a regulation against pollution had to be disregarded.

Jesus added "love thy neighbor as thyself" to the set of ethical commandments (Matthew 19.19) and thought it second only to "love the Lord thy God." On those two (he believed) hung "all the law and the prophets" (Matthew 22.37–40, see Mark 12.30). What then was the sense of the saying "the law and the prophets were until John" (Luke 16.16)? With the Baptist (as reformer and as preparer of the way for Jesus), and then with Jesus himself, there was a new era, but in what way? It is not a matter of wonders but one of ethics, for the whole passage has to do with behavior. Jesus is laying the law aside, favoring instead a simple rule to do the right thing with a generous intent. He continues to heed the old commandments as guidelines, but he does not obey them mindlessly.

Paul too held that you may eat all things or only herbs, just as you wish, and that you may regard all days as alike or honor one above the others (Romans 14.2–5); what matters is a good heart. To him "love thy neighbor" supplemented the ethical commandments (Romans 13.9) and fulfilled all the law (Galatians 5.14, see James 2.8). To the contrary he does say, "if thine enemy hunger, feed him . . . for in so doing thou shalt heap coals of fire on his head" (Romans 12.19–20), the idea being not that you will cause your enemy to feel shame as intense as fire, but that you will further his perdition (Deuteronomy 32.35 and elsewhere). Paul is being harsher than Jesus would have been. The lesson of the sermon on the mount (or the plain) has reached him nevertheless. He does not entirely heed the Jesus rule of loving your enemy, but at least he has forsaken the iron rule. In two thousand years we have not taken the new commandment any closer to heart. Paul is also charitable in asking no more of us than our character allows: "as much as lieth in you, live peaceably with all men" (Romans 12.18); Jesus himself did not invariably do more than that. To Paul as to his savior, the new commandment, to love one another, even your enemy, is conditional on what the situation calls for. We are to love within human nature. It is not the whole truth that a Christian, in contrast with a Jew or a Muslim, ought to turn the other cheek. The truth is that a Christian ought to turn the other cheek *when that seems the right thing to do.* And the *whole* truth, by the teaching of Jesus, is that everyone should behave like that— Christian, Jew, Muslim, or freethinker.

Did Jesus and Paul assume that our neighbor was from our tribe? The story of the Good Samaritan indicates that for Jesus, at the moment of his telling, there was no such limitation, and for Paul the apostle to the Gentiles there was none, either. Jesus was mindful of himself as a Jew with a mission to the Jews and not to anyone else (though he was from Galilee, "Galilee of the Gentiles"); and Paul knew himself as a "Hebrew of Hebrews" (Philippians 3.5); but both spoke of kindness to all, not just loyalty to the tribe or nation. The special covenant with one people is being put aside in favor of a covenant with everyone. The old ethical commandments are being subsumed within a new commandment, namely the Jesus rule to love your neighbor as far as you can, even when he despitefully uses you.

We are left with this: (1) the sermon on the mount (or the plain) is wise in the behavior of mankind, and gives advice about how to live on earth; (2) it is not a matter of religion, like offering your first sheaf to the Lord, or your firstborn child to Moloch; (3) it is in the idiom of the ancient poets and continues their thought; (4) it is rhetoric and not certainties; it opens prospects rather than makes promises; but (5) it admonishes us, more explicitly than anything before had done, to love our enemies; (6) we are to be like the Samaritan in the parable. As far as the iron is from the golden rule, so far is the golden from the Jesus rule.

How are these matters to be applied? I will offer some discussion, beginning with How would Jesus safeguard us in this world? and continuing with What forms of killing would he regard as murder? and When would he think murder the right thing to do?

10. Some commandments for our time What follows is a set of regulations for today. They are meant to agree with the teaching of Jesus in its two essential respects: be generous even to your opponent, and take account of all conditions. I argue as an American to Americans, but my aim is at agreement by every-one. Thou shalt not:

1. be the bully among nations (p. 91)
2. prolong life as a burden (p. 100)
3. enlarge thy estate beyond bounds (p. 104)
4. prefer one race to another (p. 106)
5. scorn woman or man for the other (p. 109)
6. legislate with intrusion (p. 110)
7. breed beyond thy number (p. 112)
8. burden the earth with pollution (p. 113)
9. deprive a creature of dignity (p. 114)
10. play thy role without honor (p. 115)

The church father Origen, who interpreted all other texts as figures of speech, understood in its literal sense that some "have made themselves eunuchs for the kingdom of heaven's sake"

(Matthew 19.12), and then cut away the manhood from his body (Eusebius *Ecclesiastical History* book 6, paragraph 8). The prohibition against seething a kid in his mother's milk (Exodus 23.19) can be regarded as forbidding an alma mater to hire her own graduates as faculty. That is, directives are liable to misunderstanding. I will accordingly comment on the ten commandments-for-our-time.

#1 Thou shalt not be the bully among nations.
The iron rule is a tendency inborn; the golden rule is learned; the Jesus rule is thought about. Should we take up arms on behalf of the just to overcome the unjust? Against courage-and-force stand cowardice-and-kindness: those are the alternatives under the iron rule. The best choice under the golden rule, and certainly under the Jesus rule, is not between them. It is for kindness plus courage, rather than for force on the one hand, or cowardice on the other.

To kill an intruder, or a nation of invaders, is the right thing to do, or may be. The waging of war abroad, openly or in disguise, for land or booty, is another matter. The term used in the 19th century to justify the massacre of the Indians (that is, the Native Americans) was "manifest destiny"—defined in the *Dictionary of American English* as "national recklessness as to right or wrong." It is an inheritance that we of the present day cannot renounce. A promise not to do the like again is empty; if we wish to make remote amends, some reparations can be worked out.

The same obligation is now seen to weigh down the Canadians, a people that most of us in the United States regard as a less rowdy version of ourselves. Urged by their federal government, the four main churches of Canada undertook to educate the children of the Cree and the other tribes. The youngsters were forcibly removed from their homes and not allowed to speak their native languages. There was general brutality by the overseers with a good deal of sexual exploitation. The mind-set of the professional Christians was no more from Jesus than from his adversary. (See the New York *Times* 2 November 2000, p.1, and *The Economist* 28 October 2000, p. 36.)

What is to be said about Joshua, the Benjamite who broke the Canaanites? It depends on whose ox is being gored. He was a great commander and in other ways a great leader. The trumpets and the shouting and the collapse of the walls of Jericho make a wonderful story, and the Lord was an ally with hailstones (Joshua 10.11). But not all that was well by the iron rule would be well by the Jesus rule. And about Jesus himself, whose name is a form of Joshua, what do we say of the wars under the sign of the cross? The campaigns to win the Holy Land from the infidels were moments of devotion. The fortress at Rhodes, with its threefold circumvallation and its engraven coats of arms, was it not a place of holy belligerence? Did not the Knights of the Hospital and the Knights Templars represent the highest ideals of Christian manliness? The crusader fought for the kingdom of heaven on earth and the remission of sins. "He might butcher all day, till he waded ankle-deep in blood, and then at nightfall kneel, sobbing for very joy, at the altar of the Sepulchre—for was hc not red from the winepress of the Lord?" (Barker). That earlier time belonged to the Lord of hosts, the Lord mighty in battle, with Michael the militant archangel. We can admire Joshua and his namesake Jesus as warlords by the iron rule, but by the Jesus rule there is more to regret.

Orthodox (that is, Eastern) Christianity—the religion of the present-day Serbs—held sway in Constantinople, now by contraction known as Istanbul. Catholic (that is, Western) Christianity—the religion of the present-day Croats—sacked the city in 1204, put its people to the sword, and carried off its treasure. Christian sects are mutually unChristian, as Gibbon remarks at the close of chapter 16 of his *Decline and Fall.*

Islam—the religion of the present-day Bosnians—then devastated the city in 1453. Had God subjugated a Greek Christ beneath a Roman one, and then beneath the Prophet? As an aftermath, the Serbs, Croats, and Bosnians of today bear towards one another an animosity that is centuries old and likely to last forever. Christianity, Judaism, and Islam pray against each other to the God they have in common.

After World War II, there were fewer hard feelings harbored by the Japanese and the Germans, because they were aware of having brought their injury upon themselves, and for a moment the United States was well liked by much of the world. Since then we have made enemies heaven knows where not. Even if our undertakings had been successful, the glory could not be compared to the heartache. We bomb armament stores, hospitals, market places, and wedding parties, and the deaths among noncombatants are put down as "collateral damage." A city section of once busy hotels and shops is made to look like a giant sand castle (Dworzak). The peacemakers among us are not called the children of God. The golden rule is not kept on earth except in a drawer of sayings. The Jesus rule is unspoken by pastors.

We assume that there will not be any revenge if the Shah, banished by his countrymen, is admitted to the United States for medical treatment. Then we are angry when in reprisal hostages are taken, and the newscaster Walter Cronkheit eggs on our commander-in-chief by saying every evening on the CBS news, "this is the 213th (or whatever) day of the captivity of Americans in Iran." With a successful Israeli raid on Uganda in mind as a model, we mount a futile raid on Iran and multiply the enmity against us. We then sell arms to Iran in its war with Iraq, to earn dollars to oppose a warlord in Nicaragua who is thought to be bringing drugs into the United States; it is a hidden action and comes to light with disgrace to all who had a share in it. When

Iraq, which had been deprived by the British of a seaport, considers action upon a contested strip of Kuwait, Margaret Tutweiler says for our State department that we have no ties with Kuwait, and April Glaspie our ambassador to Iraq says the same the next day to Saddam Hussein. So why is it surprising that he should decide to fuse the two countries into one, as Hitler did with Austria? From Saudi Arabia we then work destruction with gunpowder and chemicals, and intensify not only the enmity of all Iraqis, but also the resentment of all other Arabs, and even of all the billion Muslims on earth (see Hilsman). It was a war contrary to the Monroe doctrine ("stay out of our hemisphere").

It was also in the eyes of the wealthy entrepreneur Osama bin Laden a desecration of holy Arabia, the land of Mecca and Medina. Why had we set at naught the religious scruples of Islam? In his heart and mind, with his treasury, and from his experience in furthering the Afghan resistance to Russia, bin Laden became our chief enemy (other than ourselves) and the schoolmaster in modern sabotage. In a strike at Afghanistan and Sudan in 1998 President Clinton called him the preeminent organizer and financier of international terrorism. And on September the eleventh, 2001, the Twin Towers were brought down by his remote hand (see Jacquard among others). We demolished Afghanistan in reprisal. Was that not a triumph in getting even? It was an inflicting of starvation and general misery to no avail. The bin Laden friends and confederates, known as al Qaeda "the Base," are regrouping. United States Senators say we must clean out every cubbyhole of malice against us. But what forceful thing are we to do against terrorism, that tactic whereby the unequal makes himself equal?[24]

In war you need not fight as your enemy thinks you will. Napoleon was the master on the battlefield; the Russian general Kutuzov defeated him by retreating. After the battle of Borodino, seventy miles away, Napoleon entered Moscow and awaited a surrender (such as Robert E. Lee would make to Ulysses S. Grant). Instead he found the city abandoned and in flames. There was no food and winter would be coming on. Bewildered at the broken promise of glory, the army could only return home, through Borodino again, now a cemetery of forty thousand Russian and thirty thousand French unburied dead. All along the way to the fatherland Cossacks slashed, shot, and shelled them from the rear and from ambush, and it is a question whether they died more from assault or starvation or cold. In another time Xerxes expected to destroy the Greek fleet at Salamis, near Athens. Themistocles let the word be given, falsely, that he would try to escape by night. The Persians wore themselves out rowing to close all the waterways. And then at dawn, not as if in rout but with a shout of hurrah, the Greeks attacked. The Persian ships in front gave way, crashing into those behind them, and the enormous armament was its own undoing. Ruin for the invincible Xerxes as there would be for Napoleon. Are there lessons of history? One is that the underdog may better you in a manner unlooked for. Why say that he is unfair or dishonorable? You have been outwitted and your strength was an illusion.

So with what arms are we to overcome the terrorist? Not every question has a satisfactory answer, and this is one of those that do not. There are no effective arms or tactics. The hydra, if you cut off her head, would put out two in its place, and from each of them, if you cut them off, would come two more. That is how the weed of enmity is propagated. It is a fact that was known to him who spoke from the mount and the plain. It is unknown to those who command us today. And how are the blindness and the silence of the clergy to be understood? The United Methodists, the denomination of President George W. Bush, have declared themselves against our national bellicosity and are the exception. Is the President alert when his minister gives a sermon against American policy? And where are the

other sects of Christianity? The Jesus rule, which is to be for-
bearing and generous, would have us do the opposite of what we
are doing.

Like the Germany and Japan of over half a century ago, we
bring about our own ruin by causing world-wide animosity. We
have weapons of mass destruction, but deny them to others; the
others do not want to be denied. Few nations today can overkill,
but tomorrow is at hand. Hard feeling festers until it is ripe and
then the pod bursts. Our leaders forget that as science and
engineering develop so does the art of war. The worst is yet to
come. (1) Our communications systems are delicately strung
haywire. Every day hackers and vandals make trouble to exercise their skills; if marauders were to blame, our e-mail and
telephone lines would be frozen from overloading, radio and
television would be needles of static, financial accounts would
be erased, supplies of food and fuel would be discontinued. No
one could find out what to do (see Specter). (2) Against epi-
demics brought about by an enemy there are no safeguards.
Within living memory most Americans had been immune to
smallpox, but when that contagious scourge had been eradi-
cated, except for one storage bin in the United States and one in
Russia, the vaccinating of children was given up; a master
criminal could now take most of the young people away before
our bureaucracy supplied the doses. Anthrax is easily available
and is the fright of the moment. Most deadly of all would be a
creation of genetic engineering, which no one could cope with.
(3) Our skyscrapers have proven to be an easy target; all the rest
will be easy too. Our press and federal reports, as if laying plans
to aid our enemies, locate the Achilles heels, as numerous as the
breasts of Astarte, one among them being a decommissioned
power station in Maine: "if a tenth of 1% of the spent fuel's
radiation were released into the air it would produce lethal doses
over 1,000 square miles," and would be a menace for ten thou-

sand years, as *The Economist*, 22 December 2001, p. 26, says simply. *Science News*, 19 January 2002, p. 39, has a map showing the proposed national long-term depository for nuclear waste. Why was it necessary to tell the world? As past masters at ruination we are the instructor, and our enemies say, "The villainy you teach me I will execute." We think about defense, and that is sensible; we should also invest in good will and earn moral respect; "these ought ye to have done, and not to leave the other undone."

When the time comes, perhaps next year if not this one, we shall be with the Babylon of Nebuchadnezzar, the Nineveh of Sargon, and the Lydia of Croesus. To avert the doomday, apply the Jesus rule, the nth degree of the golden rule. Let us resolve as a country to treat others as we should like to be treated, not with force but with friendliness. Let us do good works, with no thought of return, to Iraq and Iran, Korea, Libya and Cuba, and everywhere else on earth, just for the sake of being neighborly, like the Good Samaritan.

How is the Jesus rule to be applied between the Israelis and the Palestinians? It could be that we Americans should pass by on the other side, like the priest and the subpriest in the parable. If we want to make things better there are these matters to consider. (1) In fellow-feeling for their suffering the United Nations defined a homeland for the Jews after the Second World War; those who had been living in that land were displaced by international law; their resentment was not a matter of grave concern to anyone else. (2) Aid was and still is being given to Israel by the United States; the amount is now three billion dollars a year, two thirds of it for armaments. (3) Israel has become a prosperous limited democracy of six million people (limited because the Israeli Jews have property rights that the million other Israeli citizens do not); the nations next door are less modern oligarchic or autocratic Arab states with an aggregate population more than twenty times as large (prominent among them are Egypt, Saudi Arabia, Syria, and Iraq); reasonably nearby are non-Arab but Muslim states of over half a billion all told (chiefly Turkey, Iran, Afghanistan, Uzbekistan, Pakistan, Bangladesh, Indonesia, and Malaysia). (4) The animosity is as great as ever; Israel has weaponry and fifty years of American commitments; some of the Muslim states have oil. (5) Israel is occupying certain territory that the United Nations regards as belonging to the Palestinians, some of whom have been blasting themselves to kingdom come, taking as many Israelis with them as they can. (6) Crown prince Abdullah of Saudi Arabia has made proposals for peace: the Arab countries are to recognize Israel; the Palestinians are to have a state of their own with a capital in East Jerusalem; and there is be no more terrorism; it is a dream that may come true or may give way to nightmare.

Where does morality lie for Israel? Where in our own conflicts does it lie for us? There is an answer in the refusal of 100 Israeli army reservists to serve in the West Bank and Gaza Strip because of the policy towards "dominating, expelling, starving and humiliating an entire people" (the New York *Times*, 2 February 2002, p. A1). Since Judaism was founded on a claim of special favor, those reservists are of most unusual humanity. What shall we say as an evenhanded referee in the region? We should say what our former President Jimmy Carter does in his open letter "America Can Persuade Israel to Make a Just Peace" (the New York *Times*, 21 April 2002, Op-Ed page); he is a born-again Christian by profession of faith; he may be a sermon-on-the-mount Christian as well. The American Protestant religious right, to the contrary, holds that the Jews, because they were given a promise by heaven, do have an ultimate title to the land of Canaan, and that the Israelis are accordingly to be supported without limit. It is as if some of the dogs (in the words of

Matthew 15.26, Mark 7.27) were guarding the children's bread. To my mind that view is against the teachings of Jesus from the mount (and the plain) and in the parable of the Good Samaritan— that we should regard everyone else, even an adversary, as no less worthy than ourselves. And similarly it was against those teachings that both houses of Congress passed, overwhelmingly, a resolution in favor of Israel (2 May 2002), as if taking sides regardless and forgiving wrongs in advance. And as for Palestine so for all the other regions where our country is involved. For surely we too are bent upon "dominating, expelling, starving, and humiliating" anyone who opposes us anywhere, even though most of our leaders are nominal Christians, who might have been expected to heed what Jesus said.

Some will argue that morality may not be practical. No, morality *is* practical, and the immoral impractical. The iron rule is leading to ever greater ruin. If the ongoing enmity between Israel and the Palestinians is enlarged by further brutality, then in time, when the lands rich in oil agree upon a federation, Islam will surely overcome the "Jews and crusaders" against whom bin Laden declared his jihad. The Jesus rule is the one to follow. I believe that we and the Israelis ought to help the helpless. We may not be able to *love* our enemies, but we can at least be generous to them without considering what the past has been. Terrorism against America and Israel will not end at once; the bitterness towards us will not soon be sweetened; for a while we shall have to suffer with patience. The brawlers will call us poltroons, and to bear such taunts will take courage, but that is the path to survival. Those we turn to for reports on how the war is going should not be the generals but the day-laborers of the Peace Corps. The way for the United States to weaken al Qaeda, and the way for Israel to empty pockets of Arab animosity, is to do the contrary of what we and they have been doing. Can you hope for longterm peace when you cut off your neighbor's water to parch his animals and wither his groves? That lacks the common sense, the insight into humanity, of the sermon on the mount and the plain. The matter is not an absolute one; Jesus was not an absolutist; kindness has its limits; nothing is sure to succeed; but the right course is to suffer some things without retaliating.

Ireland is an island of two countries, one of them mainly Catholic, the other partly Catholic, partly Protestant. The atheists among them are said to be of two kinds: Catholic atheists and Protestant atheists. The rather long-ago history is of oppressed Celts, Catholic in Ireland though not in Scotland or Wales, and oppressing Protestant Anglo-Saxons. Every now and then a secret society of Catholics will harm the Protestants, or the other way around, and then the debt will be repaid. But for fifty-one weeks a year the place strikes an American as peaceful. Another pair of countries uneasily divided by religion is the Subcontinent: India is mainly Hindu or secular but has a large Muslim minority; Pakistan is Muslim with many Hindus. Sometimes the one or the other will take up arms against his brother; Kashmir is a mostly Muslim province of India, and a cause of rage among Pakistani religious malcontents. The matter to be kept in mind is that both India and Pakistan have nuclear weapons. Is it possible that either would use them? All reasonable people everywhere say no. Warriors and their commanders are apt to be unreasonable, though; so time will tell. At the moment, the Subcontinent and Ireland are schools in which the Jesus rule, or its likeness, may be a part of the curriculum.

#2 Thou shalt not prolong life as a burden.
Is murder ever justified? We must be careful not to provoke a quarrel over the question. The matters to be spoken about are (1) assassination, (2) suicide, (3) euthanasia, and (4) abortion. Many people have decided and will not be budged. The thought here is that you ought not to decide once and for all. Weigh

whether you would act from hate, or for justice, or with affection. And heed the circumstances just as you do when deciding whether to break the sabbath or to disobey your parents. A primary issue for ethics is whether existence is desirable or not. "A good name is better than precious ointment; and the day of death than the day of one's birth" (Ecclesiastes 7.1). The school of Hillel and the school of Shammai disputed on the matter, the one holding it better for a man to have been created than not, the other holding the contrary. After two years and a half they came to agreement: It would be better for a man not to have been created, but once he *has* been created let him look to his deeds (*Gemara* "Erubin" 23b). It was a question calling for wisdom, and the decision was a wise one. It follows indirectly that a right to life is no greater than a right to death. Are you depriving people of a good thing, or are you doing them a favor, when you take their existence from them? And, in taking from them their existence, how have you affected everybody else? May not a good on the one hand be overbalanced by a bad on the other? The issues have to be weighed in every instance, for the answers are conditional. As in following Jesus you should love your enemy though within reason, so with Hillel and Shammai you should appraise a life for its effect upon others. What makes killing acceptable, and sometimes a deed for the better?

assassination The philosophical position known as eudaemonism holds that the greatest sum of good comes from the greatest sum of happiness. The greatest evil is the contrary sum. Not all lives are of equal value here below. The person loved is worth more to the world, if other things are equal, than the person hated. The one who makes things better is worth more than the one who makes them worse. To assassinate a Hitler or a Stalin may be a work for the good. The successor is of course likely to be even more dreadful; the people hoped for a gentler rule after the death of Solomon, but Jereboam told them, "My little finger shall be thicker than my father's loins." The question though is whether, either by ancient or by modern law, an assassination would be justified. In accord with what Jesus teaches on other matters, the commandment against killing is to be kept or not, depending on the circumstances. If there is a better formula than "harm (or sin) = suffering (or loss)," it should be followed instead, but I do not believe there is one. We the superpower America are to foresee the results and then to act on the moment; the trouble is that we generally see only a short way and make things worse.

suicide It is held here, first (with Jesus), that you should follow not a book but warmth of human feeling, and, secondly (with the schools of Hillel and Shammai after they had come to agreement), that you should value not existence but its quality. When your life is grievous to yourself or to others or both, then like Ahithophel and Cato you have the right to bring it to a close. Would that be weak or strong, infamous or noble? It would be, as many things are, all of these. Would it be hateful to God? Those who believe that yes, it might be, may withhold their hand as Hamlet did (3.1.80–90). The thought here is that sometimes suicide is best. If you can take a life on the battlefield, can you not more justifiably take your own? Those who argue to the contrary may be unqualified to judge. For why should a happy person decide for one who is not? Why should those in well-being talk of patience to those in agony? If harm is measured by suffering, in the matter of warfare, it may be so measured in the matter of suicide; the harm can be in staying alive.

euthanasia Have you the right to kill someone whose life is a burden to him? Or should you prolong life against nature? Are you furthering God's will or opposing it? Why should you engage in torture by keeping a person sentient at all costs? In this matter there is no question of whether the soul of the afflicted is put in peril. The question is whether you have the right to help a person leave a vale of tears. What should you do with a child born imperfect? Some say blasphemously that God has made a mistake and aim at making repairs as well as they can. When a child was born in ancient Sparta, "the elders of the tribes officially examined the infant, and if it was well-built and sturdy, they ordered the father to rear it, and assigned it one of the nine thousand lots of land; but if it was ill-born and deformed, they sent it to the so-called Put-away, a chasm-like place at the foot of Mount Taygetus, in the conviction that the life of that which nature had not well equipped at the very beginning for health and strength, was of no advantage either to itself or the state" (Plutarch, "Life of Lycurgus" 16, Loeb translation). Euthanasia for the imperfect newborn, the subject of Pernick's *The Black Stork*, is a matter I am unwilling to hear or read about. My own strongly held view is that you ought to end a life with kindness if it will have more pain than joy. For many of the elderly, euthanasia is an escape just as obviously. Because he was generous but tough, and given to perfect healing, I believe that Jesus thought the same.

abortion Some hold it to be wrong, and call it murder, to end a life hardly begun. The new person cannot of course be called innocent, since by instinct humanity is ruthless, and also since, if St. Augustine is right, we have been corrupted with *total depravity* (a theological term) in the original sin of our first parents. But suppose that the new person has the capability of replacing the iron rule with the golden and at length with the Jesus rule. Hippocrates the father of physicians forbade his followers to take a life in the womb, but God (so to speak) to the contrary, as if favoring the ancient Spartans, aborts many pregnancies through miscarriage. For mankind to bring about an abortion is wrong, but it is a wrong to measure against other wrongs; it may be the least bad among them. If our wish is not for existence but for an existence of quality, then the unborn child has not always been deprived of a thing worth having.

On all these matters—abortion, euthanasia, suicide, assassination—there is the question of sin. My own view is that if you are guided by love rather than by law, you will have the heart to overcome your reluctance. The Jesus rule with its amendment is that you should be kind within limits.

#3 Thou shalt not enlarge thy estate beyond bounds. Some people are far wealthier than others. Job was blessed in children and rich in animals both before the wager and afterwards, and the Lord was more than willing that he should be. But prosperity as a condition that an ordinary worker can reasonably plan for is characteristic of capitalism. And that is a system belonging to the West; the ethical ideals of the East, and the class structure, were unfriendly towards it. After the Reformation there was the Lutheran idea that every man had a calling (Beruf) at which he should labor six days a week; there was also the Calvinistic idea that those predestined to heaven would prosper on earth; and essential to both was free thought. The countries where the edicts of the counter-Reformation Council of Trent were followed lost their supremacy. The Jews, as a guest people specially protected in some countries, amassed wealth by lending money to strangers while preserving loyalty to themselves. Those are powerful conclusions by Max Weber, wholly sound so far as I can tell. Extract the religious and racial elements from them and the residue is much of the ingrained American attitude of today.

Is it ethical that some of us should have almost immeasurably greater prosperity than our fellows? It is in accord with the natural world. We look back upon critical moments in our lives, some of them fortunate and some to our regret. At an early time certain bacteria took up residence within our own and many another species; we (that is, our intestines) as the landlord, and the bacterium as the tenant, did things for each other; in time the mutual benefit became so great that neither could do without the other. A point of no return had been passed; if the relationship turned out to be for the worse, too bad! amends could no longer be made. Fish use sight in finding food, and if the sight of one fellow is dim, he ventures into deeper water, where his cousins have not gone, for why should they? why stub your fin by swimming in the dark? But to that fellow of dim sight it all looks the same, and the food is more plentiful in the depths, for it has never been taken. He finds a mate like himself down there; their progeny have still dimmer sight and venture into water deeper yet. After many generations the school is blind and at home in the bottom of the sea. There can never be recovery of eyesight; competition would prevent it; and similarly for every creature in every habitat. The wasps can do things that human beings cannot, and there is no way back to the stage where we and they were a being that could develop either in the one way or in the other. Certain steps that our grandparents took (such as mating with a cruel person, or one with a crooked face, or one with peculiar skills), and steps that we ourselves have taken (to migrate, to change our kind of work, to sign on for the duration, to marry into wealth), may affect our whole lives, to our delight or disgust.

It happens—from talent, endeavor, inherited advantage, and chance—that some of us heap up riches. Our lot does not correspond well to our goodness of character. The more fortunate among us think they deserve their hoard; the less fortunate tend to be envious. It is as if a player had gained an advantage and then without sportsmanship had crushed his opponent. You and I ought to be generous; but by what amount? That is a meaningful question, and there is no telling: one answer is "sell all that thou hast, and distribute unto the poor" (Luke 18.22,

Matthew 19.21, Mark 10.21), and that is good for a ruler to keep
in mind, though not to follow mindlessly, seeing that "ye have
the poor always with you" (Matthew 26.11, Mark 14.7, John
12.8); "half of my goods I give to the poor" (Luke 19.8) might
be a commendable portion. The last two of the prohibitions
among the 613 laws upon Jewry are against "The possession by
a king of an excessive number of horses and wives, or of an
unduly large quantity of silver and gold."

The state ought to help us with our generosity. Some sharing of assets is a matter of morality; some leveling should be
done by law. Charitable contributions ought to be (as they are)
encouraged by the income-tax system; perpetual ownership
ought to be (as to a degree it has been) prevented by estate taxes.
Alms on a large scale from one who can spare them, whether it
is a person or a nation, ought to be one of the ethical things
commanded for our time.

#4 Thou shalt not prefer one tribe to another.
Is racism absolutely wicked? *The Merchant of Venice* rests on
the verse "unto a stranger thou mayest lend upon usury; but unto
thy brother thou shalt not lend upon usury" (Deuteronomy
23.30). Here was license for a Jew at the time of Shakespeare to
lend upon interest to a Christian; a Christian was forbidden by
canon law from doing so. Shylock is a cruel, piteous, comic
figure ("I will have my bond"; "hath not a Jew eyes?"; "O my
ducats! O my daughter! O my ducats!"). Antonio had called him
cutthroat dog and spat upon his Jewish gabardine (1.3.107–8).
The speech beginning "The quality of mercy is not strained"
(4.1.187) seemingly contrasts justice (the Old Testament) with
mercy (the New), but in the play as a whole the Jew is no more
hateful than the Christian, and at the end the marriage of a
Jewish girl to a Christian boy is what we wanted. It is a play
about the worth of the Jesus rule.

If miscegenation is what we wanted in *The Merchant*, is it a sure solution? It is easier with similars than with opposites. In *Othello* the racial difference is profound: "an old black ram is tupping your white ewe" (1.1.88–9). Desdemona says she "saw Othello's visage in his mind" (1.3.253), which means that his eloquence made her blind; it is as if he were penniless and she said, "I summed Othello's riches in his mind." But the mixing does not acually occur; the marriage is never consummated. The wedding night in Act 1 is interrupted, and so is the postponed wedding night in Act 2. The wedding sheets, which by the Moorish custom would have been the "ocular proof" of Desdemona's virginity ("Lay on my bed my wedding sheets," 4.2.104; "I have laid those sheets you bade me on the bed," 4.3.21), are never stained with the blood shed in the loss of innocence. There is no coming together of the races and the end is tragical.

Miscegenation in the United States is common between Jew and Gentile and not rare between blacks and whites. Many of us are something like mainly German or Jewish but a quarter Italian (or an eighth African, or three sixteenths Native American or Pacific or Subcontinental Asian, or whatever). After a while in the melting pot we may become one human race. That is centuries away, though. At present we are not a smooth amalgam of mercury, iron, bismuth, and antimony, but a salad bowl of cabbage, endive, and spinach. Among some of us there are feelings of ethnic brotherhood, and to a degree that is all right, though it leads into temptation. Should there be *quotas* for every activity: so much spinach, so much endive? Should colleges have wobbly admission standards, for the sake of variety in the salad? The races are no more equally able to do a given task than individual people are (I myself rank last as a sprinter or gymnast or musician or artist). Nations as well as persons compete, and, so long as they do so by the golden rule, it is well. Brutal competition—as with the slogan "manifest destiny"—is damnable, but benign competition among subpopulations, in farming or in business, is just fine. If you want weight-lifters or architects, and if the best ones belong to a particular ethnic group, there is no harm in allowing that group to excel, so long as all is fair in the trials. Why should Walloons, Zulus, Aztecs, Uzbecs, Malays, Slovenes, Egyptians, and Basques have their proportional place in carpentry and seafaring? Should every twentieth person on American football teams be of Chinese racial origin?

There are however two special qualifications. The first is spoken of by James Goldsmith in *The Trap*. If you want everyone to be loyal to the state and obedient to the laws, you must find for everyone a role. There is less sedition and thievery when everyone is earning a livelihood. In a peaceable kingdom the strong do not flex their muscles. Apply that to the ethnic groupings. If the green race can do a job but the blue race can do it better, and if the blue race can also do everything else better, it may be sensible, as well as humane, to give the job to the green race. Secondly, to encourage racial and other cultural groups to do things they have not done before, so as to increase their self-respect, they may be given a measure of affirmative action, by the state or by individual philanthropists. But the measure should be a moderate one, and perhaps temporary, so that success will not be blighted by thoughts of favoritism.

Various races regard themselves as superior. To be a citizen of Japan you must be of Japanese descent. The word for the Eskimos in their own language is "the men," implying weakness in all others. I have spoken against anti-Gentilism as the photographic negative of anti-Semitism. What I admire is represented by Abraham Geiger, the founder of the Reform movement in Judaism, who labored mightily, as the chief rabbi of Berlin four generations ago, to make the culture—race, religion, customs—of his ancestors more benign to others. His theses about Jesus, the Pharisees, and the Sadducees, and about the Christian repression of medieval Jewish theology, do seem to me unfounded and unfriendly. But against the belief that the Jews had special rights as the chosen people, he thought they should regard themselves as equal to Gentiles, neither more nor less, and that they should be loyal to their country of residence rather than to any ancient kingdom of Zion. (Circumcision and the dietary laws he regarded as matters of choice.) Do not such ideas rank in originality with those of Luther and Calvin? They are also what Jesus, in the parable of the Good Samaritan, was asking for.[25]

#5 Thou shalt not scorn man or woman for the other.
The premise is that as a person, and also as a citizen, you ought to treat men and women fairly, though again you ought to accept, with moderate patience, that others may not. And you ought to favor a degree of affirmative action, but not favor balance or quotas. The sexes differ; not many women, perhaps because they lack the y chromosome, perhaps not, are on death row; fewer women than men, possibly but not certainly for cultural reasons, excel in mathematics. All the same, society should offer to women what it does not withhold from men. Some change in status has already been wrought, and with it the Bible has become old-fashioned. In Genesis (2.18) woman (*ishah*) is made for man (*ish*), which sounds reasonable, for the one word comes from the other (in Hebrew and English, but not in Greek or Latin, nor in French or German; the Norwegian *kjerring* and *kar* must be admired). There is subjugation, though, not equality. After woman eats of the forbidden fruit and man does as well, she is told that he shall rule over her (3.16). The adultery commandment is broken only if the woman is married; if a married man comes into an unmarried woman, it is merely fornication. The covet commandment regards the woman as property; nothing is said against a woman's wishing she had her

neighbor's husband. Jesus chose twelve men to be his followers; St. Paul would have a woman "learn in silence" and not teach or usurp authority over the man (1 Timothy 2.11–12). God is addressed as a father (not a mother) and as "he" (not "she"); God also has a son (not a daughter). In its customs and theology Christianity began at a time when those things were acceptable. They are not acceptable now, and accordingly the entirety of New Testament theology—like the entirety of Old Testament law (because of its ethnic character)—will be set aside as a guide for life today. It is true that Christianity is no harsher to women than Judaism is, and not so harsh as Islam, but it is unfair all the same. The view taken here is that the Jesus rule, more than any other aspect of biblical theology or law, would serve to lessen animosity about gender and race, and would accordingly be for the better. Biblical antifeminism and anti-Gentilism are not to be regarded as aspects of eternal truth. The teaching on the mount and the plain, the highest form of the golden rule, *is* an eternal truth, so far as we can penetrate into the nature of things.

#6 Thou shalt not legislate with intrusion.

The first of two matters here to be spoken of is the law in the United States against the possession and distribution of narcotics (marijuana, cocaine, heroin, LSD, amphetamines). There used to be a constitutional amendment against the use of alcohol (beer, wine, gin, whiskey), and until it was repealed the consequence was the enrichment of crime lords. Nowadays narcotics are outlawed and alcohol merely regulated, even though the experts agree that alcohol is the greater problem to society. We are in danger of drunk drivers, not of drivers in a narcotic haze. Alcohol and drugs ought to be treated alike: either both should be permitted, for the sake of consistency, or neither should. The next-best solution would be to change things about: outlaw alcohol once again, but end the penalties against narcotics. At present we give permission for the larger menace but forbid the lesser one. What would happen if narcotics were cheap and commerce in them no longer a crime? The rest of us would be safer: 80% of what addicts pay for drugs "is financed by crime, mainly mugging, burglary, robbery, shoplifting, and car theft" (*The Economist*, 12 January 2002, p. 51). And besides, a million prisoners in our penitentiaries (that is, half of them) would be outside in the labor force, adding money to the commonweal rather than taking from it. We would like anyone who lives in our country to be loyal rather than hostile; so why do we imprison those who only want to be left alone with their pain-killers? If a giant step would be too daring for us, let a small one be taken to see what would happen: let marijuana become as available as beer is. The next step would be to make cocaine and heroin as available as gin and whiskey are. The question is not whether the government ought to encourage anyone to escape from life. The question is whether, at great cost to everyone else, anyone should be prevented from escaping.

The second of the two matters here addressed is whether sexual behavior between people who know better (if it is better) ought to be condoned or condemned. Some countries other than ours look the other way, and we might do the same, so long as no one is damaged. The Roman historian Tacitus (of a few decades after Jesus) was impressed at the customs of Germany, where a woman would have carnal knowledge of only one man in her lifetime, and a man of only one woman. In our day of wide-spread disease, that system seems commendable. But the Rome of Tacitus, with its legal prostitution, was satisfactory too, practically speaking; and where prostitution is legal today its medical dangers have been guarded against. On behalf of those among us who are drawn to their own sex, mention must be made of the Theban "sacred band" *hieros lochos*. It was a contingent of three hundred men, pairs of lovers, each man of whom wished above all that his partner should think well of him. Philip of Macedon, the enemy commander, when afterwards he surveyed them dead, burst into tears at their heroism (Plutarch *Pelopidas* paragraph 18). Love between man and man or woman and woman, though unnatural as not furthering the race, is natural as being multicultural and untaught (the best author on the subject is still John Addington Symonds). If you condemn the union of man with man because you take your morals from St. Paul (1 Corinthians 6.9–10), do you share his view that women are unfit to be teachers? The thought here is that the state ought to protect, not interfere with, those whose behavior in affection or desire has the bent heaven gave them. The predator or corrupter, though, even if a Socrates, is among the last we should forgive.

#7 Thou shalt not breed beyond thy number.

Life is easier and character may be nobler if the number of children is not greater than resources can provide for. The New York *Times* (8 March 2002, p. 1) reports of an Afghan who was forced to sell a son for wheat. Overpopulation is a problem for all the earth, though not everywhere with the same severity. The solution is not that one country should absorb another through immigration, but that one country should be an example for another, to be admired or shunned. The words "beyond thy number" (in this section's title) do not say what the number may be. In some lands a man and a woman should (if they like and if their wish is granted) have two children; in some, a single child only; in some, three children or more. What follows here will not be theoretical, but practical, and it will be for the United States (which now has a large enough population, though of course we could crowd more closely together). One proposal: for the 1st child there is a large tax deduction; if a second child is born, the deduction for the first is kept, but there is no additional deduction; if a third child is born, the deduction for the first is lost; for the fourth and each additional child, there is a payment due. And another proposal: the state offers, at no cost, comfortable retirement homes (1) for single persons 80 years old, and (2) for partners of that age who have been together for ten years and do not have more than one living capable child (if they have more than one the children shall pay towards the costs of the home). These two proposals would encourage the wealthy and fit, more than the poor and infirm, to have children. The proposals are accordingly discriminatory; but are they unjust? The wealthy are entitled to pay for more grandiose mansions and garments, and more costly legal advice, than the poor are able to do; so there is no unusual reason why the wealthy should not, at their own expense, be entitled to support a larger brood of heirs. Why should the state not further evolution towards self-sufficiency?

What should the wealthy do for the destitute? Give them alms but also help them to help themselves. That is true for persons and also for nations. It may be better for the poor to amass funds than to use them up in feeding hungry mouths. We the wealthy do not want any of the poor to starve, and we can afford to support hordes at survival level, but such care makes them dependent forever. If independence is what we favor, then charity is uncharitable. Some nations are called developing; a better term would be noncompetitive. One example is the Gypsies (see *The Economist*, 12 May 2001, pp. 29–32). They have by far the lowest standard of living, and by far the highest birth rate, of any group in Europe. When I spent six months in Greece, thirty years ago, Gypsy girls in downtown Athens would get on the train for the Turkish harbor and ride back and forth, dancing for donations in one car or another; it was good entertainment, and I was glad to contribute; but alas the Gypsies had no prospects for any other life. What was, what is, to be done? The kind thing would be to give them incentives towards education and also towards negative population growth.

#8 Thou shalt not burden the earth with pollution.
When you walk through the woods you find the path strewn with debris; when you drive through the country you come upon acres

of the embalmed awaiting the last trump. On a larger scale the planet is being ruined. The Arctic ice is thinner every year. We harm the ozone layer that absorbs cosmic death-rays; we pollute the water that every living thing drinks from; we store masses of radioactivity to glow for ten thousand years. Once in a while there is developed a process that puts old tires to use, or there is found a bacterium that devours uranium. But in general we follow the iron rule of heedlessness. The golden rule would require us to leave nothing worse than before, and some things better. The Jesus rule would require that for the next generation we should clean up even the lands of our enemies, and even at great expense. It is an urgent matter, though not yet widely thought so.

#9 Thou shalt not deprive a creature of dignity.

"And God said, Let us make man in our image, after our likeness: and let them have dominion over the fish of the sea, and over the fowl of the air, and over the cattle, and over all the earth, and over every creeping thing that creepeth upon the earth" (Genesis 1.26). In the Jewish and Christian view only mankind has rights. "And the fear of you and the dread of you shall be upon every beast of the earth" (Genesis 9.2). The Buddhist or Hindu view is that every creature should be respected. A hundred years ago cows would walk about a farm, chewing the cud and dividing the hoof, and then at sunset you would see, as the poet Thomas Gray says, "The lowing herd wind slowly o'er the lea." Cows are now kept in stalls all day as milk-making contrivances. Hens would try in vain to lay their eggs where the housewife would not find them. Grain would be scattered for them, and every hen would know her place in the pecking order. Nowadays to keep one sister from injuring another for pecking out of turn, their beaks are broken by the breeder. Since the mule, as a hybrid between a horse and an ass, is sterile, mules are given no chance to copulate with each other, though they have the same desires as the rest of us. To me it is abhorrent; I would not abstain from eating meat, but I do wish the animals were thought, by those who raise or use them, to have a glimmer of feelings. "Great God! I'd rather be a pagan suckled in a creed outworn!" says the poet Wordsworth, with my voice as well as his own. Under the Mosaic code a man that sins with a beast shall be cursed by all the people (Deuteronomy 27.21) and put to death (Leviticus 20.15, see 18.23); death is also the penalty under the Hittite code; perhaps it is a matter of the natural law, this punishment for the unnatural act. I approve of the punishment from a sense of brotherhood with the creature being defiled. Fifty years ago it was found that a second notochord implanted into a frog would develop monstrously; now it is found that jellyfish genes implanted into monkey DNA will thrive as well. I find it of heartbreaking ghastliness.

#10 Thou shalt not play thy role without honor.

Like the ancient commandment against coveting, this modern one against being dishonorable is less distinct, and more inclusive, than the nine others in its group. It is a law adjustable to needs. Sometimes a principle will have to be broken; we might need to commit adultery while performing espionage on behalf of our country. We may have a good reputation, like Simon the Just or Aristides the Just, but we ourselves know best if our motives are blameless. So now by a subdivision of this honor commandment (as coveting is subdivided among our neighbor's house, wife, servants, and animals), we may consider ten things not to do:

a) Thou shalt not pollute another for thyself. Do not ask a favor that ought to be refused. It is remarked in *The New Yorker* for 5 March 2001 that corruption among politicians is as everywhere present as the background radiation from our world's beginning. Depravity in the priesthood is common though by no means everywhere present. Good character can be shown in a hundred ways; bad character in a thousand. An aspect of this regulation is: Do not coax from a woman her virginity (or ruin anything else for a low purpose). Another aspect is: Do not make love pretending affection (except in marriage or another lasting union); the pretense is the wrong, not the unlawful lovemaking.

b) Thou shalt not enshroud a rainbow of inspiration. Do not describe noble things ignobly, or make parodies or commonplaces of them. That is the unforgivable sin—blaspheming against the Holy Ghost. The original is not so impressive afterwards; it has been harmed; you have done damage. An example is to play classical music behind your advertising (Bank of America plays "Swan Lake"; Quaker Oatmeal, "La Mer"; the Kohler company, the "Largo al factotum"; Energizer, a Strauss waltz; Listerine, "The Ride of the Valkyries"; Starz, "The Ode to Joy"; Best Buy, "The Thieving Magpie"; American Express, "In the Hall of the Mountain King"; and Honda, the "Elvira Madigan" theme from Mozart). Similarly with being humorous at the expense of a famous painting. The Mona Lisa has been much abused; no one can any longer see it as it deserves. To be clever in recasting sayings of folk wisdom—such as "if a thing's not worth doing, it's not worth doing right"—is less wicked, but to do the like with a line from a play or a poem diminishes art in one of the worst forms of theft.

c) Thou shalt not think thyself deserving but others not. Do not be competitive in your heart unless you know that justice is in your hand. Do not scorn the lot of another or find joy in someone else's pain (the Hindu believes you might come back as a scorpion). And do not broadcast the sins of another; instead tell the world (if you like) of your own failures.

d) Thou shalt not touch a child in anger. To discipline your child may be the right thing to do, even if you would rather not. But to use violence, physically or mentally, against one who cannot grasp the reason—that is another instance of loving yourself too much. To pummel your fellow with small cause is not so bad, though bad it is still.

e) Thou shalt not risk thy limb for the thrill. It is better though to maim yourself than another. A craving for excitement is one of those urges that we are too full of. Hold the craving under reins until it subsides; if you must yield to it, do not take chances with any one else. If you have to point an "unloaded" gun, let it be at yourself; if you wonder what an electronic worm would do to a computer, try your own, not the internet.

f) Thou shalt not wager a day's pay in a day. It is another kind of thrill-seeking. They say that, to a gambler, winning is the greatest feeling in the world, and the next-greatest is losing. Those who make a living by taking the losses of others are hooligans. They are to be tolerated if the harm they do is negligible, but are to be tarred and feathered if they bring ruin. And rather similar to running a casino is making trial of someone else's character in everyday encounters. Small gambling or tempting is a small fault, though, and may be an oasis in a desert of days alike.

g) Thou shalt not ruin thy senses with poison. Why would you do it at all? One reason is to enliven the humdrum. Another is for the pleasure in being wicked: "stolen waters are sweet, and bread eaten in secret is pleasant." Once more it is a matter of degree. Small poisonings (daily, a few grains of opium, a pocket flask of whiskey, a few packages of tobacco) are a small fault; you can live like that, hardly damaged in the short term. Doing great harm to yourself (a week crashing about in a blind stupor) is not a small fault but a good-sized one, though in general it is less wrong than doing any harm at all to another.

h) Thou shalt not let nourishment be a pleasure. Anything beyond satisfaction is a danger. Jesus himself (unlike the Baptist) came eating and drinking, but only at special times, and not as his interest in life.

i) Thou shalt not yield to obsessive compulsion. Do not avoid the crosslines in the sidewalk just because you have to. Above all do not injure someone else just because that is what your demon enjoys. True, if we manage ourselves too carefully in one way, the flaw in our character will appear somewhere else. And, if Jesus did not always control his temper, why should we regard all our own misdemeanors as felonies? But a certain amount of spiritual exercise gives tone to our nature.

j) Thou shalt not make gloom thy contribution to the mood of the day. Keep to yourself stories of unhappiness, unless you are uncovering a moral. A corollary is: Do not prefer the unliving to the living. To bury your dog or cat in a pet cemetery is all right, but do not pay for daily masses over the creature.

Besides these commandments for our time, there are (or may be) special regulations for special faiths. What is religious to Jews may be wicked to Christians, and the other way around. To Christians it is strange that anyone should regard the loins as the place to show a covenant with God, and strange too that anyone should take care not to seethe a kid in his mother's milk, nor to eat of a beast that cheweth the cud but divideth not the hoof. To Jews it is damnable to drink human blood in a rite and to worship in a room of images.

There has been a movement in the United States towards posting in the public schools the Ten Commandments (swollen though they appear to be from an earlier succinct utterance). That would be divisive because the notation (which ten?) could not be agreed to, and undemocratic because many Americans do not recognize the commandments at all. The motto "do as you would like to be done to" would be highly satisfactory for a posting, so long as there were not thought to be any limitations (as under the Jesus rule there would not be). "Love your neighbor as yourself" would be fine too, so long as the various interpretations of "neighbor" were not discussed in school (where they might provoke hard feeling), but were kept for the place of worship and the home.

Many countries, though opening their womb to non-believers, have a state religion. The United States does not. Is there any accord among us? Our Declaration of Independence refers to a Creator, and many say we should all be expected to believe in God.[26] My own view is that for us as Americans there should be no expectation one way or the other. The golden rule, as a principle of fairness from the beginning of civilization, could be agreed upon as a minimum ethical basis for our laws. If Christians in their own affairs wish to follow the Jesus rule, that may be well for them; it may even be well for everyone. The difference between the golden rule and the Jesus rule lies only in whether, towards your enemy, you bear malice or good will, and the commandments-for-our-time that have been offered here would recommend (1) good will (2) within reason. What then does the Jesus rule say about punishment, and about breaking the law when it is unjust? If killing, even against the command-ment, is sometimes the thing to do, at other times the right thing is to act against other scripture by not killing.

11. Your turning of my other cheek   If the law is contrary to what you think best, then like Jesus in the gospels, or Socrates in the *Apology*, you should be guided by your sense of right and wrong. Before you break the law, though, you should consider, as Socrates does in the *Crito*, your debt to the state. Obedience to the law is your regular duty. So even if you follow a "higher" law, you may be held to account. Let us assume that you are to blame for a crime, either because you did what you thought best or because you yielded to human nature. What ought to be, by the Jesus rule (love even your enemy) and by his own practice (heed conditions rather than absolutes), your punishment? In the story about the woman taken in adultery (John 8.3–11), an

absolute gives way to a conditional, as elsewhere the commandments to keep the sabbath and to honor your parents, and the
ordinance not to touch a dead body, also give way. Is there any
sure footing in the matter of law? No, every step must be
watched for pitfalls. If we read the adultery story like a judge
with no aesthetic sense, what do we say about the prosecutors
and the accused? Those who did not cast the first stone, were
they also guilty of adultery? If they were, then part of the moral
may be that we are not liable for a deed done by everyone, and
that laws against such deeds ought to be repealed. No, that
conclusion cannot be allowed to follow. Laws that distinguish
the ignoble from the noble should be kept; they are a catechism
from the state, doing more good than harm even when unheeded,
since they lead to hesitation. For breaking some laws, no one
need be punished, except in reputation. A law against the smok-
ing of tobacco might be an example; let tobacco be forbidden,
but let not any smoker be punished. Adultery (or polygamy)
would be a more serious example; let adulterers be guilty under
the law, but let them not pay for their guilt if no one cares. A
third example is pornography; the tooth of the law ought to be
upon anyone who corrupts another, but not upon anyone who
mercly reaches the already corrupted. A fourth example is the
imbibing of beer or inhaling of marijuana: anyone impaired who
harms a person or property ought to pay a huge sum; anyone
impaired who merely endangers another, as by driving reck-
lessly, ought still to pay a huge sum; anyone who keeps to
himself need not pay at all. A fifth example is the same, but with
whiskey or cocaine; the gravity is not in the substance but in the
danger to others; the escapist who stays in his chambers is
harmless. "What is that to thee?" (John 21.22). A sixth example
is the killing in kindness of a disabled child or parent; courage
would be required, but love might provide it; love in the heart of
society might forgive it. A seventh example is the killing of a

stranger disabled beyond mending. Some people speak of a right to life. A right to death is greater. The absolutists who outlaw mercy-killing or drug addition or adultery, under any circumstances, are lacking in charity.

It might be that those who withheld their stone, against the woman taken in the very act, regarded themselves not as adulterers but simply as wrongdoers in one way or another. Sarpedon in Homer says that ten thousand ways of death lie about us; so do ten thousand kinds of sin. The question now is whether only a sinless person has the right to punish a sinful one. The answer is that the state makes the law, and the agents of the state enforce it; he sheriff and the hangman are only jobholders; or else the populace does its job collectively if that is the custom; the hangman was not hired as a person with no guilt in any corner of his life. What if the woman had been taken in the act of murder? Would those who once had wished they could hire their neighbor's maid (against the coveting commandment) be disqualified from serving on a jury? No, they would not be disqualified from a large matter because of a small one. It follows that if anybody *was* disqualified from casting a stone in the Bible story it must have been for a large matter. So all the crowd in the story must have been adulterers or worse. That is a conclusion from reasoning. It must be withdrawn at once. It pays no heed to the art of the storyteller. Really, little can be set down as certain, other than an admonition not to be self-righteous. The story does not even say clearly whether repentance is important. My own view is that heart-felt regret might count for much, but ought to do so in whatever life may follow, not in our life on earth.

From the story of the woman taken in the very act, and from the proverb "Judge not, that ye be not judged" (Matthew 7.1), are we to gather that Jesus would not find fault at all and would not punish anyone for anything? That cannot be thought; he was practical-minded; "stay out of prison" was his advice (Matthew

5.25), not "do away with prisons." Those who follow him
would seem obliged to engrave a code of punishment. Was it his
wish that we should reform the felon? Should a culprit pay a debt
to society and be turned loose? The ethical teaching of Jesus—a
combination of (1) love even your enemy, and (2) be aware of
what the world is like—is here held to say that kindness to the
guilty would mean harshness to the guiltless. The commonweal,
to "establish justice, ensure domestic tranquillity" and "pro-
mote the general welfare," as in the preamble to the American
constitution, should take away the menace from our midst. Some
sociologists think they can cure the psychopath; it is like giving
freedom to a toxin you have rendered "harmless"; for safety's
sake keep it stoppered in a bottle. Anyone who has done serious
harm with malice, and not simply from rage at a fig tree out of
season, must be thought likely to do more malicious harm if
given the chance. In private I may choose to turn my other cheek
to one who wrongs me, though like Jesus among the moneychangers I will not do so always. The public custom must be
stricter, to care for the common good. In religion the United
States is a mixture of Christianity, Judaism, Islam, Buddhism,
Confucianism, Taoism, the lore of the Native Americans (who
as the earliest known inhabitants might be given primary consideration), atheism, agnosticism, indifference, and ignorance. The
general law for us all should be the golden rule. Those who are
able to go further ought to follow the Jesus rule—to love their
enemies as themselves—in their own affairs. I do not have the
right to turn *your* other cheek, though, nor do you have the right
to turn mine.

What is to be done with the felon? "If there be any cunning
cruelty that can torment him much and hold him long, it shall be
his" (*Othello* 5.2.342–4). Cruel and unusual punishment should
not be applied for revenge, though, but only as a warning.

William Prynne, a Puritan thought to have slandered Henrietta Maria the Queen, had his ears lopped off and the initials for Seditious Libeler cut into his face. That was unusual punishment, though not really cruel. Endless incarceration at hard labor may be less cruel than the crime it punishes. And the death penalty is certainly not cruel. (The *method* can be cruel: in ascending order of pain there are, among others: beheading, 2 Kings 6.31; hanging by the neck, Genesis 40.22; stoning, Leviticus 20.2; and burning, Leviticus 20.14.) Being magnanimous we may allow death to anyone who would have it, as Joan of Arc would in Shaw's play. One of the most famous opponents of that penalty, Clarence Darrow, though he agreed that the child-murderers Loeb and Leopold should not again be accepted into our world, argued all the same (if his plea can be described as an argument) that they should not be put to death. Did he have any reason, either moral or religious? The only one he offered was that the deaths of Loeb and Leopold would bring grief to their parents. It follows that when the parents died, then the murderers could be put to death. Did they have a right to live at all, when Bobby Franks remained dead? Even if you can love your wicked enemy, you may love your family and friends even more. Punish the bad as kindness to the good. Confiscate the fortune of the banker who has ruined the lot of the trusting; let him bequeath nothing to his heirs until the debt is paid with biblical damages. The teaching of Jesus is not to flail about with slogans ("turn the other cheek," "whoso sheddeth man's blood, by man shall his blood be shed: for in the image of God made he man"). Instead, look for the right thing, hard to find though it may be.

12. Turning the thumb screws   A hard sentence for hard crime (such as solitary confinement for life) is here advocated, as a deterrent and to protect society. The inflicting of pain as punishment (such as a breaking of bones) is not advocated. What about the inflicting of excruciating pain to further a right cause? How far will a follower of Jesus turn the thumb screws to gain information? To save your life is one thing; to save your family, or your country, or the human race, is another. Some will say that Almighty Providence would never allow the cause of goodness to depend on torture. That is an unsatisfactory reply, for evil is widespread in the world; if we do not face it the evil will prevail. If we can only undo evil by doing evil on our own, then evil is what we must do (but be careful! think again, and then once more). The argument of this monograph is that: (1) Jesus himself was not an absolutist but was heedful of conditions, neglecting the sabbath when there was need and not honoring his parents when he had a greater duty; (2) to walk in his way we too ought to heed conditions and violate a code in time of peril; (3) the end can justify the means; we may have to act against our conscience; cruelty is wrong for punishment but may be right from other motives.

Should we inflict torture to save the world? It would be a trial for me; whether it would even be possible I cannot tell; I expect that I could do it, now that I have thought about it; I do not believe I would ask someone of thicker skin to inflict the torture for me; it remains to be seen what I would do. As an advocate of Jesus—first in being generous even to the enemy, and secondly in taking account of what the moment calls for—I am in favor of the most dreadful things when there is no alternative. How then has the Old Testament, for me, been reformed by the New? In Judaism there are traditional enemy nations and a foreigner is not to be regarded so favorably as the tribes of Israel. But in the parable of the Good Samaritan, and in the words of Jesus after the resurrection (as his disciples remembered them), no nation or person is to be harmed as a matter of policy; only when other replies fail should a hand be raised in reproof. Under the Jesus rule it is harder to turn the screws than before, but not impossible.

Are such ethical decisions of major or of minor importance to a Christian? Is not faith in the central miracles, rather than good behavior, the mark of those who follow Jesus most truly? That matter is the issue of the chapter to come.

III. Passover to passion to eucharist

When people are asked whether they believe in God, they may ask in reply, "God who manages our lives on earth? God who will judge the lives we led? or God who was the creator?" Those ideas of God dominate three eras, though each is at home in the other eras as well. The first idea belongs to a time of miracles (the age of the Bible), the second to one of theology (the age of the fathers, doctors, and reformers of the church), and the third to one of discovery (the present moment). The first of them is the subject of this chapter. The finding will be that miracles take place in the believer; they are not the foreground, but the background of the faith; the foreground is goodness of heart; and for the followers of Jesus the goodness is made better by a sense of camaraderie with their master.

1. The miracles of Elijah and Jesus   The miracle stories of the Bible were meant to be astonishing. Afterwards we believe them or else have second thoughts. The voice of God is heard through a burning bush; the Red Sea parts for a people to pass through; the sun stands still; Shadrach, Meshach, and Abednego walk about in a fiery furnace. Elijah and Elisha, and then Jesus, feed crowds with small provisions, heal the sick, and raise the dead; Elijah and then Jesus are taken up into heaven. Sometimes a miracle has been to show the power of the worker. Was the man blind because he had sinned or because his parents had? He was blind for the sake of being healed by Jesus, "that the works of God should be made manifest in him" (John 9.1–3). In speaking to the men in Judea, Peter described Jesus as a man approved "by miracles and wonders and signs" (Acts 2.22). How did Lazarus profit when he was caused to live again? Surely that event (or the story about it) was to glorify the magus who had brought him back.

A miracle is not just a heartwarming surprise, like the change of a caterpillar into a butterfly. It is a happening through intervention. Spinoza doubted that miracles could exist, since they would show the world to need adjustments, discrediting the mechanic who had made the machine. No, that argument need not be agreed to. The mechanic might have wanted special effects from time to time. We as mere cogs and pulleys cannot well say. The world is not a structure of perfection like a dodeca-hedron, but a collection of perfect and imperfect forms within chaos, and the Regulator, if there is one, might take pleasure in altering things, either to fix them up or to ruin them. It is better to ask whether miracles actually do happen than to ask whether in theory they *might* happen.

The argument of Hume in his essay on miracles is that: (1) a miracle is believed, by those who witness it, only upon the report of their senses; (2) when they recount the matter to others, part of the truth will surely be warped; (3) our own senses do not similarly warp matters in recounting them to our own mind; (4) so our own senses are more credible than a report from the senses of others; (5) these senses of ours tell us that miracles do not ever happen; (6) so there is greater reason to disbelieve in miracles than to believe in them. (Finally Hume says that no one can believe in a miracle except through another miracle, but that is mere rhetoric, since it is no miracle that people are easily deceived.) Is it a good argument? Really it went without saying. The story of doubting Thomas (John 20.25–27) is better.

Another consideration is that some Intelligence may work miracles that do not even come to our awareness. Cosmic rays may change things because some Will has made them to, with-

out our ever having any idea that the mutation was for a purpose.
I grant that it is not helpful to speak in this fashion. A miracle in
the religious sense of the word can be taken as a contravening of
nature to reveal a power that pays heed to us.

Are then the supreme miracles of Christianity to be credited? That is a question asked by those who neither believe nor
disbelieve but are in doubt.[27] It is not the question to be considered here. The question here is whether the past and its future in
Jesus were a two-part design. If they seem to have been so, then
the accounts of the resurrection and the virgin birth are easier to
believe than they were. If the past does *not* seem made for its
future, then belief will be even harder than it was.

It was around the year 30 when Jesus died. About ten years
later Paul was converted by a vision on the road to Damascus;
about ten years after that he began to write his letters. Twenty
years later yet, in the year 70, the Romans overcame the rebellion of the Jews and destroyed the temple in Jerusalem. Many of
the survivors were scattered, and the annual flesh offerings were
at an end. Later still (I believe much later) the authors of the
gospels, writing in Greek, put together materials, some of them
from Aramaic, about the life, teaching, and death of their master.
The church father Papias tells that Matthew was the first of the
gospels, and that the evangelist Mark had been a companion of
Peter; it may have been so or it may not. What can be agreed to is
that the gospels, even if they were written later than the letters of
Paul, seem the closer to the events. The evangelist Luke may
also (though I doubt it) have written the book of Acts, about
some of the early apostles; the Revelation may be the last book
of all. Can the dating be given greater precision? Does the verse
"and Jerusalem shall be trodden down of the Gentiles, until the
times of the Gentiles be fulfilled" (Luke 21.24) refer to the
destruction of the holy city forty years after the death of Jesus?
There is no telling; the words are vague, and those that follow—

"And there shall be signs in the sun, and in the moon"—are visionary, not historical. Our wish to know more may never be gratified. We would like to place biblical alongside secular events, but those of the gospels cannot be located in time.

Things promised long ago were thought to be happening here and now. Writings formerly seeming to be towards one purpose had been *prophecies* that were coming true in a manner no one had foreseen: the psalmist had said, "I have cleansed my heart in vain, and washed my hands in innocency" (73.13, 26.6), and Pilate "took water, and washed his hands before the multitude, saying, I am innocent" (Matthew 27.24). Persons and deeds, known as *types* "originals" (in the sense of rough drafts or blueprints), were being completed by antitypes "copies" (in the sense of perfect executions by the master builder): "after the similitude of Adam's transgression, who is the figure of him that was to come" (Romans 5.14). These prophecies and types are for us a key into the inner chambers of the faith.

2. A prophecy of betrayal at bread   The verse "mine own familiar friend, in whom I trusted, which did eat of my bread, hath lifted up his heel against me" (Psalms 41.9, John 13.18) is deeply embedded. It is an element in all four gospels and was known at least in part to the author of Acts (1.16–18). It was also known to Paul (1 Corinthians 11.23), who is not likely to have been the one who brought it into the tradition, for the coming true of prophetic words did not interest him so much as it would the evangelists. The accounts of the Last Supper are as follows (after Bernard, vol. 2, p. 457):

(a) As they eat (Matthew 26.21, Mark 14.18) or after the consecration of the cup (Luke 22.21) or after the supper (John 13.21), Jesus announces to the disciples that one of them will betray him, or that the betrayer's hand is on the table.

(b) Judas asks, Master, is it I? (Matthew 26.25). The disciples ask Jesus one by one, Is it I? (Mark 14.19). The disciples inquire among themselves who it is (Luke 22.23). The disciples wonder who it is, and Peter beckons to the beloved disciple, that he should ask (John 13.22–24).

(c) Jesus replies to Judas, Thou hast said (Matthew 26.25). Jesus identifies the betrayer only as one of the twelve, who dippeth with him (Mark 14.20). (Not in Luke.) Jesus replies to the beloved disciple, It is he whom the morsel (*psomion*) will be given to after it has been dipped; the morsel is given to Judas; Jesus tells him (to the incomprehension of those at the table), That thou doest, do quickly; Judas goes out at once (John 13. 26–30).

(d) Taking the bread and the cup of wine, Jesus says that they are his body and his blood (Matthew 26.26–28, Mark 14.22–24, Luke 22.19–20). (Not in John, but see 6.51–54.)

(e) Jesus tells that he will drink no more of the vine until he does so in his Father's kingdom (Matthew 26.29, Mark 14.25, Luke 22.18). (Not in John.)

(f) After the supper, the disciples dispute about who is the greatest among them, but Jesus serves them, an example of humility (Luke 22.24–27). After the supper, Jesus washes the feet of the disciples, an example of humility (John 13.4–10). (Not in Matthew, Mark.)

(g) Jesus tells Peter that he will deny him (Matthew 26.34, Mark 14.30, Luke 22.34, John 13.36–38).

Of these, (d) is inharmonious with (a)–(c), seeing that the traitor, having (evidently) partaken of the body and the blood, has not gained grace from them, but commits the crime that had been foreseen. Was (d) omitted by John for that reason, or was it added by Matthew, Mark, and Luke? We ought not to require consistency, since the accounts are less a chronicle than an assemblage of sudden realizations. All the same it may be asked, Is the truth with John or with the others? Actually, the question is not so simple, for we realize that (d) is from another legend, one that lies at hand.

3. The lamb, the bread, of the passover The sacred name of God, Yhwh, is explained (as if it were otherwise obscure) as a form of the word for existence. The sabbath has meaning from four words that sounded much alike: full (moon); seventh; finish (Exodus, Genesis); and captive (Deuteronomy). The process is known as folk etymology. It is the common man's way of understanding why a thing or a person is called such and such. If usually false by the science of language, it is true in the study of ideas. The buffetiers who tasted the king's meat became the Beefeaters of the Tower of London. Adam "the color of clay" was made "of the dust of the ground" (Genesis 2.7); Noah "rest" fell asleep from the wine of his vineyard (Genesis 9.21); of Peleg "division" it was said that "in his days was the earth divided" (Genesis 10.25); when the name of Abram "a lofty father" (*ab* + *rum*) was changed to Abraham "father of multitudes" (*ab* + *hamon*), the *r* was unaccounted for. Abraham laughed when told that Sarah should bear a son in her old age, and the son was named Isaac "laughter" (Genesis 17.17); when Jacob "take by the heel, supplant" was born, his hand took by the heel his twin brother Esau, whom he afterwards supplanted for birthright and blessing (Genesis 25.26, 27.36); after he had wrestled with an angel, Jacob's name was changed to Israel "wrestle" (Genesis 32.28); Moses "draw out" was drawn out of the river by the pharaoh's daughter (Exodus 6.10). In Homer it is told how Penelope "weft" + "peel" put off remarriage by weaving a shroud by day and then undoing it by night (*Odyssey* 2.96–102 = 19.141–7 = 24.131–7), and similarly such bywords as "horse-breaking" for Diomedes or "helmet-flashing" for Hector are justified in episodes (*Iliad* 23.287–513, 6.466–73).

The root *psh*, for an ancient ceremony of sacrifice, was

obscure. How should it be understood? what did it bring to mind? Various sets of vowels could be added, yielding various words. The one that prevailed was *pesach* "pass over." The story is that the Jews, in bondage in Egypt, marked their houses with lamb's blood, so that the Lord, bringing death to the first-born, might *pass over* them (Exodus 12.13). Amid the lamentation among the Egyptians, the Jews fled to a promised land, eating their bread unleavened (Exodus 12.37) since they could not wait for bread to rise. Afterwards every household would journey to the temple in Jerusalem every year (Deuteronomy 16.5–6) to sacrifice a lamb in gratitude and homage and perhaps in expiation of sin as well. It would be eaten with unleavened bread as if in haste, with the loins girt and the feet shod for flight.

It is a religious story, commonly called (without disrespect) a myth. And it is well made, referring to an enmity and a destiny, accounting for the traditional feast upon both a lamb and unleavened bread, and making sense of the traditional word for the custom. Among the instances of folk etymologizing in the Old Testament, none is any finer.

4. The passion at passover by etymology   There are two biblical senses of *passover*: (1) the Lord's passing over the houses at the exodus, and (2) the sacramental meal eaten afterwards as a memorial. The senses are not likely to be confused, either in the Old Testament or in the New. Two other matters, though, must be kept distinct from each other: (1) the last day of Jesus was at the keeping of the passover, and (2) Jesus as the passover was himself the lamb and the bread. Christian doctrine holds that the former of these was a happening in history and that the latter is a religious mystery. I believe to the contrary that the happening was man-made for the sake of the mystery. That is, the early Christians first regarded the death of Jesus as a sacrifice and only later came to think it had been at the time of the annual ceremony. Where the gospels are at odds with each other is on what Jesus represented. In John he is the lamb of the sacrifice; in Matthew, Mark, and Luke he is the bread of the ceremony. And it is in the difference between the two that we see how both can be justified.

Paul spoke of the bread and the lamb together when he said, "Purge out therefore the old leaven, that ye may be a new lump, as ye are unleavened. For even Christ our passover is sacrificed for us" (1 Corinthians 5.7). It was an urging to feast upon "the unleavened bread of sincerity and truth" (same verse). The words are in accord with the customs of the day, for leaven was still being purged and lambs were still being sacrificed. By the time of the gospels, though, the temple had been destroyed, seemingly a great while ago. The word for unleavened bread, *azuma* (Luke 22.1), was no longer used in the ceremony; the ordinary word for bread, *artos*, was used instead (Matthew 26.26, Mark 14.22, Luke 22.19); the forbidding of leaven would seem to have been forgotten. And *there was no lamb*, though one may have been represented by a bone. The dipping of a hand in the dish (Matthew 26.23, Mark 14.20, see John 13.26), to judge from Ruth 2.14 ("eat of the bread, and dip thy morsel in the vinegar"), says nothing about meat. The phrases "they killed the passover" (Mark 14.12) and "the passover must be killed" (Luke 22.7, see Matthew 26.17–19, Mark 14.12) are heirlooms. As Nineham says, it is *Hamlet* without the prince. Bread and wine answer to flesh and blood with perfect neatness. The ceremony in Matthew, Mark, and Luke is complete without the lamb. If there had been a lamb at the Supper, it would have had no role to play.

The Last Supper and the crucifixion (at Jerusalem, where the passover was to be sacrificed) were on the same sunset-to-sunset day; but which day was it? According to Matthew, Mark, and Luke—in their accounts of the Supper—it was the day of the feast. According to John—in his account of the crucifixion—it was the day before (when the lambs were killed). If the one chronology is right, must not the other be wrong? Those who have held with Matthew, Mark, and Luke include Lightfoot in 1635 and seventy other eminent theologians through the year 1960. Those with John include Renan and sixty others. (The two companies are cited with precision by Jeremias, pp. 177–183.) That is, many have thought that Matthew, Mark, and Luke were in error, and many have thought that John was. Surely a Christian would be happier if error did not have to be found either here or there. Lightfoot and his followers should be rejected and so should Renan and his.

Can both accounts be right, the one by one calendar, the other by another? Did the fourth gospel follow the reckoning of the Sadducees, and the other gospels that of the Pharisees? Even if there was a second calendar, it will not quiet every doubt. For John thinks of Jesus as the lamb (killed the day before the passover); Matthew, Mark, and Luke think of him as the (passover) bread. Which of the two days does Paul speak of? He does not associate the death of Jesus with the passover feast day at all. We should have thought that he would, since the matter is of such moment to the evangelists. There are these things to consider: (1) Paul says that Christ is our passover (1 Corinthians 5.7), (2) above almost all else he is minded towards promise and fulfillment (Romans 5.14), and (3) in general he strengthens his arguments with allusions, as to Oedipus of Corinth (1 Corinthians 5.1) and Epimenides of Crete (Titus 1.12). From his silence about which day it was, I gather that the death of Jesus at the time of the passover was an idea he did not think of; the idea belonged to a later generation or otherwise to traditions that he was unaware of. We are left to assess, from the gospels, not only two days but two timely happenings, two coincidences, each between an emblem (or embodiment) and the day of its special meaning. Neither coincidence by itself would seem utterly improbable, but the two together do seem so, if we weigh the matter. The wish here is to make both traditions seem absolutely probable.

The passover as the sacrificial feast of the lamb had merged with the feast of the unleavened bread (Exodus 12.8–17, 23.15, Leviticus 23.5, Numbers 28.16). The lamb and the bread would each bring the other to mind and each could be regarded as an emblem of Jesus. By and by the emblems were *elaborated*. The lamb became, as a person, a lamb of God, not a bone of which was to be broken (John 19.33, Exodus 12.46). The bread became the body of a person, with wine as his blood, at a supper in the company of a betrayer (1 Corinthians 11.23–25, Matthew 26. 20–21, Mark 14.18, Luke 22.21, Psalms 41.9). The *further* elaboration must have been later yet, namely the dating of the crucifixion (the fourth gospel) and of the Last Supper (the other three gospels) to the time, the very day, of the annual passover. If either the one report (Jesus as lamb) or the other (Jesus as bread) must be doubted, it is fair to doubt them both. The intention here is to affirm them both.

In the third and second centuries before Jesus, the scriptures were rendered from Hebrew into Greek. The version is called the Septuagint, and it is the Bible known to the authors of the New Testament. (They read and wrote in Greek as the language of learning; Aramaic was for some of them the mother tongue; Hebrew had been forgotten; it is as if a French scientist of today would read and publish—on the genome, say, or cryogenics—in English rather than in French or Latin.) The Hebrew word *pesach* "passover," used for commemorating the most important event in Judaism, was not translated in the Septuagint, though, but was merely turned from the one alphabet into the other, letter by letter. It was now written and pronounced *pascha*, a foreign word to readers of Greek. What it referred to they could gather from the story, but again a popular explanation of the word itself was needed, since again the original sense was obscure. If you are at home in Greek and hear or read *pascha* (Exodus 12.11 and elsewhere), what do you make of it? What other Greek word can it be associated with?

The word that accompanies it (Exodus 12.13) in the Septuagint, *skepazein* "cover, shelter, protect," has the similarity of an anagram but no more than that. As a speaker of Greek you could, though, believe that *pascha* was a form of *paschein, pathein* (different tenses of the same word, both being from the root *path-sk-*), which means "suffer" and is the source of our word *passion*. That is, *the passover came to be thought somehow connected with the suffering, the passion, of Jesus*. The association of those *ideas* is an instance of typology: a person or event in the past, as a *type*, foreshadowed one in the future, the antitype. The association of *words* is an instance of folk etymology: Greek *paschein, pathein* "suffer, endure the passion" gave its meaning to *pascha* "passover," because the two sounded alike. Together they are a profound instance of etymological typology and the most momentous word play there has ever been: *touto to pascha phagein meth' humon pro tou me pathein* "this passover to eat with you before my passion," that is, before I suffer (Luke 22.15).[28]

The etymological typology is confirmed by the church fathers: "the word comes from the happening: the passover is from the passion" (Melito, paragraph 46); "the Lord in his passion fulfilled the passover" (Irenaeus, *PG* 7:1000); "the passover, which Jesus desired to be his passion for us" (Hippolytus, *PG* 59:743); "it is called the passover from the passion" (Lactantius, *PL* 6:531); "for without the passion, it would not have been called the passover" (Eutychius, *PG* 86:2393).

The emblems are not at odds with each other as the days are. And each of the traditions has been imbued with the other. It is not in the fourth gospel but in Matthew, Mark, and Luke that the heavens were dark from the sixth until the ninth hour, when the lambs were killed (Philo *Questions and Answers* 1.20). And it is not in the first three gospels or Paul, but in John (6.48–63), that Jesus is the bread of life. The two emblems, the two embodiments—Jesus as lamb and as bread—are both primary. And both dates, even if secondary, are right as well, though not historically, not by the calendar, but religiously. To the evangelists the passover was the type; the passion in twofold fashion was the antitype. And what had been thought about the passover—the lamb, the bread, the freedom from bondage, the expiation of sin—came to be thought about the passion.

Instead of preferring the one day over the other, or trying to reconcile them, we ought to accept them both as we do the truths of the parables. In that way we can believe them both together. The suffering, the *passion* (Greek *paschein, pathein*), because of *the sound of the word*, was what brought the *passover* (Greek *pascha*) to mind. All the matter about the lamb and the bread, including the twofold dating—by the one reckoning (where the ninth hour has meaning) and by the other (with a communion upon the body)—is a story rather than a history. It is of an earthly agency. A promise was kept in the mind rather than in the events. It is all true in the greater way and need not be true in the lesser one.

Along with the question for historians whether the passover was on the day before, or on the very sunset-to-sunset day of the supper and the crucifixion, there is the question for theologians whether the sacrifice was twofold or single. An answer is that in a single sacrifice (1) the supper was the oblation and (2) the crucifixion was the immolation (McHugh, p. 179). My own reply is compatible but different. It is as if in synonymous parallelism there might be one event or two: "They ravished the women in Zion, and the maids in the cities of Judah . . . or ever the silver cord be loosed, or the golden bowl be broken . . . he was wounded for our transgressions, he was bruised for our iniquities." There is a shimmering between the two half-verses. And similarly there is a shimmering between the embodiments. A single thing is viewed in different aspects. The matter is not a factual but a religious one. The scriptures sometimes (Judges 5.26, Matthew 21.5–7, John 19.23–24) fail to see that through parallelism the same thing is said in different ways; some of the followers of Jesus (Lightfoot and his school, Renan and his) fail to see that he can be the passover in different ways.

The crucifixion and the Last Supper were both of them more profound by being the passover. It is not that what had been (the passover from Egypt) had prepared for what had now come into being (the passion of Jesus), as Christian doctrine would hold. It is instead that what had now come into being (the passion) was understood from what had been (the passover). Or, it is not that marking the day (a matter of record-keeping) entered the tradition before the typology (a matter of pattern-discovery), but that the typology was first and then the marking of the day. The fathers and doctors of the church, and the theologians of later times, are accordingly not to be followed. The two explanations may seem almost the same, like the North pole and the South pole, but there is a world of difference between them.

The Oxford Dictionary of the Christian Church under "passion" says: "The word 'Pasch' or 'Passover' (Gk. *Pascha*), commonly applied in the early Church to the joint annual commemoration of the Redemptive Death and Resurrection of Christ (i.e. to 'Good Friday' and 'Easter' together), was often held by a false etymology to be derived from the Greek *pascho* ('to suffer')." This implies, if it does not assert, that the occurrence of the *passion* at the time of the annual *passover* was a primary or historical matter, and that the connection between the two words was secondary or interpretative. I believe to the contrary that the connection between the words was primary, and that the fulfillment of the passover ("the Lamb of God," "this is my body") was interpretative and secondary.

It follows also that the gospels were not at first written in Aramaic and then translated into Greek, as Philo's *Jewish Wars* was, and as Black among others has argued. For the etymology—the passion at the time of the passover—was not Aramaic but Greek. All the matter about Jesus as the passover lamb and bread (as the lamb he atoned for the sins of the world, as the bread his body was eaten at a supper) is a Greek understanding of things and was written in Greek from the beginning.

5. Are the 14th and 15th lunar or solar? The two accounts— whether Jesus was the passover in the bread or in the lamb, may be reconciled. Neither Matthew, Mark, and Luke on the one hand, nor John on the other, is in error. They merely tell a religious matter in different ways. The 14th day and the 15th can be reconciled as well. There are several facts and texts, some of them contradicting others: (1) in both Assyrian (or Babylonian) and Hebrew, the day had come to be, or had been from the beginning, from sunset to sunset ("And the evening and the morning were the first day," Genesis 1.5); (2) in Assyrian ritual the full moon on the 15th and the new moon on the 1st were special days; on the 15th the moon would rise as the sun was setting, roughly, and on the 1st they would rise together; (3) in Assyrian, *shabattu* (from *shebu*, feminine *shebitu*, "full, filled") denoted the 15th; in Hebrew the word was *shabbat*; that is, the original meaning of *sabbath* was the day of the full moon; (4) the Hebraic feast of tabernacles was on the 15th day of the 7th month (Leviticus 23.34 and 39 and Numbers 29.12); (5) meat and flour offerings were enjoined for the sabbath (Numbers 28.9) and for the 1st (Numbers 28.11), those days being balanced the way the 15th and the 1st were in Assyrian; (6) in accord with the Egyptian veneration of the sun, the day of the Hebrews was at some time from sunrise to sunrise (Segal p. 131, n. 3); (7) the lamb was to be kept until the 14th day of the 1st month and killed in the evening (Exodus 12.6, Numbers 9.1–5); the passover bread was to be eaten beginning at evening on the 14th day of the 1st month (Exodus 12.18, see Numbers 9.11); (8) the 14th of the 1st month in the evening was the Lord's passover (Leviticus 23.5, Numbers 28.16), and the feast of the unleavened bread was from the 15th (Leviticus 23.6, Numbers 28.17); (9) the Israelites departed from Rameses on the 15th, the morning after the Lord's passover (Numbers 33.3).

All will be understood if a few matters are agreed to (and the discordant verses toned down).[29] Two ancient feasts, one upon a lamb, one upon bread, had been brought together. The resulting feast, the passover, was on the 15th day of the 1st month, beginning at moonrise and sunset (the 15th being the day of the full moon and once known as the sabbath); it answered to the feast of tabernacles on the 15th of the 7th month. Both the lamb and the bread are accounted for, and so are both the 14th and the 15th, on two conditions: (1) the meal of commemoration, upon the lamb and the bread, renewed an exodus meal that was not upon a lamb but upon bread only, and (2) the 14th and the 15th had at one time (though not at first) been separated by the rising of the sun rather than by its setting. In the exodus the lambs were killed on the 14th and the Lord passed over the houses of the Israelites that same night of the 14th; the sun rose and the number of the day changed; the people fled from Egypt and ate unleavened bread by daylight on the 15th. When by a different custom the day came to change at sunset, the lambs were killed at the 9th hour on the 14th and the meal was after dark a few hours later on the 15th.

John is in accord with the sunset-to-sunset dating: the Last Supper in his gospel is after sunset at the beginning of the 14th and is not a passover meal; the crucifixion is nearly an entire day later, towards the end of the 14th, when the lambs were killed; the passover meal, upon the lamb, will follow after sunset at the beginning of the 15th, but that meal is not spoken of. In Matthew, Mark, and Luke the two days cannot be accounted for together, and the bread is not eaten in the morning as it was in the departure from Egypt, but in the evening (Matthew 26.20, Mark 14.17); if the time of the Last Supper is after sunset early on the 14th, the bread (if we think of the departure) is eaten a night's length too soon; if (better) the time of the Supper is early on the 15th, balancing the feast of the tabernacles, then (by the departure story) the bread is eaten late by a daylight's length; the Supper is a passover meal, but the lamb is not spoken of. The resolution is to take all four gospels together, understanding them now in one way, now in another. I would have the Supper as in John, for the sake of having the crucifixion when the lambs were killed, a few hours before the passover meal; but I also regard the Supper as being a passover meal, as in Matthew, Mark, and Luke. In the Orthodox rite a loaf, called a lamb, is pierced, and from it run blood and water (as they did from Jesus pierced by the soldier's spear); then the blood and water are drunk (as the wine was drunk at the Supper). Those who ask what *really* happened should be aware that they are paying homage to Clio, the Muse of history, a minor deity from a foreign culture.

6. *"To eat in haste" (Luke 22.15)*   Did the fusion of the Greek words *pascha* "passover" and *paschein* (a form of *pathein*) "the passion, the suffering" come into the tradition before the gospels had been written down? That would seem so but cannot be shown with finality. It remains to tell why at the Last Supper Jesus said: *epithumiai epethumesa touto to pascha phagein meth' umon pro tou me pathein*, "With desire I desired to eat this

passover with you before my suffering." The emphasis on the wishing is false; something is wrong; and yet the words seem very fine. Happily we can displace the false emphasis and can in doing so recover the ritual being enacted. The *epithumiai epethumesa* "with desire I desired," though Greek, is a word-for-word rendering of a Hebrew idiom, the adverb strengthening the verb by repetition, so as to mean, "I greatly wanted." Another example of the two words together is *epithumiai epethumesas*, the Septuagint version of Genesis 31.30, translated as "sore longedst" (see Numbers 11.4, Psalms 106.14). I would argue though that *epithumiai epethumesa* in Luke is really a late rephrasing of the authentic words, *spoudei epethumesa* or *epethumesa spoudei*. Was there any reason for the change? Yes, an editor was minded to make a New Testament conform to the Old. So he altered *spoudei epethumesa*, or *epethumesa spoudei*, to match the *epithumiai epethumesas* of Genesis. It was a mistake to do so; the *spoudei* ought to have been kept. For it also means "in haste," yielding the sense "in haste I wanted" or "wanted . . . in haste." And now, working only with the Greek, we have recovered the formula used in keeping the passover. For the haste was a crucial element (Exodus 12.11). The resonant, *thrilling* words of Jesus, at an earlier stage of transmission (before the false "normalization") had been: "I wanted to eat this passover with you in haste before my passion," *epethumesa spoudei touto to pascha phagein meth' umon pro tou me pathein.* It is a high moment in human chronicle or legend, and it confirms that *pascha* "passover" and *paschein*, *pathein* "the passion, the suffering" implied each other in the mind of the evangelist.

It is told in Acts that the disciples paused to observe the feast of the unleavened bread. There is no mention of Jesus; the author did not think of him as the unleavened bread at the Last Supper. So the ceremony of the eucharist, a reenactment of the

Supper, cannot have been developed yet. Surely then Acts was not written by Luke (to whom it is credited on the basis of the reference to Theophilus in Acts 1.1 and Luke 1.3). For Luke would speak of the supper as a passover, that is, as the feast of the unleavened bread, a promise (*pascha*) being fulfilled (in the *paschein*). The only way that Acts and Luke can have been by the same person is that the idea of Jesus as the passover bread was unknown to him when he wrote of the Acts but then profoundly known when he wrote the gospel.

There are other types, or foreshadowings, that scripture explains, and to the persons then alive—and alert to that manner of thinking—there may have been hundreds *not* explained. The interpretations that we can identify are often arresting. Jesus tells a generation wanting a sign that none should be given except for the sign of Jonah, who had been "in the belly of the fish three days and three nights"; it is as if the time between the crucifixion and the resurrection had been regulated in an adventure beforehand. In the centuries to follow, the church fathers will see, as many among the earliest Christians may have seen all along, that Jesus was not only a second Jonah but even more tellingly a second Isaac. In that type there was again a three days' lapse of time, and also a beloved only son, the wood of sacrifice, and an offering in the place of a lamb—a lamb under thorns like a ram within brambles (Genesis 22.4–13). But among all the types, or models, the passover is the supreme one. The passion is the supreme antitype or perfect product.

7. Prophecies of death and resurrection As the types (such as the lamb and the bread of the passover) were seemingly being completed by the antitypes, passages (such as Psalms 41, the betrayal at bread) were seemingly coming true as foretold. That is, prophecies in words were being fulfilled. One of the greatest among them is Isaiah 53:

4 he hath borne our griefs, and carried our sorrows (Matthew 20.28, to give his life a ransom for many)

5 the chastisement of our peace was upon him; and with his stripes we are healed (Luke 23.16, I will therefore chastise him; Matthew 27.26, when he had scourged Jesus)

7 as a sheep before her shearers is dumb, so he openeth not his mouth (Luke 23.9, he questioned with him in many words; but he answered him nothing)

7 he is brought as a lamb to the slaughter (John 1.29, the Lamb of God, which taketh away the sin of the world)

9 And he made his grave with the wicked, and with the rich in his death (Matthew 27.57, there came a rich man of Arimathea)

12 he was numbered with the transgressors (Mark 15.28, the Scripture was fulfilled, which saith, And he was numbered with the transgressors)

12 he bare the sin of many, and made intercession for the transgressors (Luke 23.34, Then said Jesus, Father, forgive them)

Two of these verses (it would seem) had brought the passage forward in its entirety: 7, "as a lamb to the slaughter," Jesus being here regarded as the passover lamb; and 12, "he bare the sin of many," taken with the name of Jesus, "the Lord is salvation."

Another passage regarded as a prophecy being fulfilled is Psalms 22, with six verses that seem to come true at least once in Matthew 27, Mark 15, Luke 23, and John 19:

1 My God, my God, why hast thou forsaken me? (My God, my God, why hast thou forsaken me?, Matthew 27.46, Mark 15.34)

7 All they that see me laugh me to scorn: they shoot out the lip, they shake the head: (They bowed the knee before him, and mocked him, Matthew 27.29, Mark 15.18–19, John 19.2; reviled him, wagging their heads, Matthew 27.39, Mark 15.29, Luke 23.15–36)

8 He trusted on the Lord that he would deliver him: let him deliver him, seeing he delighted in him (He trusted in God: let him deliver him now, Matthew 27.43)

14 I am poured out like water (forthwith came there out blood and water, John 19.34)

16 they pierced my hands and my feet (they crucified him, Matthew 27.35, Mark 15.24, Luke 23.33, John 19.18)

18 They part my garments among them, and cast lots upon my vesture (parted his garments, casting lots, Matthew 27.35, Mark 15.24, Luke 23.34; in John 19.24 the synonymy of the Psalms verse is misunderstood)

The best way to account for the evidence (I believe) is to say: (1) that Jesus was crucified (Acts 5.30, 10.39, and 13.29 have him hung on wood—the King James has "hanged on a tree"—but hanging by the neck was not the method, for the agony was to be long-lasting: see Hengel, p. 121; the cross gives us the word *excruciating*), (2) that stories about Jesus were told and retold, (3) that in time Psalms 22.16—"they pierced my hands and my feet"—was thought to have been a prophecy of the crucifixion, (4) that other verses from the psalm then seemed prophetic also, and (5) that the elements of the gospels were written piecemeal and only at length put together.[30]

To Christians the first verse of Psalms 22, as spoken in Matthew and Mark, is the most troublesome utterance in history or legend. "And about the ninth hour Jesus cried with a loud voice, saying, Eli, Eli, lama sabachthani? that is to say, My God, my God, why hast thou forsaken me? Some of them that stood there, when they heard that, said, This man called for Elijah. And straightway one of them ran, and took a sponge, and filled it with vinegar, and put it on a reed, and gave him to drink. The rest said, Let be, let us see whether Elijah will come to save him" (Matthew 27.46–49). The evangelist (I believe) is combining the cry with the idea of scoffing. Jesus calls out, My God (*Eli*);

the crowd say in derision, He is calling on God the Lord (*Eli Jah*); and then they complete their jest by turning this name of God (*Eli Jah*) into the name of the prophet (Elijah).[31]

Some of the questions remaining are these (my answers are in parentheses and may of course be wrong): (1) did it all happen as told? (the evangelists are often unreliable elsewhere); (2) is not the twofold fulfillment of the psalm, in the cry of Jesus and in the scoffing, evidence of authenticity? (the fulfillments may be human handiwork); (3) does not the use of Aramaic seem authentic? (Aramaic is used because the wordplay is Semitic; in the Greek version, as in English, the passage is unsatisfactory); (4) does not the mention of Elijah seem contrived even in Aramaic? (the wordplay could not have been made with Elisha or Isaiah, and the mention of Elijah is convincing for three reasons: Jesus had identified the Baptist as Elijah; Elijah had been taken into heaven; and it had been said, Malachi 4.5, that Elijah should return before "the great and dreadful day," whereas nothing of the kind had been said about Elisha or anyone else); (5) is there in sum an indication that the gospels were first created in Aramaic? (this one story was created in Aramaic; that does not speak to other stories; the folk etymologizing of *pascha* as the Greek *paschein*, *pathein* "suffer, endure the passion" was not Aramaic but Greek from the beginning and is at the core of the gospel narratives); (6) what is the tone of the passage, with its cry and then wordplay? (the tone is of solemnity and then of utterly unexpected savage humor; the storytelling is highly effective); (7) does the passage as a whole do more good than harm to the Christian story? (it does more harm than good).

When Judas, repentant, threw down the thirty pieces of silver and went and hanged himself, "the chief priests took the silver pieces, and said, It is not lawful for to put them into the treasury, because it is the price of blood. And they . . . bought

with them the potter's field, to bury strangers in . . . Then was
fulfilled that which was spoken by Jeremy the prophet, saying,
And they took the thirty pieces of silver, the price of him that
was valued . . . And gave them for the potter's field" (Matthew
27.3–10). (Our whole understanding of this passage is due to
Strauss, pp. 350–2.) The gospel has referred to Jeremiah, who
does have a parable of a potter (18.2–6), but the prophecy being
referred to is Zechariah (11.13), about the price of a man: "And I
took the thirty pieces of silver, and cast them to the potter in the
house of the Lord." But *yasar* "potter" cannot be the right
reading, for there is no potter in the house of the Lord that you
would cast silver to. The word must be a copyist's mistake for
osar "treasury" (the key words resemble each other closely in
Hebrew). Which of the variants, potter or treasury, did the
evangelist use? He used both of them! It is as if the elements had
been combined in a dream! And the death of Judas as told in
Acts (1.18), "now this man purchased a field with the reward of
iniquity," supplies the potter's *field*.

Another verse that came to mind was "They gave me also
gall for my meat; and in my thirst they gave me vinegar to
drink" (Psalms 69.21, Matthew 27.34). And yet another—one
soon to be at the center of Christian belief—was "After two
days will he revive us: in the third day he will raise us up, and
we shall live in his sight" (Hosea 6.2, Luke 24.46, 1 Corinthians
15.4). These verses and passages—Isaiah 53, Psalms 22, Zechariah 11.13, Psalms 69.21, and Hosea 6.2, along with Psalms
41.9—may be the promises of the Old Testament that are kept
best in the New Testament. The evangelists, through hearing or
reading, knew them all, and discovered still others (I assume) in
the course of their writing. And they often called attention to
them, as Mark does to Isaiah 53.12 ("the Scripture was fulfilled,
which saith, And he was numbered with the transgressors"), or
as Matthew does in speaking of Jeremiah (though he means

Zechariah). It must be allowed all the same that the completions are a patchwork without a pattern. Some figures (and events) that might have been types—such as Joshua when the sun stayed still for him, or Jacob when he defrauded Esau—do not actually correspond to any antitype. And many verses are left unfulfilled, such as "he shall see his seed" (Isaiah 53.10, which cannot refer to Jesus, though the rest of the passage may be thought to do so) or "All they that be fat upon earth shall eat and worship" (Psalms 22.29). And the sands of reference are soft footing in "he was numbered with the transgressors . . . and made intercession for the transgressors" (Isaiah 53.12); for the two sets of transgressors are not the same: some are malefactors, others are persecutors.

The composite of an Old Testament with a New had a lofty place for what had been, but a loftier one for what was coming to be. Certain things were fathomed immediately, others only by and by. The gospel tells that after the resurrection, now as the Christ, Jesus appeared to the wayfarers bound for Emmaus, "And beginning at Moses and all the prophets, he expounded unto them in all the scriptures the things concerning himself . . . Then opened he their understanding, that they might understand" (Luke 24.45).

8. Who spoke the magnificat?   The death and resurrection of Jesus, together, are the foremost Christian story, commemorated at Easter. The wonder of his birth is next, the story of Christmas. And here too both the type and the prophecy are profound. A woman has been been told by an angel that she will conceive a son of great worth. She replies, "My soul doth magnify the Lord" (Luke 1.46). The passage is known as the magnificat from the words in Latin, "Magnificat anima mea Dominum." In nearly all manuscripts the woman is Mary the mother of Jesus; in some manuscripts it is Elizabeth the mother of John the

Baptist. For which of the two are the words the more suitable? Raymond E. Brown, to whom I am indebted as he is indebted to others, believes the answer on balance is Mary. I myself believe it is Mary as things now are, but was Elizabeth as things once were. The elements of my argument are these: (1) that the typology leads to the Baptist rather than to Jesus, (2) that the thrust of the Zechariah story is blunted if the name John is not called for in some special way, and (3) that the Baptist is being replaced by Jesus, a process underway in the scriptures, but not completed.

The passage is an isolable hymn, Hebraic in the parallelism of its clauses. This is a byroad that must be traveled. On result of the form is that, though the halves of a verse combine well with each other, a verse in its entirety often does not combine well with its fellows. When the verse comes to a close, so as a rule does its matter. If in a tour de force a thought is sustained throughout a passage (Job 4.10–11, about lions; 18.8–10, about traps), the passage is still abrupt at its ends. When we learn biblical poetry by heart we remember each verse easily but go wrong in putting the verses together. The poetry is lyrical or proverbial; it is unsuited to continuous stories. And it describes the lot of mankind, not a unique happening or person. Job disputes with his companions in generalities, and his words are often hard to tell from theirs: "Is not destruction to the wicked? and a strange punishment to the workers of iniquity?" (31.3). If there are names or other details, they are twofold like Tyre and Sidon, or Sodom and Gomorrah; they do not seem highly specific. There are differences, but there is sameness. There is sometimes even an exact sameness, for in the poetical parts of Job, the psalms, and the prophets, many an element recurs as if it were from a treasury owned in common: "on all their heads shall be baldness, and every beard cut off" (Isaiah 15.2, Jeremiah 48.37). The general nature of the poetry is evident in Psalms 3: it

is said in the prose of its first verse to be a psalm of David when
he fled from Absalom his son, but it has in its poetry nothing at
all about David or Absalom, or about the disloyalty of a son to
his father. Similarly the words of the magnificat are not acutely
relevant to either Mary or Elizabeth. They had not even been
acutely relevant to Hannah the mother of Samuel when she too
was told by an angel that she would conceive a son of worth:

Luke 1.46–55: My soul doth
magnify the Lord, And my spirit
hath rejoiced in God my Saviour.
For he hath regarded the low estate of his handmaiden: for, behold, from henceforth all generations shall call me blessed . . . he
hath scattered the proud . . . and
exalted them of low degree. He
hath filled the hungry with good
things; and the rich he hath sent
empty away. . . .

1 Samuel 2.1–5: My heart re-
joiceth in the Lord, mine horn is
exalted in the Lord . . . Talk no
more so exceedingly proudly . . .
The bows of the mighty men are
broken . . . They that were full
have hired out themselves for
bread; and they that were hungry
ceased: so that the barren hath
born seven; and she that hath many
children is waxed feeble. . . .

Both passages are noble but vague. An item from an ancient
storehouse of phrases has been used without much shaping to
the event. Neither Mary nor Elizabeth can reasonably say,
under the circumstances, that the Lord has put down the mighty,
and Hannah cannot reasonably exult that the barren has born
seven. Brown believes that if the evangelist had meant to speak
of Elizabeth he would not have omitted such a vaunt, since
Elizabeth like Hannah will now conceive the child she had long
hoped for. I agree that because there is no vaunt the speaker is
Mary. But in an earlier draft of the gospel, I believe, before a
vaunt was omitted, the speaker was Elizabeth. The story was
changed in favor of Mary when the glory upon the Baptist was
thought to belong more rightly to Jesus.

A number of barren women, some of them past the age of

childbearing, had been specially favored. Sarah the mother of Isaac was one (Genesis 16.1–17.21); Rachel the mother of Joseph was another (Genesis 30.1–24); the mother of Samson was yet another (Judges 13.2–24); Hannah was a fourth; Elizabeth would be a fifth. The births of Isaac, Samson, and Samuel had been foretold by an angel, as now the birth of the Baptist is foretold (Luke 1.13). Samson was to be specially consecrated to the Lord as a Nazarite, a holy man who would not drink of the vine or cut his hair; and the same must be true for Samuel (who was not to cut his hair) and for the Baptist (who was not to drink of the vine). And since the name Hannah means grace, and the name John means the Lord is gracious, it would seem that the Baptist was once, more explicitly than he is now, meant to be a second Samuel.

Is this supersubtle? Are John and Hannah truly related in both sound and sense? The angel tells that a son will be born and is to be named John; Zechariah the father is made mute because he does not believe it; the people do not think that "John" is suitable, seeing that it does not belong to any forebear; and Zechariah writes out, "His name is John." It is a good story, but it has no moral, and it does not relate to anything. Surely there ought to be another element, one to tell why the name was John rather than something else. The missing element is the typology: the Baptist was to be another Samuel, born of Elizabeth another Hannah; the name John would refer to the name Hannah. If the story was once like that, it was better; for "John" was then not just one name among many, but one that showed the past to have come true.[32]

In the scriptures as they now are, written not by the followers of the one but by those of the other, the Baptist is in every way less than Jesus. "I indeed baptize you with water; but one mightier than I cometh, the latchet of whose shoes I am not worthy to unloose; he shall baptize you with the Holy Ghost and with fire" (Luke 3.16, Matthew 3.11, Mark 1.8, John 1.33). Both were charismatic, but the Baptist did not work miracles (John 10.41), while Jesus was famous for them. There were prophecies that as a voice crying in the wilderness (Isaiah 40.3) a messenger should come to prepare the way of the Lord (Malachi 3.1); Elijah should be sent before the dreadful day (Malachi 4.5). It was all fulfilled in the Baptist; he was the voice, the messenger, the Elijah (Matthew 11.14, 17.12, Mark 9.12, Luke 3.4); and the Lord whose way should be prepared was Jesus. As Samuel anointed David, a greater than himself, the Baptist baptized Jesus, a greater than himself: the recurrence was manifold.

The Baptist as a second Samuel is a Nazarite. Jesus is said to fulfill the verse "He shall be called a Nazarene" (Matthew 2.23). No earlier verse says Nazarene, though; there are only the verses that say Nazarite (Judges 13.5, 1 Samuel 1.11). The two words sound alike and that is enough. Jesus has become a Nazarene, a man from Nazareth. The origin has been made up and it serves incompatible ends. By a mingling of like-sounding words Jesus has the sanctity of a Nazarite (an ascetic holy man), not yielding to the Baptist in this respect. At the same time, by an exact interpretation of the words, Jesus is not a Nazarite after all, but a Nazarene (which merely says where he came from), and need not abstain from strong drink. "John the Baptist came neither eating bread nor drinking wine . . . The Son of man is come eating and drinking" (Luke 7.34, Matthew 11.19).[33]

Now in one way, now in another, the Baptist was losing to Jesus most of the force that had once been his. "He must increase, but I must decrease" (John 3.30). And yet not every dyne would be lost; the Baptist continued to cast shadows. Some of the followers of Jesus knew of baptism as done by the Baptist (Acts 19.3) but did not know of baptism in the threefold Name (Matthew 28.19, see John 4.1–2). And baptism, the rite of the Baptist "for the forgiveness of sins" (Luke 3.3), was remembered, but the eucharist, the rite of Jesus "for the remission of sins" (Matthew 26.28), might be forgotten (as in Acts 20.6). Jesus himself did not baptize with water (John 4.2, but 3.22); had he done so it might have seemed a borrowing from his forerunner; but the disciples baptized as a great part of their mission. And after the resurrection, without speaking of the eucharist, Jesus said that baptism (along with belief) was needed for salvation (Mark 16.16).

What has happened behind the magnificat (if my argument is sound) is that Elizabeth the mother of the Baptist was once regarded as a second Hannah the mother of Samuel. Elizabeth was accordingly given words to say that Hannah had said before. But at a late moment the evangelist, from devotion to Jesus, made Mary the speaker. In doing so he omitted the verses about conception by a barren woman, for they would not now apply. Other changes were then made as well, though the passage still did not become wholly appropriate. The reader senses hurry in the assembly of fragments, and also senses that, to those who left the gospels as we have them, a man more than holy, and greater than the Baptist, had come upon the earth. It could be held that a truth was at first misunderstood (as referring to Elizabeth) but at length understood rightly (as referring to Mary). A Nazarite is born of a barren women; a type is completed (the Baptist is a second Samuel, Elizabeth is a second Hannah); and a vague prophecy is fulfilled ("they that were hungry ceased," "filled the hungry with good things"). But then the Nazarite, the Baptist, is replaced by a Nazarene, Jesus, born even more wondrously.

9. *"A virgin shall conceive"*   In the Hebrew text a verse from Isaiah (7.14) means "a young woman shall conceive." In the Greek version at the time of Jesus the word is *parthenos*, and the sense is "a virgin shall conceive" (confirmed by Luke 1.34). So

to one who was thinking in Greek (Luke more than Mark) there was authority for the idea that Jesus should be born of a virgin. Other women—Sarah the mother of Isaac for one, and Elizabeth the mother of the Baptist for another—had conceived in their old age, but no other woman in scripture had conceived intact. The Baptist was great in the eyes of the followers of Jesus though not so great as Jesus himself, and accordingly the birth of the Baptist was special but that of Jesus was unheard of. Still, as the eucharist, in comparison with baptism, is not yet in the heart of the early Christians, neither is the virgin birth. From his failure to comment upon it, the fourth evangelist seems no more aware of that wonder than the crowd are when they say, "Is not this Jesus, the son of Joseph, whose father and mother we know?" (John 6.42). And if Jesus was born of a virgin, then the descent of Joseph from God (as in Luke) or from David and Abraham (Matthew) is meaningful in an empty way.[34]

The first evangelist also says of Joseph and Mary that he "knew her not till she had brought forth her firstborn son" (Matthew 1.25), which means that he did know her afterwards. That is, a woman who had been filled with child by the Holy Ghost would afterwards be entered by a man. What appalling bad taste! The evangelist here must join Tertullian (*PL* 2.835), who thought it indifferent whether Mary lost her virginity to a man coming into her from the outside or to a manchild coming out of her from the inside.[35] The brothers and sisters of Jesus (Matthew 13.55–56, Mark 6.3) may have been the children of Joseph from an earlier marriage (as in the protoevangelium of James), or may have been the unrelated housemates of Jesus in an extended family. But the verse that Joseph did not know Mary *until*—that cannot be explained away. Nor can it be explained away that Jesus was her *firstborn* son (Luke 2.7, see 7.12, 8.42, 9.38), which means, unless it is meaningless, that she might bear another child later on. Better to say that the tradition, as written by Matthew and Luke, is incomplete. Let us not be Sadducees about this (who say that the truth lies in scripture alone), but Pharisees (who give weight to unrecorded tradition). Some branches of the church will improve upon the text; the gospel need not be the final word. If Mary the mother of Jesus was a virgin when she conceived him, she was one for ever afterwards and is a virgin now in heaven.

10. "Prepare ye the way of the Lord"   The Greek word *kurios*, translated as "Lord," was used in the time of Jesus as a title of respect—by a disciple for his teacher, by a son for his father, by anyone for a man of eminence, and by worshipers in the mystery cults. It is also how the evangelists and Paul spoke of Jesus, sometimes with his name as well, sometimes not. The word had been used countless times in the Septuagint, the Greek version of the Old Testament, to render the Tetragrammaton, the name of God, Yhwh or Jhvh. In obedience to the commandment the name had not been uttered in Hebrew, *Adonai* "Lord" being said instead; and the Septuagint was reverent in the same way. (Similarly with *Dominus* in Latin, *Herr* in German, *Seigneur* in French, *Lord* in our language, and so forth.) To the early Christians the two meanings of *kurios*—God and Jesus—would fuse. Paul (formerly Saul) tells Agrippa that he was journeying with others to Damascus when he saw a light from heaven: "And when we were all fallen to the earth, I heard a voice speaking unto me, and saying in the Hebrew tongue, Saul, Saul, why persecutest thou me? it is hard for thee to kick against the pricks. And I said, Who art thou, Lord? And the Lord said, I am Jesus whom thou persecutest" (Acts 26.14–15; the Greek has "And the Lord said" or "And the lord said," but the King James version, which I have modified, has simply "And he said"; in the parallel passage, Acts 9.5, as if being fair, the King James supplies the *Lord*, or *lord*, where the Greek does not have it; the

Greek proverb spoken in Hebrew, or Aramaic, means "do not (you donkey) injure yourself by kicking at the goad.")

Paul (or else the author of Acts)—in the words "And the Lord said, I am Jesus"—is here taking Jesus to be an aspect of God. It is as if the Father implied the Son, and the Son the Father. And now it was clear, to those who would see it, what had been meant by "For unto us a child is born, and unto us a son is given . . . and his name shall be called . . . the mighty God, the everlasting Father, the Prince of Peace" (Isaiah 9.6), namely that the Father and the Son are one. The Lord who is the shepherd in the twenty-third Psalm had become continuous with the Lord who would dwell as a good shepherd (John 10.11) among men on earth. It was a grand fulfillment. When the Baptist quotes from Isaiah (40.3), "Prepare ye the way of the Lord" (Matthew 3.3)—and in a moment tells of Jesus: "he that cometh after me is mightier than I, whose shoes I am not worthy to bear" (verse 11)—it is as if God the Son had been foretold by the prophet eight centuries before.

11. Fulfillment a mark of invention   The evangelists (taken together) believed (1) that Jesus had been (at least figuratively) the lamb and the bread of the passover, (2) that he had risen from the dead, (3) that he had been born of a virgin, and (4) that he was the Lord incarnate. They also believed that these and other elements of the present (as antitypes and fulfillments) had been prepared for by the past (in types and prophecies). That is, as the gospels tell of them, the supreme miracles differ from annals not just because they are wonders but also because they keep promises. And this coming true, this working out of plans made before the beginning of time, is itself a wonder. For (as a rule governing everything else) when an uncommonplace happening has been foretold, it belongs to art, not to life; life has no pattern. When histories are full of purpose, they are really legends;

history has nothing in view. The biblical correspondence of past to present is the most impressive design in literature when seen at a distance. Does it seem just as good upon scrutiny? The answer arrived at here is no, it does not. The design is a rough assemblage; the pieces do not fit together. The before and after—of the Old Testament and the New—are to be explained away.

The fulfillments are not unaccountable works of divine providence (creations), but can be accounted for as the work of mankind (inventions). A human agency can be seen behind the curtain, fine-tuning the effects. The evangelists (and those who had somehow supplied them with ideas and materials about Jesus) believed that the most important events there could ever be had just taken place, but their writings appear less a report from heaven than a manufacture on earth. To judge with detachment from what has been held to be miraculous in Christianity, commerce with God as manager is not to be found in the workaday world.

The detachment however is what has kept the commerce from taking place. Historical truths are one thing; religious truths are another. It is not to reason but to faith that miracles belong. Do not look for them in the book of knowledge, but on a different shelf. They can be believed in as things that happened, but they did not happen in the world of hustle and bustle.

12. Miracles wrought by ourselves   Jesus gave the power of healing to his disciples (Mark 16.18) and to seventy others (Luke 10.1–17). It is a power that Simon Magus tried to purchase (Acts 8.18). Peter used the power to restore health to Aeneas and to raise Tabitha from the dead (Acts 9.34–40, 3.1–10). Has not all of that diminished the miracles done by Jesus himself? Is there much worth in a coat of many colors when everybody has one? The matter is again one of typology—of moving in cycles rather

than like an arrow. The world may be thought to show foreshadowings of the incarnation (the central moment of time) and
then to show afterglimmerings. Elijah as healer prepares for
Jesus; Peter as healer looks back to him, and so do those who
heal in his name today. And, if other cultures are foreshadowings
or afterglimmerings of Christianity, healing done not in the
name of Jesus, but by the emperor Vespasian (attested to by
Tacitus), can be a kindred good, not a good in rivalry.

Is it not all superstition and a hoax? Is there truly faith-
healing by anyone? Yes, just as one person can do surgery as if
by an occult extra sense (see Gladwell), another may seem able
to lay hands on the spirit. Faith-healers are not charlatans one
and all. The real miracle-worker, though, is the patient, not the
physician. The healing takes place in the mind and the heart of
the believer. If the belief is infirm, the miracle does not happen.
And as for faith-healing so for prayers. Jesus may be held to
promise that the prayers of the faithful or the chosen will be
heard: "whatsoever ye shall ask in prayer, believing, ye shall
receive" (Matthew 21.22; "shall not God avenge his own elect,
which cry day and night unto him?" Luke 18.7). Are those words
promises? I do not believe they can have been intended as
promises in the usual sense of that word. But if they *are* promises, then it would seem that the prayers not granted were of the
disbelieving or the unchosen. Or it may be that the prayers were
not worthy, for the models are "thy will be done" (Luke 11.2)
and "nevertheless not what I will, but what thou wilt" (Matthew
26.39, Mark 14.36). The believer is likely to feel that the prayer
has been granted to a degree, just as the Good Samaritan is likely
to have been rewarded in his heart.

Faith-healing and prayer—like the other miracles—belong
mainly to the earlier age, though. To walk on the water was for
then; to walk on the moon is for now. Things comparable to

the resurrection and the virgin birth are done today in sterile laboratories.

13. The idea of the Second Coming   There were two related expectations in Hebraic thought at the time of Jesus. The first was that a messiah (Hebrew for "anointed," Greek *christos*) should lead the chosen people over the nations: "there shall come forth a rod out of the stem of Jesse" (Isaiah 11.1–4, see 9.2–7, Ezekiel 34.23, 37.24, Psalms 2.7–9, 89.35–36, 132.11). The second was that "the end shall be at the time appointed" (Daniel 11.27–12.2, see Malachi 3, 4). The gospels throb with immediacy on both matters (even though they were written long after the death of Jesus). ". . . we trusted that it had been he which should have redeemed Israel," say two of the disciples, and "to day is the third day" (Luke 24.21). "Repent ye: for the kingdom of heaven is at hand," warns the Baptist (Matthew 3.3). "This generation shall not pass, till all these things be fulfilled," says Jesus himself (Matthew 24.34).[36] We may imagine that on the day of the crucifixion one bystander said to another: "Jesus suffers now, the way the prophets foretold, but he will return as the messiah, the Christ; his coming will be like a refiner's fire; there will be judgment upon the good and the wicked; the last page is being written, and the book will soon be closed." It was only a matter of hope, though, not one of firm faith or belief; the three Marys went to visit the tomb thinking that their master was dead. And the final events that had been looked for did not happen. Though Jesus (it was believed) did arise from the dead, in the midst of signs and wonders, the world remained the same; time continued to run.

What pattern would be created to replace the one that had failed? With heightened awareness the past was regarded as an umbra that had been thrown forwards. Things said or written long ago about one matter had happened again in another. Types had been completed by antitypes. Jesus paid the debt of his foreshadow: "after the similitude of Adam's transgression, who is the figure of him that was to come" (Romans 5.14). Prophecies had been fulfilled: the words "I am poured out like water" (Psalms 22.14) had come true in Jesus as "one of the soldiers with a spear pierced his side, and forthwith came there out blood and water" (John 19.34). The passion had revealed the primary sense of the passover. The old law and stories were thought to have been preparations for what should be.

It was a grand design, but the flaw remained. Jesus had risen from the dead, but had not returned with cataclysmic glory and finality. What was the value of the antitypes and fulfillments if they made no difference? The story of the resurrection was not so compelling when it was fraught with disappointment. The design was salvaged by Paul through a new conception. The resurrection was still the great event but it was not the final event. There would be a *second* coming of Jesus as the messiah (the first coming being the thirty years of his life *including* his brief stay after he had risen from the dead). The end would be at the second coming, and the wait for it would not be long. ". . . unto them that look for him shall he appear the second time" (Hebrews 9.28); "the time is short . . . the trumpet shall sound, and the dead shall be raised incorruptible, and we shall be changed" (1 Corinthians 7.29, 15.52; the sense is "we the living shall be changed," see 1 Thessalonians 4.16–17). In looking for the messiah and the end, Christianity was still like mainline Judaism, except that Christians believed the messiah had already lived once and had, after death, come back on earth for a short while, giving heart to his followers. Would he not return soon, perhaps this very hour? It was an urgent thought, and it led to the central rite of Christianity.

14. The origin of the eucharist Hebraic meals were solitary, or within the family, or communal. Some were annual feasts like the passover; some were banquets; most were casual meals at short intervals such as every day. They were usually meals of sobriety but not always (1 Samuel 25.36). A pattern for the Last Supper can be found from the Essenes, a sect not mentioned in the New Testament (nor in the *Mishnah* or *Gemara*) but known to us (probably) as the people of the Dead Sea scrolls. They were a celibate community, perhaps hasidim, who looked for the end of time, and their meal was one of moderation and composure: "when as many as ten solemnly meet together, the priest shall bless the bread and the wine, and then all the gathering, each according to his rank, shall give thanks and partake" (Cross, p. 87, condensed).[37] The supper in the gospels is like that: there are ten or more, a master, a blessing, bread and wine, and even an awareness of who "should be accounted the greatest" (Luke 22.24). But one difference overwhelms these similarities. The central words of the supper in Matthew, Mark, and Luke are more powerful than the ritual of the Essenes or anyone else ever.

At the Last Supper in Matthew, Mark, and Luke, Jesus gave the bread "to the disciples, and said, Take, eat; this is my body," and similarly with the wine, "Drink ye all of it; for this is my blood" (Matthew 26.26–28, Mark 14.22–4, Luke 22.19–20). These are among the most shocking words ever spoken. In Judaism to eat human flesh, or to drink blood, was an utter abomination. Converts to the religion of Jesus, though they might not keep the old sabbath or endure a cutting on themselves, did "abstain from meats offered to idols, and from blood, and from things strangled" (Acts 15.28–29). The invitation at the Supper—to eat his body and drink his blood—was like a beckoning by Moloch or an introit to a black mass.

In the fourth gospel the same dreadful, wonderful idea

occurs in another conception. "Your fathers did eat manna in the wilderness, and are dead. This is the bread which cometh down from heaven, that a man may eat thereof, and not die. I am the living bread which came down from heaven: if any man eat of this bread, he shall live for ever" (John 6.49–51). "Whoso eateth my flesh, and drinketh my blood, hath eternal life" (6.54). We may gather that both traditions—Matthew, Mark, and Luke being the one; John, the other—always had a sacrament upon Jesus in mind, an eating of his body, a drinking of his blood.

The Last Supper (in the evening) and the crucifixion (the following afternoon) took place on the day between the sunset closing Thursday and the one closing Friday. Then came the sabbath, the seventh day of the week. The resurrection was (thought to be) on the day after that, between the sunset closing Saturday and the one closing Sunday. That is, the resurrection was on the first day of the week, the third day after the crucifixion by inclusive reasoning. Afterwards—though those among them who were Jews kept for a time the sabbath as well—the followers of Jesus honored the weekly day of the resurrection, which became (perhaps at once) regarded as the Lord's day (Revelation 1.10, see 1 Corinthians 16.2). It was the day of Jesus, not the day of God, except that Jesus and God were thought somehow the same. The disciples would break bread (Acts 20.7) on the day of Jesus, even though they did not (evidently) remember their master when they kept the feast of the unleavened bread (20.6). It was also on the day of Jesus that converts, such as Corinthians or Thessalonians, would hold fellowship meals of their own.

The Jewish Christians would have been decorous by custom. The Gentile Christians were rowdy, as we learn from Paul's censure. After asking rhetorically, "The cup of blessing which we bless, is it not the communion of the blood of Christ? The bread which we break, is it not the communion of the body of

Christ?" (1 Corinthians 10.16), he changes the subject to the creation of woman for the good of man (11.9). Then, returning to the subject, he reproves those who are dishonoring Jesus, for whose sake they have assembled: When you gather together the way you do, that is not how to eat the Lord's supper. For instead of sharing, you start eating at once, and while one is going hungry another is already drunken. If you want to eat like that, stay in your houses instead of going to church. I have already told you what happened (1 Corinthians 11.20–23a, rephrased). ". . . the Lord Jesus the same night in which he was betrayed took bread . . . and said . . . this is my body . . . this do in remembrance of me . . . also he took the cup . . . the new testament in my blood" (11.23b–25). To the words "in remembrance," regarded as having been said by Jesus, Paul now adds in his own voice, "For as often as ye eat this bread, and drink this cup, ye do shew the Lord's death till he come" (11.26).

The faithful would go from house to house daily "breaking bread" (Acts 2.42, 2.46) "with gladness and singleness of heart." On Sunday they would gather to eat in church. The hour on that day may have been after the sunset closing Saturday, in accord with "the same night in which he was betrayed took bread" (1 Corinthians 11.23); but daylight would seem more likely, for the primary observance was not of the Last Supper, but of the resurrection. Was there a tradition that Jesus actually said "in remembrance" (for a remembering of events that were not yet finished)? I believe that Paul is putting into words what he thought had been implied, and by so doing is causing the Last Supper, in a memorial that he calls the Lord's Supper, to be the high moment within the weekly fellowship meal, if not within the daily meal as well. Paul is not thinking of Jesus as the passover bread, for he alluded to that bread without mentioning the Last Supper when he said, just a few hundred words earlier, "Purge out therefore the old leaven, that ye may be a new lump, as ye are leavened. For even Christ our passover is sacrificed for us" (1 Corinthians 5.7, where the passover, as a sacrifice, must be the lamb). So it follows that: (1) Paul is reflecting upon the Last Supper, in chapters 11 and 10, but is not regarding it as the yearly passover meal, the way that Matthew, Mark, and Luke do; and (2) it is to Paul, and not to the evangelists, that we owe the words of Jesus "in remembrance."

The words "in remembrance" are also in some manu-scripts of Luke 22.19–20, though not in others. If they are authentic, how could they ever have been lost? That is why the editors Westcott and Hort, followed by others, do not allow them. (The edition of the Greek text for the New English Bible argues besides that the words are not in the style of Luke.) No doubt a scribe took the "in remembrance" from a ceremony of his own time, or from Paul, rather than from the oldest stratum of the gospel. Accordingly (to offer again the conclusions from the preceding paragraph, but now in reverse order), (1) it is to Paul that we owe what the gospels do not have (except for this interpolation), namely the thought of reenactment, and (2) to the evangelists we owe what Paul does not have, namely the thought that the passion was at the time of the passover. Both Paul and the evangelists tell what they know in their heart to be true, even though they may not know any of those things for a fact.

Jesus would be remembered at meals but would also be worshiped in a rite with the elements of bread and wine or perhaps even without them. Forty years after the destruction of Jerusalem (that is, sixty years after 1st Corinthians, or eighty years after the death of Jesus), Pliny wrote to his emperor asking how to treat the Christians. They were meeting before dawn (he said) and singing hymns to Christ as if to a god, promising not to commit fraud or adultery; afterwards they would meet for a regular meal (*Letters* 10.96, to Trajan). So by now there was a ceremony in memory of Jesus, and also a meal in common to satisfy hunger, and the two were separate. They do not seem to be separate in 1st Corinthians. For in that letter Paul is adding the idea of the Last Supper to a meal that the followers were eating in riotous fellowship.

Why are the words "in remembrance" not in the gospels (except for the insertion into Luke)? It is because the evangelists tell a story that ends at the resurrection or shortly afterwards, as if they were unaware that the world had continued to exist. Paul was earlier than the gospels (much earlier, I would say), but he sounds later, for he speaks of a time well after the resurrection, even while he expects the second coming at any moment. It is because of him, and not because of the evangelists, that the reenactment is the main ceremony of Christendom. If "in re-membrance" were an element in the gospels, it would seem out of perspective, like the words "take up his cross" in "let him deny himself, and take up his cross, and follow me" (Matthew 16.24, Mark 8.34, Luke 9.23).

Paul next warns the Corinthians to eat and drink worthily, so as not to "be guilty of the body and blood of the Lord" (11.27). The thought is of Judas among Philip, Thomas, and the others of the eleven. "For he that eateth and drinketh un-worthily, eateth and drinketh damnation to himself, not discern-ing the Lord's body" (11.29). Paul is seeing—unless I am mis-taken he is seeing *just now*—why some are dying before the second coming. "For this cause many are weak and sickly among you, and many sleep" (11.30). The cause is that they are eating and drinking without remembering the master. And the effect is not commonplace; it is a heaven-sent affliction of illness and death and hell. The eucharist has (I believe) its origin in these verses (11.23b–30). The meal is no longer merely in fel-lowship, one with another, but is now in remembrance of Jesus, with the thought of not betraying him by unworthiness.

There are ten elements in the argument I have offered; the

fourth and the sequence seventh through ninth are my own widow's mites of a contribution. (1) The bystanders at the crucifixion are not thinking of the passover. Among them the followers of Jesus believe he will presently come again as the messiah in the midst of the final things. (2) Half a generation later Paul says that Christ our passover has been sacrificed (1 Corinthians 5.7), but does not suggest that the sacrifice was at the time of the passover feast. (3) Meanwhile, legends about what Jesus did, and matters that might have looked forward to him, are being assembled. Some things are written down, others are told and retold. One of the most powerful of these things is an ancient verse about a betrayal at bread. It is taken as a prophecy that came true at a last supper. (4) With the annual keeping of the passover, the word itself—*pascha*—comes to be understood, in Greek, as a form of *paschein* (*pathein*) "passion, suffering." For that reason the passion of Jesus is thought by all the evangelists to have been at the time of the passover. (5) One tradition (John, in harmony with 1 Corinthians 5.7) takes the Supper to have been in the evening at the beginning of the sunset-to-sunset day of preparation; the Supper was accordingly a night and a morning before the lambs were killed; Jesus crucified was the Lamb; the passover would begin a few hours later. Another tradition (Matthew, Mark, and Luke) regards the Supper as a passover meal, where Jesus offers the bread and wine as his body and blood (as he does in 1 Corinthians 11.24–25, where the day of the passover is not mentioned). (6) Sometimes not (John), but sometimes (1 Corinthians 11.23, Matthew, Mark, Luke), the traitor is thought to eat of the bread that Jesus gave as his body. As the traditions mingle, the bread of the Supper (Matthew, Mark, Luke) becomes the bread of life in the fourth gospel, and the ninth hour (John) becomes a part of the three other gospels.

(7) Long before these beliefs about the passover are worked out in the gospels, Paul looks for epochs, and wonders why people are dying before the end. It is from their dying that the idea occurs to him: the Last Supper was not an event at the end of time, but one at the close of an era. A part of the idea is that Jesus said the supper was to be eaten then and there by the disciples in forward-looking remembrance of his death, which he knew to be at hand. (8) Another part of the idea is that the Supper should be renewed in backward-looking remembrance of his death until he comes again (1 Corinthians 11.26). (9) It is from this renewal that Paul sees why some people are dying. The reason is that those who eat unworthily at the meal of remembrance are being afflicted for doing so. (10) The gospels (except for the seeming interpolation into certain manuscripts of Luke) do not have the "in remembrance" because, though long after Paul, they do not look beyond the resurrection as he did.

To the mind of the faithful, Judaism has been completed. The bread and the lamb of its annual offering have become God incarnate, and the followers of Jesus, while they are waiting for his second coming, can commune with him through bread and wine, and through the honoring of a lamb that will take their sins away.

15. Why a meal was called a love-feast The letter of Jude has to do with the larger of the communal meals but not with the smaller. It is as if the writer were following Paul in speaking about the hooligans, and as if the eucharist (the Lord's Supper, a memorial of the Last Supper) had not yet become a reason for Christians to gather together. The meal as Jude (12) speaks of it seems to have later been called an *agape* "charity, love." Clement of Alexandria (*Paidagogus*, that is, "Educator," 2.1.5: *PG* 8.386) and Tertullian (*Apology* 39: *PL* 1.538) used the word (or *dilectio*) in this special sense (meaning common fare, not the virtue), and Orthodox Christianity does so even now. In English we add an explanation and say love-*feast*, for to call a meal a "love" is about like calling it a "hope" (Dix, p. 104).

One of the three primary manuscripts, instead of *agape* in Jude (12), has *apate* "deception," a fraternal twin by looks in Greek; and in 2 Peter (2.13), which resembles Jude in its phrasing, there is a like choice in the manuscripts between *apate* and *agape*. Jude was a source for 2 Peter, or the other way around, or they had a source in common; 2 Peter, because it is the less precise and the more full of words, would seem to have been the borrower, but there is no being sure. The Codex Vaticanus has the dative plural *agapais* in both Jude and 2 Peter; the Codex Alexandrinus has *apatais* in both; the Codex Sinaiticus has *agapais* in Jude and *apatais* in 2 Peter. Vaticanus and Alexandrinus have the definite article *hoi*, but Sinaiticus does not, and the *hoi* must be authentic, for there is no reason why it should have been added but just the contrary.

The contexts do not help us to decide between the words; neither passage flows well. The *agapais* or *apatais* combines with *spilas* or *spilos*, meaning spot or reef, and the translators do their best:

> These are spots in your feasts of charity (Jude 12, King James)
> Spots they are and blemishes, sporting themselves with their own deceivings (2 Peter 2.13, King James)

> These are blemishes on your love feasts (Jude 12, Revised Standard Version)
> They are blots and blemishes, reveling in their dissipation (2 Peter 2.13, Revised Standard Version)

> They are a dangerous hazard at your community meals (Jude 12, New Jerusalem Bible)

they are unsightly blots, and amuse themselves by their
trickery (2 Peter 2.13, New Jerusalem Bible)

These are the hidden reefs at your love meals (Jude 12,
Anchor Bible)

they are spots and blemishes, reveling in their dissipations
(2 Peter 2.13, Anchor Bible)

These men are a blot on your love-feasts (Jude 12, New
English Bible)

they are an ugly blot on your company, because they revel
in their deceptions (2 Peter 2.13, New English Bible)

The two passages (in any translation) make sense to the
same extent as they agree with each other, which is: almost but
not quite. Finally it should be said that *houtoi eisin hoi en tais
agapais humon spilades suneuochoumenoi* "these are the spots
on your love(-feast)s when they gather together," besides yielding strange English, is unacceptably strange Greek. By word
order the *hoi* goes naturally with *spilades* (only a foreigner
would reach over the *spilades* to take it with *suneuochoumenoi*),
but *hoi* and *spilades* cannot go together, for they disagree in
gender.

My answer (with a touching up of *agapais* or *apatais* and
an exchange of one diphthong for another) is *houtoi eisin hai en
tois achatais humon spilades*, "these are the spots on your
agates." That is grammatical, and it is attested besides, for in
the poem *Lithica*, attributed to Orpheus, the agate is said to
have *spilades* "spots," while (from a computer search into the
Thesaurus Linguae Graecae) no similar authority for *spilades*
with either *agape* or *apate* can be found in the first thousand
years of our era. I assume: (1) that a scribe of Jude, reading the
dative plural *achatais* "agates," or else hearing it from dictation,
wrote down *agapais* and then for grammar transposed the diph-

thongs, and (2) that 2 Peter, because *agapais* did not make sense to him, "corrected" it to *apatais*. That is more than a possibility; I believe it is a certainty. Aside from the philology, what is the moral? It is that the bad reading in Jude gave the word *agape* "love, charity" a special sense, one used for centuries and much in use today. In my opinion the sense (and the phrase love-feast) ought to be kept, both for the Eastern ceremony and for a Western church social with food. That the text of Jude is wrong seems unimportant, "for the letter killeth, but the spirit giveth life" (2 Corinthians 3.6).[38]

16. The Jesus rule in the eucharist Why were people still dying before the second coming and the end? Paul seems to have become aware, suddenly, in writing to the Corinthians, that the reason lay in their disrespect for the Last Supper at their communal meal. Some of them (he held) were betraying Jesus anew by eating selfishly and drinking to drunkenness. And the thought was solemnized (later than Paul, later than Acts) by the agreement among Matthew, Mark, and Luke that the Last Supper was at the time of the passover. A summary might be as follows.

The *passover* had been within the *passion* in a twofold manner: (1) at the words (here amended) "I wanted to eat this passover with you in haste before my passion" (a grave play on the words, implying in ritual phrasing that the passover as a promise was being fulfilled), and (2) at the ninth hour on the cross, when the heavens grew dark (a meaningful happening, for the lambs were killed at that time).

The *passion* would then be within the *remembrance*: (1) at the words over the bread "this is my body," and (2) in the "lamb of God, which taketh away the sins of the world."

There would somehow have been for the twelve (or at least for eleven) disciples at the Last Supper, and for the believers at the crucifixion, a real presence of the passover in Jesus. And in exactly the same way there was to be for the faithful (in accord with Matthew, Mark, and Luke) a real presence, not merely a figurative or emblematic or otherwise symbolic presence, of Jesus in the eucharist. Catholics believe there has been a transubstantiation; Anglicans believe that, though there has not been a transubstantiation, the elements, besides continuing to be bread and wine, have also become, for the true worshiper, not for the false one, the body and blood of the savior. It is like believing in the resurrection as a real happening (as required by 1 John 4.2–3), rather than as merely a symbolic one. But what is the meaning of "real" or "somehow"? Your heart and eyes must first be opened (your third eye, as some say), and then you can see that it was not a spectre (nor a gardener, John 20.15) but Jesus from the dead. That is how it was with the followers then (Luke 24.16, John 21.4) and how it is with many followers today.

The truth is not the same for everyone, though, and does not have to be examined. We should be content with saying that it is a mystery how the presence of Jesus in the eucharist can be actual and physical ("It is the spirit that quickeneth; the flesh profiteth nothing," John 6.63). If analyzed by science the body and blood of the ceremony would prove to be bread and wine; if analyzed by faith the bread and wine would prove to be the body and blood; and similarly with the crucified lamb. As with the resurrection and the virgin birth, there can be a real presence by faith if not by science, and as a result of the faith there may be an effect within the believer. Some trust with hesitation; others trust wholeheartedly. Some are wrought less; others, powerfully.

And what was formerly Judaic has become universal. The sacrament of the Lord's Supper, or eucharist, reenacts a Last Supper which, together with the killing of a Lamb, commemorated an exclusively ethnic matter, namely the deliverance of a chosen people from bondage. But the Last Supper, reenacted in the Lord's Supper, was and is ethnic no longer. For at its heart was and is the teaching of Jesus, to love even your enemy as yourself. The ethnic feast and sacrifice had become, and they are now, a feast and sacrifice for all peoples, in friendship with all peoples.

There is an argument, a self-evident one, that has not often (or ever) been made against the existence of a real presence in the eucharist. Paul holds that the communicant who "eateth and drinketh unworthily, eateth and drinketh damnation to himself, not discerning the Lord's body," and gathers that for this reason many are taking ill "and many sleep" (1 Corinthians 11.29–30). The thought is (1) that Jesus is within the bread and wine of the remembrance, and (2) that the heedless, but not the upright, will see death before the messiah returns. Since #2 proved to be false, is not #1 disaffirmed? And if the apostle to the Gentiles, the prince of theologians, was utterly wrong, may not the barons and knights—Augustine, Aquinas, Luther, Calvin, and the Council of Trent—have been just as wrong in whatever they said?

What is the rejoinder? It comes from a study of Paul as elsewhere sometimes sound, sometimes not. If we had to either accept or reject the entirety of what he says, we should reject it; but we do not have to make that choice; the matter is not an absolute one, just as the teachings of Jesus, on right and wrong, are not absolutes. It was a good idea of Paul's that the followers of Jesus may have rapport with their master in commemorating the Last Supper; it was a bad idea that those who take communion unworthily are punished by death for their betrayal. We may believe in a real presence without thinking that some of us will die because they do not discern the body.

Another argument pertaining to the idea of a real presence in the eucharist is this. If it was rightly said of the Baptist, in comparison with Jesus, that he did no miracles (John 10.41), there cannot be the miracle of a "real effect" in baptism. And yet Jesus after the resurrection said, "He that believeth and is baptized shall be saved" (Mark 16.16), which implies that in baptism there truly is a real effect, one needed for salvation. So how can it be that the workings of baptism are merely symbolic while those of the eucharist are earthly real? The answer is that the miracles of the Baptist were not sensed outwardly; they were miracles wrought within; there was a real effect even though the bystanders did not see any. It follows that the rite of the Baptist was and is, to the believer, just as real as that of Jesus. The faithful may take from the Baptist the thought of repenting for the past. From Jesus they may take the rule of being kind towards their enemies in the future. It is a rule that Jesus himself kept (the gospel says) by praying for those who were crucifying him. And it is a rule that may change our intentions and behavior for the better. If it does change them, then in the eucharist (or through other forms of remembrance) there is a hidden miracle and a real presence of him who was, for his followers, the way, the truth, and the life.

IV. The ways from here to where God is

When the world did not end as expected, punishment in an after-life became an urgent thought among Christians, and the nature of God—divine but also incarnate in the form of humanity—became a matter to be defined. The creed, expressed with a bygone world view, locates the faith within its miracles. A different creed—about loving your neighbor, even your enemy, as yourself—would be truer to the teaching of Jesus. The study of God nowadays must also take a new account of biology (Is there a genetic basis for evolution in ethics?), of physics (What was the beginning like? what will the end be like?), and of psychology (Are there enduring values in religious or other intense experiences?). We ought to make at least a restless peace with these questions if we are to speak of God at all.

1. One after-realm or two or three   Was there to be the same allotment after death for everyone, or were there to be two different allotments, or three? I believe the answer changed with the changing expectation that the messiah and the end would come (1) the day after tomorrow, or (2) within the lifetime of the living, or (3) only when Providence at length decided. Under the first of these time schemes there was no need for long-term thoughts since there would be no long-term future. Only when the end did not come were other speculations worked out. Under the second scheme, those who were dying must have been disloyal to the master. But when people continued to die, the good as well as the bad, the third scheme seemed to hold the truth.

Some of us deny that any higher power metes out retribution. Others of us believe in retribution from a sense of fairness. Surely a scoundrel will be made to pay for his wrongdoing. If for some reason he is not made to pay, then surely his descendants will pay instead. "The fathers have eaten sour grapes, and the children's teeth are set on edge" (Ezekiel 18.2, Jeremiah 31.29). No, fairness cannot allow that guilt is inherited. ". . . the soul that sinneth, it shall die" (Ezekiel 18.4). The retribution must be upon the doer. If it is not in this life, it must be in an afterlife. But some deny that there *is* any afterlife; only nothingness awaits us. "All things come alike to all: there is one event to the righteous, and to the wicked" (Ecclesiastes 9.2), "the living know that they shall die, but the dead know not any thing" (9.5), "there is no work, nor device, nor knowledge, nor wisdom, in the grave, whither thou goest" (9.10). So held the Sadducees, who followed the written law. The Pharisees to the contrary believed in an afterlife from the unwritten tradition. And that belief prevailed in the gospel when the world did not end. The thought was that if the wicked do not make amends now, they will be miserable later, as they "go away into everlasting punishment; but the righteous into life eternal" (Matthew 25.46; 5.29, 10.28). In figurative speech or else as revelations (and how can you be sure which?) Jesus tells of the sheep and the goats in the world to come, and of the poor man in Abraham's bosom who is implored by the rich man in flames below to moisten his finger and reach it down to cool his thirst. After the crucifixion, during the time of waiting for the master to return, the two realms were regarded as the workings of justice: the one a garden for the good, the other a furnace for the wicked. "If thine enemy hunger, feed him . . . for in so doing thou shalt heap coals of fire on his head" (Romans 12.19–20).

Hell then became a great concern of Christendom. It is true that some of the foremost figures in Dante's *Inferno*—

Francesca, Farinata, Ugolino—still think so intently what they
last thought as living persons that they suffer the wind or fire or
cold as if inured. Their torments are nevertheless to the reader a
cause of shuddering. A motto of the middle ages was "Remember that you must die" *memento mori*, and the spectacles of that
age were the pageant of the seven deadly sins and the danse
macabre. The dread of the next world has by our own time gone
away, but it returns as we lie dying, and it may be warranted.

The early theologians came to realize, or to persuade themselves, not in contradiction but with a supplement, that the two
realms are not enough. There has to be a third realm for the
wicked who repent. They do not belong in heaven, but they also
do not belong in hell, for they can be redeemed. We are now
reasoning our way into the mind of God. Jesus speaks of the sin
that will not be forgiven, either in this world or in the one to
come (Matthew 12.32), and that is a new idea: forgiveness in the
world to come. Neither hell nor heaven can be the locale where
this late forgiveness takes effect. Another locale, a temporary
one, a whereabouts of purgation—a state of consciousness in
which sin can be sloughed off—is the place for those who will
be salvaged. But how are they to put their sins aside, and make
themselves worthy, after they have died? If they truly were
repentant at their moment of death, the prayers of the living, and
the friendliness of those in heaven, might be availing.

The holy objects that we had grasped or seen could be
availing as well. The ark holding the tables of the commandments harbored sanctity; David danced before it (2 Samuel
6.14); a man who touched it was struck by a thunderbolt (6.6).
The mantle of Elijah divided the waters (2 Kings 2.14); the bones
of Elisha revived a man being buried (2 Kings 13.21); hand-
kerchiefs from St. Paul's body cured the diseased (Acts 19.12).
Those on return from the holy land in a later age would bring
with them relics of like power: a drop of the Virgin's milk and a

piece of the earth that Adam had been made from, the bones of St. Mark (now in Venice) and those of the wise men Caspar, Melchior, and Balthasar (in Cologne).[39] Why then should there not be intercession by the souls in bliss whose relics the sinners had honored? If you believe in heaven and hell, is purgatory any more distant? When the end of the world was no longer really looked for soon, heaven-or-hell was thought to be the end, with purgatory as an interim home for those being made better. One allotment had become two and then three.

2. One person of God or two or three   Another instance of three-from-two-from-one followed when the world went on as before. Judaism thinks of God as one and alone. In summing up the commandments as "love God" and "love thy neighbor," Jesus begins by saying, "The first of all the commandments is, Hear O Israel, the Lord our God, the Lord is One" (Mark 12.29, Deuteronomy 6.4, not the King James wording). St. Paul holds that God is the head of Christ, as Christ is the head of man, and man the head of woman (1 Corinthians 11.3), and that too is unitarian, for it regards Christ as a middle term, not as an aspect of God; and the same is true for the verse that at length "shall the Son also himself be subject unto him that put all things under him, that God may be all in all" (1 Corinthians 15.28).

This oneness is a duality, though, when the Son of man is regarded as the Son of God (John 6.69); for within that thought the messiah is divine. Jesus speaks of God as the Father of us all ("Our Father, which art in heaven"), but as his own in particular ("of my Father," John 15.15). In theology the Father and the Son as persons of God are the type, or else the antitype or perfection, of Abraham and Isaac.

The third person of God is spoken of when the resurrected Christ (as his followers recount the matter) enjoins baptism "in the name of the Father, and of the Son, and of the Holy Ghost"

(Matthew 28.19; 2 Corinthians 13.14, 1 Peter 1.2). Before his death Jesus had promised to send to his disciples the Holy Ghost as an advocate (John 14.16, 14.26, 15.26, 16.7, 1 John 2.1); and the Holy Ghost—the Spirit of God which moved over the waters at the Creation—was then (seemingly) to participate in the remitting, or retaining, of sins by the disciples (John 20.23). A Trinity (including the Holy Ghost)—from a duality (of Father and Son), out of a unity ("the Lord is One")—is now complete to our understanding. As with the afterlife, one has become two and then three.[40]

(Do not Christians here set themselves apart? The Trinity can be regarded as God in heaven, God on earth, and God within the illumination from heaven to earth. It is the ultimate vision of the *Divine Comedy* and a mystery: three in one, one in three. The idea should be taken figuratively or as myth; it should not be defended in religious warfare. Nor should the name of the Trinity be allowed to make baptism a cause for resentment. The rite ought to be regarded as a custom practiced in one way by one people, in another way by another; the washing away of sin had been an element in Judaism, and cleanness is more important in Islam than in Christianity, Matthew 15.2, Mark 7.2. Baptism is a good but not if it causes enmity, and similarly with the idea of the Trinity. The denominations that allow freedom of thought seem to me admirable in this respect.)

3. The Jesus rule as the creed From St. Paul onwards the church has held (or has come to hold) this canon of beliefs: (1) through our first parents, sin came into the world; (2) it infected everyone and was manifested in sexual awareness; (3) being an infinite crime it would need an infinite atonement; (4) mankind bore the obligation, but only God had the capability; (5) so the atonement was made by Christ in his two natures as man and as God; (6) from time to time sin offerings of lambs had been made to appease God; (7) Jesus was the supreme such offering as he carried away the sins of the world; (8) thanks to him, those who did good works—or had faith, or had been chosen—might be united with God again.[41]

It is an argument that justifies heaven and condemns mankind but gives him hope. It is theology, not religion, nor ethical philosophy. And it seems to me man-made, as scripture seems to me man-made, not God-made. To me, the argument is like the one behind the sacred texts of the *Iliad* and the *Odyssey*. Hera, Athene, and Aphrodite vie with each other, Who is the fairest among them? The Trojan prince and shepherd Paris is to decide, and each of the goddesses (hoping he will choose herself) promises him a favor: dominion or prowess or the most beautiful of women. Of course he names Aphrodite as the fairest. The reward is Helen, wife to Menelaus the brother of Agamamnon. And that is why for nine years and more the war is fought at Troy.

In the early centuries of our era the sin-and-atonement theology was made more substantial with matter implied or explicit in the gospels, and a profession of faith was created for the faithful to say aloud as well as in their hearts. There are two versions, the Apostle's Creed of the Western church, the Nicene Creed of the church in the East. The former of them (from Philip Schaff, and without "begotten") goes like this: *I believe in God the Father Almighty; Maker of heaven and earth. And in Jesus Christ his only Son our Lord; who was conceived by the Holy Ghost, born of the Virgin Mary; suffered under Pontius Pilate, was crucified, dead, and buried; he descended into hell; the third day he rose from the dead; he ascended into heaven; and sitteth at the right hand of God the Father Almighty; from thence he shall come to judge the quick and the dead. I believe in the Holy Ghost; the holy catholic Church; the communion of saints; the forgiveness of sins; the resurrection of the body; and the life everlasting.* Here "suffered under Pontius Pilate, was crucified, dead and buried" is a matter of history (whether it happened or not). And "the communion of saints"—from a Greek phrase meaning "communion through the (two) holy things," that is, the bread and the wine as the body and the blood (Elert, p. 9)— also belongs to our world, though to the other world as well. But most of the formula belongs to the other world entirely. Should it be kept or modified or replaced?

Rudolf Bultmann—who was known for such work as an analytical commentary on the fourth gospel—had the prestige half a century ago to astonish German Protestant Christianity. And even today some of his argument is accepted as beyond question, though the more important part of it is not. Towards a newer statement of the Christian message he warned that the Bible stories had been told in terms now outmoded. And then, with appalling (because seemingly willful) Teutonic obscurity, he said what he thought should be believed instead. The good and easy elements in his thesis are: (1) that the earth can no longer be regarded as a middle locale between heaven above and hell below; (2) that remarkable isolated happenings, such as a rising from the dead or a walking on water, are not greater wonders than those of modern science and technology; and (3) that Judaic legends ("Satan hath desired to have you, that he may sift you as wheat," Luke 22.31) and mystical ideas of the time ("In the beginning was the Word," John 1.1) are now to be put away.

What remains for Bultmann is an existentialist understanding of the events as they apply to us. The myth of the dying and rising god is one thing; more important are the narratives of a miracle beyond all others; more important yet is the belief of the early Christians that through a savior their wrongdoings had been forgiven; most important of all is the decision we can make to participate in that redemption. Bultmann's own creed might then be phrased like this: *I believe that God caused the suffering of Jesus Christ to be an event not merely in time but also beyond time, and that the sins of those who have faith today were atoned for.* The matters at fault here are: (1) that God manages the earthly world (which may be true but cannot be shown), (2) that the agony of Jesus was a singular happening (when Alexander the Great captured Tyre he crucified two thousand men in a single day), (3) that the non-mythic part of the gospel story is accurate (the evangelists as historians do not inspire trust), (4) that Jesus was God or the messiah or in some other way more than human (which may be true but ought not to be assumed when the testimony has been impugned), (5) that through another being we can be cleansed of sin (again, merely asserted by Bultmann, not argued from premises: his word is *Heilsereignis* "healing event"), (6) that Christianity, alone among religions, can rid its worshipers of sin, and (7) that there is some reason why to be rid of sin is a benefit. Bultmann made it acceptable for a Christian to deny what many regard as the fundamental article of Christianity, but what he has left us with is meagre and unavailing.[42]

In *The Myth of the Magus* E. M. Butler laid down that, with some exceptions, a worker of wonders had these things in common with others of his kind: a supernatural or mysterious origin, portents at his birth, perils menacing his infancy, some kind of initiation, distant wanderings, a magical contest, a trial or persecution, a last scene such as a supper, a violent or mysterious death, and a resurrection or ascension. Her chapters are devoted to: *the wise men of the East* (the magi, Zoroaster); *the Hebrew holy men* (Moses, Solomon); *the sages of Greece* (Pythagoras, Apollonius of Tyana); *the downfall of the magus* (Christ, Simon Magus); *post-pagan shades* (Virgil, Merlin); *beneath a black sun* (Zyto, Joan and Gilles, Faust, Friar Bacon); and *in the light of common day* (Dee and Kelley, Gauffridi and Grandier). "Both as god-man and as the hero of a mystery tale, Christ represented a limit beyond which human imagination could not go in developing the magus legend" (p. 66). It is a remarkable treatise, contemporaneous with Bultmann's essay and, really, subsuming it.

Only part of the reason why I am doubtful of the miraculous elements in scripture[43] is that all miracles are against the law of nature, that is, against the laws of God. I would also say that scripture itself tarnishes the miraculous elements (by saying such things as that Joseph did not come into the body of the Virgin Mary until after Jesus had been born). Truly the miracles, like those of Elijah and Elisha, are enhancements. In the days of the ten commandments the emphasis was on honoring God and on not being wicked towards man. The Christian church wrongly caused the emphasis to be on magic. I would return the emphasis to ethics, but unlike Bultmann I would retain the magical elements, though in storage and not on the workbench. One advantage with the return to ethics is that we can take to heart the Good Samaritan parable and the sermon on the mount without affirming that they were ever uttered. Another is that the will of God need not be affirmed either. A third advantage is that, since the world did not end as foreseen, the realm of magic was to a degree discredited even on the day of resurrection, whereas none of the ethical matter has ever been diminished in any way at all. The creed might then go like this: *I believe that Jesus, who taught us to be generous even to our enemies, knew eternal truth, and that if humanity follows the Jesus rule it may live for ever.* Can any of us be without error—that is, infallible— in faith and morals? It would surely be in affirming these words. And the Bible as biography makes the words more meaningful in two ways. (1) Jesus himself prayed for his enemies just as he had bidden others to do ("Father, forgive them"). The foremost summary on how to live in the world—a bare commandment to love even those who may not love in return—is confirmed in a narrative of ultimate triumph. (2) In communing with their master as he had asked them to ("this do in remembrance of me") the disciples had a sense of oneness with him, and Christians today can share that sense, and can at the same time think of themselves as Andrew, James the Less, and the others who heard the words "this is my body . . . this is my blood." No driving of devils into swine can compare with any of that. After the new creed is said, the rite with both elements should follow, and the communicant will then be a better person. It is a friendly religion and wishes well to those who are committed elsewhere.

4. Why not to fear God as a judge　The creed has the words ". . . from thence he shall come to judge the quick and the dead." The *Dies irae*, used in the mass for the dead, implores Jesus for mercy. Michelangelo's *Last Judgment* in the Sistine Chapel shows Christ as inexorable.[44] Against those warnings, and to further hope, I would offer ten more-or-less distinct reasons why it does not (to me) seem likely that we shall be condemned to everlasting hellfire no matter what. The last of the reasons is the most important. (1) Jesus says that God is of the living (Matthew 22.32) and that goodness is rewarded on earth (Luke 6.38; alms in secret, repayment open, Matthew 6.4, 6.18); it is an idea imbedded in Judaism, arguing against any justice to come. (2) Since God does not appear to notice most of us now, in any kind way, we are not led to think he will notice us later. (3) In favoring Jacob and David, God was arbitrary; if those two were deserving, most of us are not so bad. (4) That the wicked should be punished, and the good rewarded, may be a merely human idea, unworthy of God. (5) The stories of Jesus teach great moral truths, not great facts about any hereafter. (6) The evangelists and theologians are unreliable; they cannot even be reconciled with each other. (7) Since much of the Bible is mythic (God is no more overhead than anywhere else), the words about the judgment may be mythic as well. (8) Mayhem, adultery, theft, and disdain of parents are common among dogs, cats, and birds; one species of ant enslaves another; will God punish any of these in an afterlife? (9) How can the codes for Christians and Jews apply to other nations? the Native American asks the missionary why the Great Spirit did not give the good book to the red man. (10) Jesus speaks of love and of forgiveness; if God practices the Jesus rule, loving those who will not love back ("he is kind unto the unthankful and to the evil," Luke 6.35), then no one—no lost sheep or prodigal son—will fail to be forgiven, repentant or not.[45]

5. Compelling God through a wager   A prisoner is told that a hangman will come for him by Saturday, but that the particular day will be a surprise. The day cannot be Saturday, he reasons, for if it were Saturday, then it could not be a surprise when the hangman came. And by the same reasoning, once Saturday has been ruled out, it cannot be Friday either. And similarly backwards through Thursday, Wednesday, Tuesday, and Monday. The prisoner concludes that, by the terms announced, every day is impossible. Then the hangman comes on Wednesday.

Where is the fault in the problem? It lies in thinking that the surprise would be a complete one, when it would be only partial. Even if the hangman came on Saturday, that would still be something of a surprise, as contrary to reasoning (Ian Stewart in *Scientific American* June 2000 may have come to the same conclusion). We are like the prisoner if we claim to fathom what is utterly beyond us. I have given ten reasons why we should not fear God as judge; they may all be effaced by a more powerful reason why we *should* fear.

Pascal offers us this wager (here modified). If we lead good lives, we have a chance to win an eternity in heaven. The likelihood may not seem great, but the reward would be infinite.

And if the gamble does not pay off, nothing has been lost other than some wicked pleasures. And besides the matter of winning, there is the matter of not losing. The fellow who leads a bad life may have to pay his debt forever.[46] Many people wager like that, or at least think they do. They pay some attention to the sabbath and try to be patient with their parents. They are uncharitable, but they have excuses, they think. Others know themselves with greater awareness and recognize their depravity. I was friends with a man who fearfully regretted that he had not wagered on goodness. The nurses said they had never seen anyone who resisted death with so strong a will. Such a dread of a last judgment improves our behavior while there is still time. The thought of hell deters some of us as the thought of prison does others.

Suppose however that God is displeased when we try to purchase his favor. Here is a reason not to make the wager. The error of Oedipus in Sophocles was that, like Pascal, he thought he could control his fate. When the gods told him he would marry his mother, he put land between her and himself, as if to make the prophecy a lie. That was a challenge to the gods: when they have told you such and such, should you try to prove them mistaken? It was a crime to flee from his mother. It would also have been a crime not to have commerce with any woman at all. We may think that Oedipus had a choice, as we may think that Achilles could choose between a short glorious life and a long life without glory, but those thoughts are wrong. Oedipus did not have a choice whether to marry his mother or not, and his wickedness lay in thinking he did. He might with humility have asked the gods for advice; the story would then have been different; the oracle might have said that his "mother" was really something other than Jocasta; when Deucalion and Pyrrha were told to throw the bones of their parents over their shoulders, they threw boulders from mother earth. But as things are in *Oedipus the King*, the hero has forgotten the maxim *know thyself*—know that thou art only a human being. The play is great aside from its moral, but the moral is great as well: Do not believe you have the mastery.

An agreement between God and man is to be made by God. If man declares the terms, he may be punished for doing so. Jephthah promises the Lord—as if bargaining for victory in battle—to sacrifice whatever living thing first greets him on his return: "Alas, my daughter: thou hast brought me very low" (Judges 11.35). Theano promises Athene, if she will break the spear of Diomedes, a sacrifice of a hundred oxen; but the goddess shakes her head (*Iliad* 6.305–11). Why are we not to speak the name of God? what is the reason behind the commandment? It is that we have no right to the power of the name, either to bring things about or to summon divinity at will. Marlowe's Faustus in conjury "racked the name of God, forward and backward anagrammatized," and if it was not God that he controlled, it was at least the devil. God might be displeased when the ascetic incessantly murmurs what is known as the Jesus prayer, "Lord Jesus Christ, have mercy on me." Are we honoring God if we seek to move him by being good?

Even if we do not think we have the mastery, may not God be angry when we declare his will with assurance? In the Book of Job the friends are rebuked at the end for speaking as if they understood the justice of things. What they said about the will of God may have been right, but they were wrong in claiming to know it. "Where wast thou when I laid the foundations of the earth?" (Job 38.4). Until we can reply to that, the next life will be a mystery. "Canst thou bind the sweet influences of Pleiades, or loose the bands of Orion?" (38.31). "Doth the hawk fly by thy wisdom, and stretch her wings toward the south?" (39.26). Knowledge of any life to come is withheld from us. It may be that there are rewards for those who have been just, and punishments for the unjust, as human ideas of retribution prevail in heaven. Or it may be that in heaven human ideas absolutely do not prevail.

So how are we to prepare for the next life if there is one? The first among the three possibilities—to be heedless—is risky. The second—to bargain with God in a covenant—may also be risky. For we are assuming control beyond our lot when we behave well for treasures in heaven (Matthew 6.19; "buy terms divine in selling hours of dross" is the phrase in Shakespeare's sonnet 146). What will eternity be like for the hypocrite who wanted to do a wicked thing but wondered whether heaven was watching? In Egyptian lore Osiris weighs our heart at our death.

The best of the three possibilities (according to my own mortal reasoning) is not to think at all about any life to come, but to be good with absolute abandonment rather than for recompense. "Be not like slaves that minister to the master for the sake of receiving a bounty, but be like slaves that minister to the master not for the sake of receiving a bounty" (*Mishnah* "Aboth" 1.3). Nowadays in an unbelieving culture there are persons who generally do the honorable thing without reflecting about hell or heaven. And the stoics (such as Epictetus, Seneca, Cicero, and Marcus Aurelius) were noble as a habit of mind. Do as you would like to be done to, even when you know it will not help you. That seems to me better than (a) the Mosaic idea of a pay-and-repay agreement with God where the worst sin is the worship of any other deity, (b) the idea of St. Paul's that by good behavior you can heap coals upon the head of your enemy, (c) the Catholic idea that good works earn a reward, (d) the Lutheran idea that all depends on faith, and (e) the Calvinistic idea that all was ordained at the beginning. But how *are* we to be heedlessly good—noble as a habit of mind? We can resist the iron rule, follow the golden rule, and make the Jesus rule our ideal.

6. The need for evil with the good   There would be no stories about miracles, nor any thoughts of heaven, if we knew nothing but happiness. In truth we know misery just as well; many of us know it a great deal better. Jesus says that God is good, but philosophers are not so sure. Epicurus argues that: "If God is *able* to take away evil from the world but does not want to, he lacks feeling; if he *wants* to take it away but is not able to, he lacks power; if he neither is able to take evil away, nor wants to, why call him God? and if he both *wants* to take it away, and is *able* to, why does evil exist?" (The text is lost except through Lactantius.) The question is not a specific but a general one. It is not "Why has God allowed such and such a heartbreaking occurrence?" but "Why is the world a place of heartbreak?" Why is there not just good, how do you account for the evil?

There are two biblical answers, one of them clear, the other cloudy. The clear answer is a simple dualism, said to be Persian but really universal. The counterpart of God is the adversary, the Satan of *Paradise Lost*, chained along a burning lake or roaming imbruted as heaven "left him at large to his own dark designs." In Christian religious thought Satan is also the Antichrist with seven heads and ten crowns. The ultimate battle will be in the valley of Jehoshaphat (Joel 3.12) or on the mount (*har*) of Megiddo, that is, Armageddon (Revelation 16.16), and victory will be with the good, or else it will not. St. Augustine holds that evil is not an independent enemy, but only a deviation from the good, and other fathers would say that the good, through Christ outside of time, was the victor before the war began. But the devil's theologians disagree, and who can dispute against them? The myth of scripture is more glorious than the ingenuity of commentators and should be followed at least in our imagination until we find out differently.

Which battalion have we been conscripted into? Are we with the Lamb or with the Dragon? We were born into the iron guard with its iron rule. Our natural preference is not for the benign but for malice. The good is bland, the evil has flavor. (Ashley shows us vistas into the other kingdom, but in seeing them we feel that we knew them already.) When we sign a pledge with blood it is not for devotion and purity but for power and pleasure. As we study the felons and their felonies, though, we hear a voice of counsel, "Let us not reason about them, but look and pass on" (*Inferno* 3.51). If we heed the warning, then our enlistment into the regiment of the wicked comes to an end. The iron coin is turned to its obverse of gold.

The cloudy answer to the problem of evil in the world lies in the sustained conception of God as willful and otherwise human: ". . . the mouth of the Lord hath spoken" (Jeremiah 9.12); "the Lord came down to see the city" (Genesis 11.5); "I will set mine eyes upon him" (Amos 9.4); "the Lord's hand is not shortened" (Isaiah 59.1); "written with the finger of God" (Deuteronomy 9.10); "I will make the place of my feet glorious" (Isaiah 60.13); "the Lord God walking in the garden" (Genesis 3.8); "the Lord shut him in" (Genesis 7.16); "will rejoice over thee with joy" (Zephaniah 3.17); "in these things I delight, saith the Lord" (Jeremiah 9.24); "the anger of the Lord and his jealousy" (Deuteronomy 29.20); "it repented the Lord that he had made man" (Genesis 6.6); "This is my beloved son" (Matthew 3.17, 17.5, see Mark 1.11, Luke 3.22).

Since these passages are figures of speech, causing the abstract to become concrete, is it not also by a figure of speech (1) that God is good and his adversaries evil, and (2) that God rewards or punishes *us* for being good or evil? In answering these questions we should distinguish between the matter of results and the matter of motive. A farmer's crop is burnt up by a Samson who has turned foxes tail to tail and put a firebrand in the midst of each pair (Judges 15.4), or it is ruined by hail. The result is the same, and we call both bad. But only the fire-setting is bad as judged by the motive; the hailstorm is just the way things are. There is goodness in our nature and also wickedness; and there is also good luck and bad. The goodness in our nature we associate with good luck and God; the wickedness, with bad luck and the devil; but that is only a conventional way of speaking. God does not give us good luck as a reward (so far as I can tell), nor is bad luck either a punishment or a trial of character. God and man are not alike even though man has written that they are. Was man made in the image of God, or was God made in the image of man? There is at any rate a way that man may remotely come to resemble God, and it is in accord (1) with the Jesus rule, (2) with Jesus' thought that God is good, and (3) with the word godlike. Namely that as a creature we are likeliest to survive forever if we become generous beyond our first tendency.

7. Survival of the fittest in ethics   The types and prophecies, with the resurrection and the virgin birth, are elements of Christianity. Altogether distinct from them there is an element—or ability or impulse—that may be called godlike. The idea lies within "God created man in his own image, in the image of God created he him; male and female created he them" (Genesis 1.27); it is also within "ye shall be as gods, knowing good and evil" (Genesis 3.5). The godlike element is to know good from evil, and then to choose the good. It is of course a myth or figure of speech that mankind resembles God; for God is abstract, like existence. All the same, the argument here is that mankind has a share in God—or in infinite everlasting existence—and will have an even greater share tomorrow, not through magic but through what we call godlike behavior. Treat your neighbor squarely (not by the iron rule but by the golden)—even treat your enemy with kindness (not by the golden but by the Jesus rule). The Bible has been thought at odds with the theory of evolution, but there is no need to choose between them. In ethics, as in other ways, we have evolved from simpler forms of life, and are evolving still. It is true that the sciences are cumulative but the humanities not; when you compose a poem or a sonata of your own you cannot begin where those of yesterday left off. But if there is more kindness than there used to be, then humanistic scruples accumulate after all. Those who hold that God made all creatures as they now are will deny this evolution; but the days of creation (Genesis 1.3–31) are times kept on a cosmic watch, and within the times there may be changes towards the better.

Living things are apt to learn from experience. Once we have touched a hot stove we do not touch one again, and for a while we do not touch even a cold stove. Those who can adapt to challenges, such as the stove, are likelier to have descendants cthan their fellows are, and by degrees the trait of adapting becomes ingrained. It is the same as with the speed of the hound, the strength of the gorilla, or the left upper incisor of the nar- whal. Within a species, there is evolution in accordance with the iron rule of self-interest, and similarly for the species within a genus, for the genera within a family, and so forth. But thanks to an awareness of good and evil, there is also evolution in accor- dance with the golden rule. When the impulse in favor of good- ness comes too late, the feeling is remorse, and we think, "The good that I would, I do not: but the evil which I would not, that I do." As with the hot stove, once we have said painful things, we are careful not to do so again, and for a while we hardly say anything at all. Those who most quickly sense the stove, or the remorse, are the likeliest to bequeath the ability to do so, with the result that (after many generations) their descendants sense a stove, or remorse, by second nature. The slow to learn, physi- cally and morally, are selected against.

It is an argument towards predestination. If God has all

knowledge, including all foreknowledge, then all has been determined already. The doctrines of the theologians may be recon-
sidered. No, they are inadequate and otherwise unacceptable.
Did St. Paul, Calvin, or the Jansenists ever tell whether Christ
died for those predestined to damnation? Is there a reasonable
meaning to "no man can come unto me, except it were given
unto him" (John 6.65)? I would take the verse to say that unless
you have a disposition towards kindness, you cannot follow the
Jesus rule by second nature. If you have the genetic material of
foresight and hindsight, you were endowed with an advantage
over those who do not have it. You can come unto Jesus in the
sense that you can more easily follow his rule than others can. Or
you may be converted even now, towards the sermon on the
mount and the parable of the Good Samaritan, and the change
may be gradual or it may be sudden.

If our own species has evolved as the most complex, we
could be expected to have become the most generous too, sur-
passing in nobility of character even the vampire bat (which
regurgitates some of her supper for a hungry comrade). Not
many of us are so friendly as that. The exemplar of self-sacrifice
is not the vampire, though, nor ourselves, but the social insects.
What has led the worker bees to feed and groom the queen with
no prospect of repayment? Why do they want to help another
female lay hundreds of more eggs? Why would they rather have
sisters than lay their own eggs to make daughters? That is not a
question for an individual worker of today, but one for a nation
and ages past; the behavior of bees is as much a part of them as
their body type. Still, something like an answer can be found.
Though the female allotment of genetic material in bees is
divided in the usual way (with some genes going here and some
there in various assortments), the male allotment is not like that,
but is the same in all the many offspring of one mating. The
workers are half like each other with respect to their mother's

donation, but wholly alike with respect to their father's. They have accordingly a ¾ genetic resemblance to each other, and would have the same resemblance to any more sisters of theirs that the queen might make (using sperm she had stored). But the workers if they mated would have (as we human beings have and as our dogs and cats have) only a ½ resemblance to offspring of their own. So in furthering the production of the sisters, the workers are actually "begetting" more of their likeness than they would do if they were queens themselves.

The author of the primary paper on the subject is W. D. Hamilton,[47] who believed that the bees were controlled by a gene for altruism. Some will say as Descartes said of God, "I have no need of that hypothesis." It seems to me that the bees sense an affinity between their ¾ likenesses and themselves. They are stimulated by chemicals and behave from olfactory tropisms. Eons ago that came to be their way of life. We are the same as the bees in responding to pheremones and through neurons, for we too are machines, though our own tropisms we call instincts and thoughts. The mind is a part of the body, in ourselves as in the bees, and any decision we make is the result of (1) our inborn wiring + (2) synapses made by our experiences + (3) countless stimuli from the present moment. What then of a gene for altruism, in bees and in ourselves? I believe that such a factor (whether a gene or a complex of genes) does exist, as surely as a factor for mania depression or obsession compulsion. But instead of altruism I would call it awareness of our identity in others.

It is a part of the human condition that has been developed in the last ten millennia, a twinkling of an eye. If you and I go so far as to love our neighbor as ourselves, it is—to rephrase the three numbered items in the previous paragraph—(1) partly because we have inherited an ability to do so, (2) partly because we have learned to do so, and (3) partly because we respond to the situation. If that love of neighbor furthers the survival of those in whose bosom it lies, it tends to be favored in the selection of the next generation. The iron rule is still an element in our nature; the golden rule is replacing it; our parents were slightly more iron, slightly less golden, than we are, and similarly for *their* parents. Our species alone seems capable of becoming what I have called godlike; in ethics the finest product so far, thanks to this capability, is not the bees but ourselves; after ten more millennia the product may not need an apology.

Bloodties are a cause of loyalty. They are not the *sole* cause of it; parents love their children more than children love their parents; and some of us love our friends—even our pets, even our jobs—more than we do our families. All the same, we sense affinity with our kindred owing to similar dispositions, and the degree of closeness is important. One identical twin, unless suicidal, will never harm another, for they are really the same person (I was reading of a pair who had been separated in childhood; when they met, each was wearing seven rings and four watches). Brothers sense their brotherhood; cousins are affectionate. Behind our relative comes our neighbor, for whom we do favors with the idea, though not the feeling, that the debt will be remembered. It is true that Cain slew Abel, that Jacob defrauded Esau, and that the property line between my house and the next one is in dispute. But ordinarily we follow the golden rule towards those who are nearest to us. Farther away than the family, friends, and the neighborhood, there is less decency, less fairness.

The same applies to the Jesus rule of treating even our enemies with generosity. Those who are much the same—such as the Protestant Irish and the Catholic Irish, or the Hindus and the Muslims of the Subcontinent—will perhaps be reconciled after centuries; between the Tartars and those they butchered the ties were less binding; a few generations ago our forebears in the United States were massacring the Native Americans; not long ago we ourselves were doing the same to the Vietnamese; just yesterday we demolished both the God-made and the man-made structures of Afghanistan. It was and is a violation of the golden rule, unless the rule is a tribal matter as in the Old Testament. It was also, and is, a crime of magnitude by the Jesus rule, even when that rule is tempered (as I would say it always ought to be) by taking account of the circumstances. The fittest to survive the brutality of today will be those against whom the fewest bear hard feelings. That the Jesus rule will prevail is here believed, but its victory lies a distance away. It is not a matter of tender-hearted piety, or not *only* such a matter, but also one of power politics. A clothing of good will is not impenetrable, but it is better armor than any other. The argument is this: (1) when we lived in caves, survival depended on the iron rule (to look after ourselves); (2) in the era of civilization, survival came to depend not just upon the iron, but also upon the golden rule (to be friendly to our fellows); (3) in a distant realm of time the Jesus rule (of having charity even towards our enemies) may become imprinted within us; (4) the direction of change is towards an ever broader recognition of ourselves in others; and (5) the process is an evolutionary one because it favors those who can "learn" (or adapt) over those who cannot. It is only in this way that I find God as manager to be at work in the world.[48]

Our enemies are the human beings we are at odds with. In a different way our enemies are the rodents and weevils. In a different way yet they are the amebae of dysentery, the bacteria of diphtheria, and the viruses of papilloma. There is a diminution of affection as we go farther from ourselves. The golden rule and the Jesus rule apply less and less; before long they do not apply at all. In another era, perhaps at the end of this third millennium after Jesus, there may be found a reason to love and forgive the microorganisms. For now it will be enough to evolve in ethics at home.

8. *How the world began and will end*   Did God create the world out of nothing or out of himself? And will it last forever or be burnt up or languish in cold? The sacred name Yhwh, explained as "I am" or "I am that I am," is an affirmation of existence. What the world (as an aspect of that existence) was like at the beginning, whether there will be an end, and what the end will be like: that is the subject now to be thought about. We may not be able to go far, but no journey is more worth while.

Galileo is said to have dropped weights from the tower of Pisa to show that they would fall at the same rate, each being pulled by the earth but also held back by its own inertia; Newton wrote an equation to describe the attraction. Michelson and Morley detected no difference in the speed of light, whether the source was coming nearer or going away; Einstein accepted (against intuition) that the speed of light was constant; the measuring rod, in motion with respect to the light, had been foreshortened or lengthened. That is, some things are known from experiment (Galileo; Michelson and Morley), some from reasoning (Newton; Einstein). Other things are learned almost by chance, even ones that change our view of the world. Edwin Hubbell found, from a shift towards red in the wave lengths of light, that all galaxies are receding from us, the farther away the faster. Until then nearly everybody had thought the world would always be much the same. (Those who are careful would divide the credit for the special theory of relativity between Einstein and Poincaré, with shares to Lorentz and others. Hubbell acknowledged that de Sitter had predicted the red shift, and honor is also due to Friedmann and Lemaître.)

It now seems that all the matter we know of had once

(roughly fifteen billion years ago) been a singularity of almost infinite density. It was the moment of creation, coarsely known as the big bang. A maker may have wrought all that there is. Or a limit may have been reached. Or there may have been a collision, not of actual entities but of virtual ones (see *Science News* 20 September 2001, pp. 184–6). Nliks, mbavs, and pdofs (related as dynes, ergs, and ohms are) made contact with analogues from another system, and what we regard as the primary things— matter, energy, space, and time—came to be as they had not been before, or else as they had been (once or immeasurably often). Our universe until then had lain as a thing that might be, rather than as a thing that was. The dimensions had been in storage for when they would be useful. A nothingness was a composite of laws and of subjects to obey them. All was without form and void.

As we scan the skies by night everything looks much alike. Some places are bright, some dim, and some empty, but there are no signs of an edge. It may be that we are in a special place and that there are boundaries elsewhere. For how can you have a sphere without a surface? Assume to the contrary that we are in an ordinary place and not a special one. From anywhere the skies will look more or less as they do from here. If that is the way things are, then the world is not a sphere but a hypersphere, where a boundary in one direction is connected to one in another, so that when you leave by the north you at once come in from the south. It may be that space is not a volume where parallel lines never meet but one where they do meet or diverge. Why would we not be aware of that geometry? Because for our daily lives the three dimensions of space are not affected by the one of time. We have not evolved so as to be aware of spacetime by second nature.

Besides the macrocosmic rules and equations from relativity study, there are microcosmic ones from quantum study. It is not understood today, and seemingly never will be, why particles, such as photons of light, sometimes behave like waves. The greatest wonder under creation is that by changing a particle you can immediately change its entangled companion a light year away (see *Nature*, 11 December 1997, pp. 575–579). And if another dimension of space is needed for the hypergalactic world, six or seven more may be needed for the subatomic one (see Green). Neither the large picture nor the small one is satisfactory, and the two have not proven compatible. Since by definition "work" = force x distance, if no distance is traveled— that is, if physicists make no progress—there will have been no work; but force is being exerted by strong minds.

What will become of us? One answer, now favored by those who weigh the quantity of matter, is that the world will expand forever, to a colder and colder broth of a particle here, a particle there; gravity will prove too weak, or anti-gravity too strong. Another answer, in keeping with symmetry, is that there will be a big crunch, as gravity proves able to slow the behemoths down and bring them back, increasingly hot, with a reversal of entropy (my idea, perhaps a bad one). Either there was a single beginning with an eventual fade-out, or there has been, and will be, one beginning-and-end after another. Only a third alternative allows that a remnant of ourselves may survive for all time, namely that matter and energy are supplied, by the evaporation of black holes or in some other way, to replace whatever has receded out of reach.[49] It is all a reminder of our lowliness, but a revelation of glory as well.

And besides our world—that is, our universe, including all matter that we can know about and all energy—there may be worlds that have not yet made contact with ours, and there may be others that never will. Is there spacetime in those other worlds, or are there analogues to spacetime? It is woeful to contemplate. Infinity and eternity are not mine to talk about further. What I gather from cosmology is (1) a strengthened opinion that the miracles of Christianity—the resurrection, the virgin birth, and the fulfillment of the passover in the passion— are not for our age the great wonders that they were, and (2) a strengthened faith that the Jesus rule for human life is the best means of surviving into whatever future there may be.

9. The earthly good and the eternal   The argument is again that we may become godlike, but now it is of single sheep rather than a flock. We do not resemble God, but we may feel that we have become godlike, through exaltation or exhilaration or ecstasy. Anguish is no less common and no less intense, but survival is furthered by the heaven on earth, not by the hell. The heaven, or ecstasy, may be spiritual or physical. It is enough that we watch and listen. If we take part we are affected the more. We leave our drab human nature behind and upon return we are different than we were. That is the ethical legacy from our forebears and to our descendants. The matters following have to do with: (1) our oneness with the rest of creation, (2) our inspiration from the arts, (3) the good and bad of religion, and (4) the sovereignty of mathematics.

(1) We sense God or the eternal through light, warmth, sound, shape, motion, and the like. Some things are pleasing and some hateful; to find them so is in the character of all beings alive. There was a time when I would go into the country to see the sunrise, and I gather now that my awe was an ancient response. The naturalist Ivan T. Sanderson, in a chapter on forest rats, tells of the cascade of flowers and succulent fruits that the rats would clear away—some of them huge rats, some long and slender, some ordinary, and some small and fragile. Lying among them beneath a canopy of ants, he was moved to a prayer of thanksgiving, not as a believer in any religion, but "to all the

everlasting forces and conjunction that had combined to produce
the indescribable beauty of the present that moved before my
eyes." It was a fellowship with all other creatures, a matter of
folk memory or DNA. Judaism and Christianity cannot be right
that only mankind matters. In *Remembrance of Things Past*
Proust has told of how at a certain cloudiness, or from a haw-
thorn or a madeleine, he would find himself where he had been
before, not for any reason but from his nature. On a grander scale
every thrush or appletree among us "remembers" in its development the earlier stages of its species, genus, family, order, class,
phylum, and kingdom: in the phrase of Haeckel, "ontogeny
recapitulates phylogeny." Any living thing is a small testimony
to what has been and then to what had been before that.

One distinction of mankind is language; we say complex
things and may write them down; without language there would
be no Judaism or Christianity. I doubt however that language is
the best means to religious truth. The Sadducees denied there
was an afterlife; the Pharisees believed in one. I disbelieve in one
but am unsure; any answer proven can be disproven; discussion
seems to me unavailing; the bear and the hollyhock know as
much about the matter as we do. The Sadducees held that the
will of God was in the sacred written law alone; the Pharisees
held that the written law was to be supplemented with a traditional law construed by a millennium of sages. What seems to
me best as law is only an attitude of wary kindness towards even
our enemies (this is what I call the Jesus rule). In the same way
I have low esteem for accounts of those special events called
miracles. I do though gather that Jesus had rapport with a truth
beyond truth. My faith comes from glimmers of the fullness of
existence. And I hold that a Buddhist or an American Indian worshiping nature can be as much of a Christian as a Methodist can.

In another universe there may not be spacetime as in ours,
and its forms of life may not know of nourishment, reproduction,

and evolution. In our universe all of us—bacteria, ferns, lob-
sters, and chipmunks—share these processes as if there were no
alternative, and we respond as our tribe has slowly learned to.
Ask a toad what is beautiful, as René Wellek used to say, and he
will reply: his she-toad. I myself regard the body of a woman as
one of the most beautiful things there could be. It is not a matter
of truth but one of value; it is the result of how things came
about. Change—sometimes by small steps, sometimes by giant
ones—will proceed from here, and will go forward, sideways,
and into blind alleys. The television series *Nature* (my favorite
when it is narrated by George Page) offers the glories and pains
of the earth in a manner hardly to be equaled. The segment
"A Lemur's Tale" shows how the male ring-tailed lemurs of
Madagascar, at mating time, will rub their tails with a vile resin
secreted by their wrists, and then swat each other in the face. To
participate in this circus seems to be what we were meant to do.
Even if there has not been any creation with a purpose, there are
still arresting wonders to observe, and transcendent if commonplace pleasures such as combining our body with another. The
high moments give us courage to endure the hardships and they
further our betterment. A working definition of God is "existence," and to have a part of it is to share in time and the timeless.

Jesus (Luke 10.27) summed up the commandments into
(1) love God and (2) love your neighbor as yourself (the golden
rule). The change he wrought was twofold and dealt wholly with
our life on earth. First, he added a new commandment: to love
one other. It was new, or different from Judaism, in regarding
our neighbor as not just our countryman but even our enemy (the
Jesus rule). Secondly, he was not an absolutist but a realist. By
his teaching and example, the commandments—the old ones but
the new one as well—should be bypassed when there is need.
Do not turn the other cheek to the moneychangers in the temple;
do not keep the sabbath when you can help the infirm; bear false

witness or commit adultery if you have do. How then are we, following Jesus, to love God (the sum of the earlier command- ments among the ten)? Is it truly a matter open to will and decision? I think it is a matter of being cheerfully aware of the world and well disposed. We can resolve to be less sullen within ourselves and less of a nimbus to others.

(2) We are also made magnanimous by art. As a student of Greek one year I read the whole of the *Iliad*, and for a long while I taught six books of it to students of second-year Greek. As I once allowed to a handful of Homerists, it was not so much a job as a way of life. I became somehow a changed person as a result. It was the supremity of the Homeric conception, together with the unfailing perfection of form. All in all it was the best there can be, and then better than that. The same is true for the four great odes of Keats + "The Eve of St. Agnes." The effect is humbling but enlarging, rational but also irrational; the sense is of moral profundity, and the language is of a resonance that remains beyond its welcome, like the opening movement of the Brahms violin concerto. As Ugolino asks in Dante, if you are not moved by it, what *are* you moved by? Among motion pictures the most important to me is "Potemkin," which I see again and again for spiritual refreshment; next is "Children of Paradise," which I saw once and was so affected by that I cannot see it again; after those, on my list of 100, come (the movies of) "Carmen" (Miguenes) and "La Traviata" (Stratas). What have they to do with eternal things? I speak of them only to say that art can ennoble the least worthy among us (myself), and that the effect is permanent.[50]

(3) Even if it is a myth that God has spoken to man, and only a hope (or fear) that God will be known in an afterlife, there are moments outside time in this life when God can be brought closer. A Christian reenacts the Last Supper; a Jew commemo-

rates the passage from Egypt; the ancient Greek glimpsed the Eleusinian mysteries. Many of us regard such ceremonies as of greater worth than anything we own. We are addicted to the opium of the people. Of course with any human activity there are those who hate it; religion is not for some persons; we excuse them without lowering our esteem for them. The particle physicist Steven Weinberg thinks religion a scourge to be rid of. And I agree that it has led to endless grief. Demons congregate within religion and often take possession of us. Voltaire in the section "Religion" in his *Philosophical Dictionary*, from an age when heresy might be punished with terrible pain, allowed that the religion of his land was surely the best, and then asked, as if in an intellectual exercise, what the second-best religion would be like. His answer was, a religion that would not make threats about the next world but would advocate kindness in this one, a religion not of repression but of good cheer and generosity. Touché: a thrust against the eighteenth-century Catholicism that its author had cause to dread. The Jesus rule, if it were followed by everyone, would defend us from wars of faith and from pogroms, inquisitions, and all the other furies of self-righteousness. If we could love our neighbor, even our enemy, as ourself, then the practice of religion, in rites and stories, might without harm give us moments of escape from the commonplace, and in consequence our hearts would be enlarged. I would have a Lord's Supper in memory of a teacher of benevolence. If in its liturgy there were any thought of Gentiles against Jews, or of men as meant to dominate women, that untoward element would have to be made as though it had never been.

The great Ramanujan, who as a Hindu prepared his own meals in rooms at the University of Cambridge, once remarked that he thought all religions more or less equally true. And, yes, many a religion does serve as well for devotions as many another. Christianity has special trappings, though. The Bible in the King James version is like a natural wonder in language. *The Divine Comedy* and *Paradise Lost* are Christian poems with moments of cosmic grandeur. Handel's *Messiah* sets deathless scripture to angelic music. Leonardo's *Last Supper* will never be surpassed among paintings. Notre Dame in Paris and the other Gothic cathedrals are architecture worthy of the Lamb; St. Mark's in Venice is the most beautiful building there can ever be. Those works inspire even the nonbeliever, but for one who is friendly to the faith they are a marketplace of commerce with heaven.[51] My own thought however is that the glorious works of man are for the better only when, like the Samaritan of the parable, we give everyone else his due and regard our enemy as a brother.

(4) The mathematical physicist Roger Penrose has suggested that there are (a) the physical world, (b) the world of ideas, and (c) the world of mathematics. As an amateur I would say the same. At the moment I am held by Fermat's two-squares theorem, that every prime number of the form $4n + 1$, but no prime of the form $4n - 1$, can be expressed as the sum of two squares. 1009 (a $4n + 1$ prime) $= 784 + 225$, or $28^2 + 15^2$. I see how to prove the latter part of the theorem (that no $4n - 1$ prime is the sum of two squares), but cannot prove the former and astonishing part, though unless I deceive myself I am making progress. I mean to look for the proof by and by (after I have given up), and it may be too much for me; but for now I want to keep working. A theorem I have found for myself is that the sum of the cubes of the first n numbers equals the square of the sum of those numbers: $1^3 + 2^3 + 3^3 \ldots n^3 = (1 + 2 + 3 \ldots n)^2$: thus $1 + 8 + 27 + 64 + 125 + 216 = (1 + 2 + 3 + 4 + 5 + 6)^2 = 441$. A mathematician would no doubt find the proof an easy one; I find it terribly hard, but have not given up on that problem either.

It was discovered just yesterday, so to speak, that the radii of circles inscribed within a larger circle sometimes bear to each other simple, orderly relationships. On the cover of *Science News* for 21 April 2001 there are good-sized circles labeled *2* lying east and west, then somewhat smaller ones labeled *3* north and south, and then, on a curve, circles of the inverse sizes 6, 11, 18, 27, and so forth, all in close packing. "Where do these numbers come from?" asks one mathematician. They are the values of $x^2 \pm 2x + 3$. And besides this curve there are others, on the cover, defined as $2x^2 \pm 2x + 2, 4x^2 \pm 0x - 1, 5x^2 \pm 2x - 1, 5x^2 \pm 4x - 1, 8x^2 \pm 4x - 1, 9x^2 \pm 4x - 1$, and $10x^2 \pm 14x + 6$. The simplest of the right triangles—3, 4, and 5—is at the heart of the construction, and it may be that other right triangles generate the other numbers. Why they should all be integers is more than I can see. My advice from experience is: make photocopies of the cover and think about the matter during coffee breaks or bring it to mind during wakeful hours at night. To watch a full eclipse, when the moon exactly comes over the sun, is astonishing, a thrill of a lifetime; to look at the circles within that *2, 3* disk is no less astonishing and an experience to be renewed at will.

The value of π is the number of times the diameter of a circle will go into the circumference; its value is 3.141592653589793 ..., never ending. What does it have to do with ordinary numbers? How can you reconcile a curved line (the circumference) with a straight one (its diameter)? There is a beautiful demonstration— as beautiful as anything in the world outside mathematics—that $\pi/4 = \frac{1}{1} - \frac{1}{3} + \frac{1}{5} - \frac{1}{7}$. ... The number e represents the limit of $(1 + 1/n)^n$, and is the base of natural logarithms; its never ending value is about 2.718. The value i represents the square root of -1. What can π, e, and i have to do with other? Euler proved that $e^{\pi i} = -1$ (see Knopp). Is it not beyond belief? How can you

begin to understand it? Does any cult have a mystery more
profound?

Again, Mandelbrot has found that if you instruct a computer to draw the points satisfying the value n as it generates n^2
+ c (where c is an arbitrary complex number), you will get a
shaded figure that looks like a symmetrical heart, with a near-
circle of smaller size behind it, and then a much smaller circle,
the surface of the whole being covered by a down of filaments
with intricate encrustations; and under magnification you will
find almost but not quite the same structures here and there, in
self-similarity, and so on forever, smaller and smaller. It is
beyond imagining; it stops the heart with ghastliness and incred-
ibility. It is a truth that would have existed had it never been
discovered; it is older than any particle in the universe; it belongs
with the things that are forever.

(5) An endword. In defining tragedy as an imitation of an
action, Aristotle told of its effect. By rousing up pity and fear
within us, tragedy brings about a catharsis of those passions.
That is, the weakness accumulating in the vesicles of our mind is
purged by our response to a grand event, and we are then better
able to bear the calamities that cross our daily path. (The philosopher used the medical term catharsis since he was the son of a
physician.) Actually the experience is not like that. We are
moved by a Greek tragedy not because the story is piteous and
fearsome, but because the play as the sum of its parts is a work of
art—a Dionysian entertainment, in the phrase of Carl Otfried
Müller. *The Trojan Women* does fill us with pity and fear, but pity
and fear are not the right words for the *Agamemnon* or *Oedipus
the King*. Those great plays and the others affect us not so much
by bruising the heart as by commanding us in the manner of the
allegretto of Beethoven's seventh symphony. Similarly with the
wonders of nature: mountains, oceans, and the flying lessons

that bluejays give to their young. Our response to it all is aesthetic: there has been, in the words of the mathematician W. D. Hardy, "a very high order of unexpectedness, together with economy and inevitability." And similarly from a communion with the body and blood, or a communion of the spirit with the everlasting. From the emotion and wonder we are changed when we return to where we were. We are like the fellow in Plato's cave who is shown the world of true forms and then has different values when he comes back. We are more generous than we were, less brutal; we have greater charity for our enemy than we did; the iron rule has been transmuted somewhat to the golden rule and even to the Jesus rule. As a race we are not so bent upon destruction. We are likelier to become an element in eternity.

Summaries

I. *Jesus would have us keep the commandments unless there is a better reason not to.* The accounts of how the commandments came into being, the commandments themselves, and the rest of the Old Testament as well are not worldly truths. They are religious stories, laws, and poems, and as such they have their own truth, which is like that of the New Testament parables or the stories in Homer. Jesus prescribed the commandments as a way of life, but held that the sabbath commandment, and accordingly all the others, might be outweighed by an awareness of right and wrong.

II. *The Jesus rule is to be generous to your enemy, within limits.* The story of Jesus was created, in the decades between his death and the writing down of the gospels, with the thought that the greatest of all events had just happened. There is no being sure what parts of the story are annals of flesh and blood rather than fables from the mind and the heart. Whether there ever was a sermon on the mount (or on the plain) is a matter to be accepted freely or else not, and the same for the parable of the Good Samaritan. Those are the likeliest elements of the New Testament to be authentic (for they are the most contrary to what had been thought or foreseen), but they are not to be regarded as historical truths. Sifting the evidence is an unneeded labor, though. For (1) the instruction to be magnanimous towards your enemies—the broadest advance there has ever been in ethics—can be studied for its own sake; as the iron rule of ruthless self-interest yields to the golden rule, so the golden yields to the Jesus rule. Nevertheless (2) by the example of Jesus himself we are not to be kinder than is warranted. Those two principles offer betterments for today if we consider things and do not merely read sentences from books. As the ethical old commandments are to be followed but not absolutely, so too is the new commandment, modifying the ethical old ones. We are not heedlessly but thoughtfully to take the Jesus rule as our guide of life. Between miracles and ethics, the church made the wrong choice, and, in the same way, between the military and the charitable, governments of our time have the wrong preference. The way of Jesus—his teaching together with his life—is today neglected as unworkable, even by those who claim to be his followers. It should really be regarded as the best path, even by those whose faith is in other prophets.

III. *The passover came to be within the passion; the passion come to be within the eucharist.* God as manager of our earthly life is hardly to be found in miracles. Those wrought by Jesus and Elijah belong to a bygone culture. The stories of the resurrection and the virgin birth do not have the perfection of a mockingbird's song or a spider's web. The Jesus rule has all the same been enhanced by its matrix of mystery. When the momentous events were being told by one generation to another, it came to be thought, and is written or implied in the gospels, that the *passion* or suffering (Greek *paschein*) had commemorated and fulfilled the *passover* (Greek *pascha*, Hebrew *pesach*). That is, the ceremony upon bread and wine in the Last Supper (of Matthew, Mark, and Luke) and the sacrifice of a Lamb in the crucifixion (John) were thought the keeping of a promise. It would be the final passover and complete the divine plan. What happened however was not like that. Jesus did return after his death (it was believed), but not as had been expected of the messiah, for the world did not end with a triumph of good over evil. What was the use of the types and prophecies—what was the worth of the resurrection—if daily life went on the same as before? The thought now was that Jesus would return again, and that this later return—known as the second coming—would bring the end. (The first coming had been Jesus' earthly life, including the short while after he had risen from the grave.) Those who were dying during the middle time—of waiting for the second coming—were then held to have brought death upon themselves. For had they not betrayed their master anew by behaving unworthily at the fellowship meal? From that belief the meal became (1 Corinthians 11) a ceremony "in remembrance," engraving Jesus upon the hearts of his followers. The Last Supper, with the crucifixion, would be within a Lord's Supper, or eucharist. As with the Old Testament ethical commandments and the new commandment of Jesus, though, it is not an absolute matter but a conditional one. The real presence in communion fare is measured not by science but by faith. And within that presence, though also without it, there is the Jesus rule, the golden rule as it reaches even to our enemies and is ethnic no longer. The thought for all humanity is not that Christ died for our sins, as theology would say, but that Jesus was put to death for teaching common kindness.

IV. *God is transcendent, but "the kingdom of God is within you" (Luke 17.21).* When there was no world-ending cataclysm and Jesus resurrected did not remain long, it was believed that there would be justice in an afterlife, and that the spirit of God would remain on earth until the messiah came again. What the evangelists and theologians stressed accordingly was the miraculous element in Jesus, summed up in the creed, though what he himself had stressed was love of our fellow human being. Will God, through the Son as judge, punish us for eternity, as the creed seems to warn? Who knows for sure? Arguments are apt to be delusions. It would seem best to lead an upright life without any idea of recompense in heaven. A better creed would be one affirming the Jesus rule. There is reason to think we are evolving in ethics; by the end of time, though not before then, humanity may have become godlike, as Jesus may have been godlike within time. God—as the creator of things, including time—is the same as existence itself, which is the name of God in Hebrew, well understood as meaning the Eternal; the farther we look into spacetime, the more remote it is. Whatever moves us deeply—the rite of communion, the beauty of the world, the act of making love—may have an effect on our sense of God and on our behavior besides. That is the final answer of this monograph.

The belief of Thomas Jefferson

In defending my central thesis—that between magic and ethics the church made the wrong choice—I sometimes say what was said two hundred years ago by Thomas Jefferson, whose version of the Bible has been republished with commentary (notably by Foote, Harrington, and Roche, and by Adams, Lester, and Sheridan). I am a follower upon Jefferson's heels; the similarity between us is great. Even greater (by my estimate) are the differences.

Jefferson was among the rationalists, navigators of thought. If Bayle and Voltaire were Columbus and Magellan, Paine and Jefferson were Balboa and Vasco da Gama. We who come after may think they took the wrong turn from time to time, but they were the adventurers, the immortals.

At the beginning of my third chapter I said that a person who is asked about God may reply: God the manager? or God the judge? or God the creator? Jefferson believed chiefly in the last of these, though in the first as well and perhaps in the second. As an architect he thought of God as an Architect, a Geometer, a Mechanic.

"I hold (without appeal to revelation) that when we take a view of the Universe, in its parts general or particular, it is impossible for the human mind not to perceive and feel a conviction of design, consummate skill, and indefinite power in every atom of its composition. The movements of the heavenly bodies, so exactly held in their course by the balance of centrifugal and centripetal forces, the structure of our earth itself, with its distribution of lands, waters and atmosphere, animal and vegetable bodies, examined in all their minutest particles, insects mere atoms of life, yet as perfectly organised as man or mammoth, the mineral substances, their generation and uses, it is impossible, I say, for the human mind not to believe that there is, in all this, design, cause and effect, up to an ultimate cause, a fabricator of all things from matter and motion, their preserver and regulator while permitted to exist in their present form, and their regenerator onto new and other forms. We see, too, evident proofs of the necessity of a superintending power to maintain the Universe in its course and order. Stars, well known, have disappeared, new ones have come into view, comets, in their incalculable courses, may run foul of suns and planets and require renovation under other laws; certain races of animals are become extinct; and, were there no restoring power, all existences might extinguish successively, one by one, until all should be reduced to a shapeless chaos" (letter to John Adams, 11 April 1823).

That is given as a profession of faith against the argument that the world cannot be shown to have had a Cause, for (by the same logic) behind the Cause there would have been another cause, and so on. Jefferson's counter-argument (not really an instance of reasoning) seems to be: (1) the world had no cause, or (2) it had a Cause without a prior cause, or (3) it had a Cause deriving from a prior cause, and (4) of these the second is the most satisfying and therefore the likeliest.

How well does Jefferson in his theology withstand Darwin and Hubbell? For comparison with the two-centuries-old argument from design I will sum up where we are today. The theory of creation (perhaps ongoing) can be made to agree with the theory of evolution, but cannot be derived from it. All crawling or leafy things, and also all mineral or elemental things, are survivors of competition. It may be that God, with a plan of what would happen, or else without one, wrought a system of destruction and rebuilding. Or it may be that such a system came into being because nothingness is unstable. Instantaneous (or else continuous) creation is also compatible with an expanding universe. From an almost infinitely dense mote, or by a collision of dimensions, around fifteen billion years ago, all the matter we know of broke forth, along with energy and with space and time. One school says that God wished to have it so; another says that Will was not involved.

Why did some humanists, not believing, study the scriptures so closely? Their motive was like that of Jesus himself (with the right adjustments in scale): they sought the betterment of a world in need. Jefferson thought the sages of Greece and Rome gave good advice about personal tranquillity. On the more difficult and important problem—how to treat your fellow man—he looked to the sermon on the mount (or the plain) and certain of the parables. His religion was actually a philosophy. Why did he not make it widely known? Among the reasons were a political wariness (learned in the campaign of 1800) and a personal reticence (not even his family knew of his Bible at the time of his death).

Jefferson regarded himself as a Christian. To him the theologians who made devotion to Jesus into a mystery cult were not Christians but Neoplatonists. What he himself made, in a brief form and then in a longer one, was a scissors-and-paste abridgement of the gospels. It is known as the Jefferson Bible. The earlier version, lost but reconstructed, was inscribed as "for the use of the Indians, unembarrassed with matters of fact or faith beyond their comprehension." The later version, here regarded as the same job done differently, no doubt kept that intention while enlarging upon it. The Old Testament was not included (for it was the law being reformed), nor were the epistles (they were for those who believed already). Most strikingly the miracles (regarded as inauthentic) were not included either, not even the resurrection.

When there is a man with a withered hand, along with the question of healing on the sabbath, in the Jefferson Bible, Jesus speaks about the sabbath but does nothing for the hand (Matthew 12.9–13). When there is the question about a blind man, whether it was he or his parents who had sinned, in the Jefferson Bible, Jesus says the blindness was to manifest the will of God, but then does not restore the sight (John 9.2–3). In these two instances the material was intractable; the words of Jesus have less point when the miracle is taken away. At other times what remains is sufficient and, if we are not looking for anything else, as fine as can be.

At the end of the *Odyssey* Odysseus slays the suitors and, as we did not quite foresee, is enrobed in the garment that Penelope had been weaving by day and undoing by night; soon husband and wife are reunited in love: it is an absolute triumph. In the unabridged gospels Jesus rises from the grave in the absolute triumph that is (or may be) the most meaningful of all events. At the end of the *Iliad* the body of Hector is burnt, the bones are gathered into a golden casket, and a feast is held in his honor: it is the calm of an absolute grief. In the Jefferson Bible it is the same: Joseph of Arimathea and Nicodemus took "the body of Jesus, and wound it in linen clothes with the spices, as the manner of the Jews is to bury. Now, in the place where he was crucified, there was a garden; and in the garden a new sepulchre, wherein was never man yet laid. There laid they Jesus. And rolled a great stone to the door of the sepulchre, and departed." There is no more, and the sense is: The life of Jesus was greater than any other, and he should be honored before all who have been or will be, though there is no reason to think he was the Son of God.

Not always but usually the miracles may be taken out and the ends closed up with continuity. Jefferson has fashioned a good piece of workmanship. His composite is of more than historical interest. From one point of view it is the purest form of the best moral teaching the world has ever had.

Did he restore the gospel to how it once had been? No, that is inconceivable. The world in the time of Jesus was alive with thoughts of the End. Any happening might become a cataclysmic wonder. Things were seen and heard that in an ordinary time would have remained hidden. To his followers Jesus was the target that all the past had aimed at. If the legends about him had been only moral, without marvels, they would not have been handed down.

The fact may be that Jesus was not the Son or God, nor even a worker of wonders, but a teacher and nothing besides. He must have had about him a grace that inspired immediate devotion. Some people own this quality more than others do. Why may Jesus not have owned it more than anyone else ever? Those who believed in him would accordingly have afterwards painted the lily of his sentences. We may say that the Jefferson Bible, though it is not the gospel as it ever was, tells how things actually were before they were changed by one imagination after another. The abridgement yields for Jefferson the summary that:

"The doctrines of Jesus are simple, and tend all to the happiness of man.

1. that there is one God, and he all-perfect:

2. that there is a future state of rewards and punishments:

3. that to love God with all thy heart, and thy neighbor as thyself, is the sum of religion. These are the great points on which he endeavored to reform the religion of the Jews. But compare with these the demoralising dogmas of Calvin.

1. that there are three Gods:

2. that good works, or the love of our neighbor are nothing:

3. that Faith is every thing; and the more incomprehensible the proposition, the more merit in its faith:

4. that Reason in religion is of unlawful use:

5. that God, from the beginning, elected certain individuals to be saved, and certain others to be damned; and that no crimes of the former can damn them, no virtues of the latter save" (letter to Benjamin Waterhouse, 26 June 1822).

Those last five are strong remarks, against the dogma of the Trinity, against the underestimating of good works, and against predestination. Setting them aside I would return to the earlier three doctrines of Jesus as Jefferson has here summed them up. Let me take the three in reverse order, aligning them with the aspects of God named in the third paragraph in this section: God who manages our lives on earth, God who will judge the lives we led, and God who was the creator.

To love God and to love thy neighbor as thyself. Jefferson might have allowed that both parts of this were Judaic (Deuteronomy 6.5, Leviticus 19.18); perhaps he did not know that they were. Between them they sum up the ten commandments. Is there any clutch or brake upon the directive? Yes, your love of God has been affected by your believing, or not believing, in miracles. If like Jefferson you disbelieve in them you will not apprehend God in the same way as a believer does. With Epicurus and other philosophers you may even hold God to an accounting. To love God as an abstraction is to be cheerful towards existence. That is not easily done but it can be an end in view. No more is needed than to take pleasure in the beauty of things and not to become despondent from daily glooms.

To love your neighbor is another matter, and Jefferson's summary needs two supplements. In Judaism your neighbor is a member of your tribe. Jesus regarded himself as a Jew in comparison with a Samaritan, though as a Galilean in comparison with a Judean. His parable of the Good Samaritan has an ethnic

moral since the Samaritans had reason from history not merely
to resent the Jews but to harbor malice against them. It is an
unexpressed part of the parable. And Jefferson, to judge from his
silence, was unaware of it. The good Samaritan seemingly did
what no one in Jewry would do or ever had done: he loved his
traditional *enemy* as himself. We gather from Jefferson that
through Jesus the iron rule of Judaism was being changed into
the golden rule. Actually the golden rule within Judaism—love
your landsman as yourself—was being changed into the Jesus
rule. That is my first supplement to Jefferson. The other is that
Jesus himself set limits. He was not an absolutist but a surveyor
of what lay at hand. In following him we ought not to deliver
ourselves for massacre; we are only to put ourselves in our
enemy's shoes and then step back into our own.

The twofold directive, as we may take it from the gospels,
though Jefferson did not, is to love God and all people, even our
enemy. That asks of us our best but nothing more. In loving God
we are not to be crushed by small hardships, and in loving our
enemy we are not to say at his bad luck, "It serves him right."

On a future state of rewards and punishments. If you do not
believe in the resurrection, you cannot speak about an afterlife—
of punishments and rewards—so confidently as believers can.
Jefferson is one of the last people we should have asked to show
that justice would be meted out by and by. It may be that as a
philosopher he liked the idea of an afterlife, so that what is unjust here and now may be made right there and then (another
view is that since there is no justice in this life there will be none
in the next life either). Jefferson also had a minor reason and a
major one to speak of the world to come. The minor was a wish
to heighten the contrast between Jesus and the Jews whose law
he was revising, for Judaism was divided on the matter (the
Pharisees said yes, there was an afterlife; the Sadducess said no,
there was not). The major reason, important also to Voltaire, was

a wish to improve behavior. For even if you disbelieve in a last judgment, you may want others to believe in one, since the dread of a "weeping and gnashing of teeth" might make them better persons in this life. The most profound idea of a continuum is Dante's: that our last thoughts from earth will stay with us forever. Whether Jesus' beliefs included or could combine with that idea there is no telling; whether Jefferson's could so combine is even more uncertain. In the teachings of Jesus about a future state, so far as they have come to us, and in Jefferson's comments upon those teachings, there is no advancement to match "love your neighbor, even your enemy."

There is one God, and he all-perfect. Jefferson disbelieved that Jesus had been God the Son, and disbelieved with intensity in a Trinity of Father, Son, and Holy Ghost. By his argument from design (explicit in the letter to Adams, implicit in the one to Waterhouse) a single Designer was necessary and sufficient. That grandly simple, philosophical answer is inadequate. It accounts for only the good, not the evil. Jefferson might have spoken about the ethics of Jesus without speaking of God at all. Or he might have said merely, "there is one God," without the "all-perfect." The matter of imperfection in the world—where did it come from?—would then not have arisen. But now it has, and no answer is offered. In the unabridged Bible, spiritual forces are always near by; there are elements of evil that have nothing to do with God except for being against him. The Jefferson Bible, by comparison, is expurgated of mystery; it is stiff and stark. Jefferson was not deaf to unhappiness; the kindness of Jesus was to him the highest ideal. So ought he not to have said why there was any need for that kindness? His belief is in this way inferior to the elaborate theology of traditional Christianity. The teaching of Jesus—to love your neighbor, even your enemy—has no worthy companion in Jefferson's thought about God's all-perfection.

I disagree with Jefferson in the following ways. First: he (seemingly) took Jesus' revision in ethics to have been from the iron to the golden rule; I take the revision to have been from the golden rule within Judaism to the Jesus rule for all the world. Secondly: Jefferson (seemingly) allowed no exceptions; I regard the golden rule and the Jesus rule as only guiding principles, not as unyielding laws; to Jefferson (seemingly) the teachings of Jesus are an ideal; to me they are practical, not angelic but human. Thirdly: Jefferson (seemingly) thought that justice required an afterlife; I do not see that it does; our idea of justice may be incomplete. Fourth: his belief in one God who is perfect fails to account for evil. Fifth: he thought it easy to separate the words of Jesus from those of the evangelists, and deleted the miracles; I regard the traditions about Jesus as fitted together (though with some loose ends and snarls), and think of the miracles simply as Bible stories. Sixth: in taking away the mysteries he does not allow any emotional element in our devotion to Jesus; for me a reenactment of the Last Supper may heighten our sense of being disciples and may in that way make us better everyday persons; it is a ceremony that Jews, Buddhists, American Indians, and agnostics can find ennobling, seeing that it asks for no commitment; had he been less austere, Jefferson too might have found it worth while, and might have become friends with those he regarded as Platonists; truly, communion with Jesus is one of the nourishments to sustain us on our march.

Endnotes

1. (to p. x): Arthur Koestler has argued that the Khazars, a tribe of Central Asia who converted to Judaism in the eighth century for independence from both Christianity and Islam, entered Europe and became by weight the main element in modern Jewry. If that were so, why should the Jews of Poland have spoken Yiddish, a form of German? A merit of the Koestler argument is that it might help to account for the two kinds (here distinguished from each other more abruptly than they are in real life): (1) the Ashkenazim, who are relatively fair in eyes, hair, and complexion, relatively well educated and prosperous, reasonably tolerant of others, apt to marry outside Judaism, apt to have smaller families, and apt to be of the Reform movement; (2) the Sephardim, who are relatively dark, less well educated and less prosperous, not so tolerant of others as they might be, unlikely to marry outside, likely to have larger families, and apt to be Orthodox. The former kind is predominant among Jews worldwide; the latter kind is predominant in Israel. Some rabbis in the West would like to "de-Ashkenize" their landsmen so as to have, among themselves, one nation indivisible (the term "de-Ashkenize" was used by Alexander Schindler in 1982: see Silver, p. 35). Many rabbis in Israel would also like to de-Ashkenize Jewry, but by undoing the Reform movement altogether.

If the Khazars were an Aryan nation, and if the Ashkenazim are descended from the Khazars, then the Ashkenazim are Aryans too. But if the Khazars were Turkic-Mongolian, then they were not Aryan, and the Jews of Khazar descent, if there are any, cannot be Aryan either, except in some other way. It has been argued that if the Lord promised the land to the seed of Jacob, and if the Jews are Khazars instead, then the land has not been promised to them. The review by Grossman in *Commentary* (p. 63) mentions that from frequency of fingerprint types the Jews from all whereabouts have been shown to be related. Another search for identity would be from frequency of blood types (I have read that African-Americans as a group are two-thirds African). Yet another search could be through mito-chondrial DNA (which is transmitted in the female line) together with types of the (male) y chromosome. There is a study of the contribution to the present-day Polynesian race by "sailors, traders, whalers, and missionaries" (Hurles, p. 1802). Another study indicates that the present-day Jewish race can be traced to a few distinctly different women, but cannot similarly be traced to a few different men (Thomas). How the tribe of Sarah-and-Isaac (the Sephardim of Israel, say) compares with that of Hagar-and-Ishmael (in Jordan, say) would be of timely interest.

2. (to p. 1): The Lord called them *debarim* "words" (Exodus 20.1), and afterwards they were known as the ten *debarim* (Exodus 34.28, Deuteronomy 4.13, 10.4), as they have continued to be in Judaism. The other commandments, ordinances, statutes (such as not seething a kid in his mother's milk) were known as *miswot* (Genesis 26.5, Exodus 15.26, Psalms 78.7, Isaiah 48.18). Philo (*On the Decalogue* 9, 12) speaks of the commandments as the ten *logoi, chresmoi, nomoi, thesmoi,* or *logia* "words, decrees, laws, oracles, statutes"; to Josephus (*Antiquities* 3.90) they are the ten *logoi* "words"; the Septuagint also has *logoi* (Exodus 20.1, Deuteronomy 10.4) or *remata* (Deuteronomy 5.5). In the gospels they are the *entolai* "commandments" (Mark 10.19, Luke 18.20); in Acts (7.38) they are the *logia*.

3. (to p. 3): "Gentile scholars are confused about this first commandment and unwisely explain it as not being a command-

ment. Consequently, they ask themselves, 'If so, how are there ten commandments?' In answering that question, there are differing opinions among them. Some divide the verse *Thou shalt have no other gods*, into two commandments, while the consensus of their paltry scholars is to divide *Thou shalt not covet* into two commandments . . . . Yet the verse mentions only *the ten words*, and not the ten commandments" (Ramban, v. 1, p. 64: see Nahmanides in Works cited).

4. (to p. 5): Josephus first wrote his *History of the Jewish War* in Aramaic for the peoples of the highlands, who did not know Greek (*War* 1.3; his word for them was barbarians, the Greek word for foreigners, whose speech sounds like bar-bar, that is, gibberish). His purpose (agreeable to his patron, the emperor Vespasian) was "not so much to extol the Romans as to console those whom they have vanquished and to deter others who may be tempted to revolt" (*War* 3.108). Who were they, these who might take up arms against Rome, either for revenge or from the thought of an easy victory? They were the Parthians, the Babylonians, the Arabians, and the Judeans living beyond the Euphrates and in Adiabene (*War* 1.6). Was Josephus referring to fellow countrymen of his in Parthia? No, the Parthians were Iranians, for they had Zoroastrian names, not Jewish ones. So it is of interest that he approached them in Aramaic, a Semitic language, rather than in an Aryan one. Josephus later wrote his *War* in Greek for all those outside the interior, that is, for the rest of the empire east of Rome; readers in Palestine would evidently have had a choice, Greek or Aramaic. (Only the Greek version of the *War* survives.)

5. (to p. 6): We are all Cro-Magnons, not Neanderthals, but some of us are Negroes, some Semites, some Aryans, some Mongols, and some of other stocks. And of course many of us are of more races than one. Ethnic origin is hidden since in-

vaders, being manly and silent, leave their genes behind but not their tongues. Genghis Khan brought Finland and Hungary within his empire, and (must have) settled those territories with women from his realm, who (must have) brought up their children in Mongolian. But other tribes, from the west rather than the east, ravished their way into the blood-line, which is why that Asian language is spoken by the ethnic Scandinavians of Finland and by the Central Europeans of Hungary. Are not the Greeks of the present day more Turkic, after four hundred years of occupation, than Achilles and Odysseus had been? It would seem so, though the ancient Greeks must have had hair that was dark to at least a medium degree, since Menelaus in Homer is often said to be blond, which implies that the others are not. (The same for Harald Fairhaired: the other Norwegians must have had hair that was darker than his.)

6. (to p. 7): Richard Horsley to the contrary holds that the Galileans in the time of Jesus had been essentially Judaic for centuries; the idea of forcible conversion (with circumcision) is not one he accepts.

The Reform movement in Judaism has recently—as reported in the Chicago *Tribune*, 28 June 01, p. 1—returned to the rituals of conversion. One of these is baptism, of men and women alike. Another is the circumcision of men. (For converts who have already been circumcised there may be—the rabbis disagree strongly about this—a symbolic drawing of blood at the site.)

7. (to p. 9): What I have suggested about the letters alef and ain, he and het, may stand on a foot of clay; I have followed Bloedhorn and Hüttenmeister, and am unable to go further. A few centuries later the Judeans will disdain some pronunciations of the Galileans (*Gemara* "Erubin" 53b), and a linguist might

be able to trace the variants to Greek ancestry or some other cause. The men of Ephraim did not say *shibboleth*, but *sibboleth*, for they "could not frame to pronounce it right" (Judges 12.6), and the reason why they could not is now remote. Dialects develop when people stay put, like Immanuel Kant, who never left Königsberg in his life. One person imitates another and defects become fashionable. Every village in la Wallonie, the French-speaking part of Belgium, has its own dialect, and the pronunciation of the word for hat—*shahPO* is the standard one—ranges from *chahPEE* (ch as in church) to *KApeeo* (my authority being a permanent exhibit au musée de la vie wallonne in Liège). But behind the dialects is the grandmother tongue and you may be able to hear it if need be. I once went by freighter from Oslo to Gothenburg to Copenhagen to Hamburg, and noticed that the shipworkers and the dockworkers understood each other well enough to do dangerous jobs together. An acquaintance of mine, an American, was reared by his one grandmother in Irish and then, forgetting all his Irish, was reared by the other grandmother in German; now when he travels to where an ungainly dialect of German is spoken he listens with limited understanding for about three weeks and then can pass as a native.

8. (to p. 13): The verse is quoted from the Revised Standard Version, confirmed by a scroll (see Hendel). The King James reads, from the Masoretic text, "according to the number of the children of Israel." The scroll is to be followed, for we can see why its reading would have been changed, but cannot see the contrary.

9. (to p. 14); The Cain-giants-flood composite from Genesis, which accounts for the dreadful things, is one of the two Bible stories known to the poet of *Beowulf*, the other one being the story of the Creation, which accounts for the good things. The

myth is retold with Germanic bleakness and strength in C. S. Lewis's poem "The Adam Unparadised."

In the book of Enoch, chapter 7, a bad lot of angels take to themselves wives and beget giants, and afterwards sin against the other creatures, and devour one another and drink the blood. In chapter 86 they fall like stars into a pasture of cattle, and let out their members like horses, and come into the cows, which give birth to elephants and camels and asses.

10. (to p. 24): I gather from Jesus, and from Paul as well, that the use of strong language is not wicked in itself but in the intent behind it (such as a wish to *be* wicked or to offend or corrupt someone). Its use as an ornament is to be forgiven. The ornament goes out of fashion, though, and some words that used to take daring—such as *hell!* or *damn!*—are mild today and rare. Romuald Comtois once told me that in French Canada the most awful word was *calice!* "chalice," and I used to hear oaths like *tabernac' de Chrisse il fait froid ce matin* "tabernacle of Christ it's cold this morning." Some words had and may still have a weaker form, like *darn* for *damn*: *câline* for *calice*, *tabernouche* for *tabernacle*, and *Calvasse* for *Calvaire* (Sinclair Robinson).

11. (to p. 27): "Then Jael Heber's wife took a nail of the tent, and took a hammer in her hand, and went softly unto him, and smote the nail into his temples, and fastened it into the ground: for he was fast asleep and weary. So he died" (Judges 4.21). Truly it is a wonderful story, but it depends on a false inference. For this prose is retelling the poetry of the next chapter: "She put her hand to the nail, and her right hand to the workmen's hammer" (5.26), where Sisera is not killed in his sleep, but standing ("At her feet he bowed, he fell"). How is the change to be explained?

The words for nail and hammer really mean about the

same, as the mates do in most word pairs. A single action described twice, in chapter 5 (she clobbers him), has become, when retold without awareness of the synonymy, a two-handed action described once, in chapter 4 (she pounds a spike into him). A better rendering for "nail," in chapter 5, would be "stave, lintel, piece of lumber." (And that would also be better where the word occurs elsewhere: Ezra 9.8, Isaiah 22.23–5, Zechariah 10.4.) But then we should not have Jael with hammer and nail, and who can forget her? (The translators did not forget her when they wrongly said "nail" in the other passages.)

Similarly with "thy King cometh unto thee: he is just, and having salvation; lowly, and riding upon an ass, and upon a colt the foal of an ass" (Zechariah 9.9). The synonymous parallelism is misunderstood in the fulfillment, "And the disciples went, and did as Jesus commanded them, and brought the ass, and the colt, and put on them their clothes, and they set him thereon" (Matthew 21.6–7), where there are two animals, not one, and Jesus is placed on both of them, which is absurd. (So Wellhausen p. 94, explaining Judges 4–5, brilliantly.)

12. (to p. 29): The same must follow from the recurrence of half verses and entire verses, such as "And they shall beat their swords into plowshares, and their spears into pruning hooks" (Isaiah 2.4, Micah 4.3; see Joel 3.10). How might the word pairs and lines have become elements owned in common by all poets? The tradition must at first have been oral rather than written, for the oral poet needs ready-made supplies to help him speak on the moment, while the writing poet does not need them since he has the leisure to create phrases for himself. It is accordingly as expected that Jeremiah, as an oral poet rather than a lettered one, dictated his prophecies to Baruch (Jeremiah 36.18). The tradition would also seem to have been far larger—for the elements to have become known to all poets—than we can tell from what

has survived. That means, any word pair or verse, even if now found only once, is more likely than not to have been a commonplace at one time.

The like is true for Homer. The analogue to parallelism— as a conventional high style or problem—was a dactylic hexameter rhythm. The Hebraic poet had solutions in the word pairs, which were resources for creating parallelism. The Homeric poet had solutions in ready-made phrases of different length and shape. If *horses* or *Poseidon* needed a supplement, *single-hooved horses* or *Poseidon shaker of the earth*, would come to mind. And, as elements were repeated in the one tradition, so were they in the other: "Her fate lamenting, leaving manliness and youth" (*Iliad* 16.857 = 22.363). And analogously with *The Song of Roland* and *Beowulf*.

From the concordances to Homer (Prendergast and Dunbar), the *Roland* (Duggan), and *Beowulf* (Bessinger), the recurring lines are easy to see. From the concordances to the Bible they are not so easily seen. Some of them are: "The Lord is my strength and song, and he is become my salvation" (Exodus 15.2, Psalms 118.14, Isaiah 12,2), "I will not give sleep to mine eyes, or slumber to mine eyelids" (Psalms 132.4, Proverbs 6.4), "For their feet run to evil, and make haste to shed blood" (Proverbs 1.16, Isaiah 5.7), "on all their heads shall be baldness, and every beard cut off" (Isaiah 15.2, Jeremiah 48.37), "I have heard a rumour from the Lord, and an ambassador is sent unto the heathen" (Jeremiah 49.14, Obadiah 1), "A day of darkness and of gloominess, a day of clouds and of thick darkness" (Joel 2.2, Zephaniah 1.15), "The Lord also shall roar out of Zion, and utter his voice from Jerusalem" (Joel 3.16, Amos 1.12).

13. (to p. 48): My conclusions are similar to those of Eduard Nielsen, with these differences: (1) I suggest why "other gods" came to include "image" (namely that a supplement intended

for "other gods" was attached to "image" through heedlessness or lack of space); (2) I regard the making of an image as including (in fact as chiefly consisting in) the making of an image of the Lord; (3) I hazard a connection in Hebrew between the captivity in Egypt and the sabbath, so as to justify the phrasing of the sabbath commandment in Deuteronomy; (4) I do not limit stealing to the stealing of a man, as Nielsen does (evidently to avoid duplication with coveting); and (5) to avoid that duplication and for balance in heft, I take coveting to include the wish to break any of the other commandments.

Baruch J. Schwartz—who regards "I am the Lord . . . Egypt" as a prologue (against the common Jewish notation) and who takes "other gods" and "image" together—finds that "the number of topics is nine." I believe there are ten topics, for I would keep "other gods" and "image" separate, giving to the latter the sense "do not worship your God in any image." Schwartz also holds coveting to be of roughly equal weight with killing, adultery, stealing, and false witness; I myself do not think it is weighty enough unless it becomes more inclusive.

14. (to p. 59): The Greeks somehow remembered, through the myth of the Minotaur, that they had once been compelled to send, to Minos of Crete, a certain number of young men and women, for sacrifice to a half-bull (the Minos taurus); what the tribute really had been was bushels of grain and jars of oil, to a land where young men and women, for sport, rode bulls through a labyrinthine market place. On Barabbas see Rigg. On *The Song of Roland* and what happened at Roncevaux see Eginhardt (Einhard), paragraph 9 (Firchow and Zeydel). On the Minotaur see Dow, p. 151.

15. (to p. 66): Matthew 7 reads: (6) ". . . neither cast ye your pearls before swine, lest they trample them under their feet, and

turn again and rend you. (7) Ask, and it shall be given you; seek, and ye shall find; knock, and it shall be opened unto you: (8) for every one that asketh receiveth; and he that seeketh findeth; and to him that knocketh it shall be opened. (9) Or what man is there of you, whom if his son ask bread, will he give him a stone? (10) Or if he ask a fish, will he give him a serpent? (11) If ye then, being evil, know how to give good gifts unto your children, how much more shall your Father which is in heaven give good things to them that ask him? (12) Therefore all things whatsoever ye would that men should do to you, do ye even so to them: for this is the law and the prophets. (13) Enter ye in at the strait gate. . . ."

Verse 7 is a threefold promise of what God will do; 8 is a threefold affirmation; 9 tells what any one of us would do; 10 says the same in other words; and 11 draws the conclusion: if we being evil can do a good thing, will not God being perfect do the good thing even more surely? The structure was built up and now in 11 the capstone is emplaced. But the "therefore" (Greek *oun*) beginning 12 is jarring; there is a change in thought; the whole is no longer rhetorically admirable. The Anchor Bible suggests that 12 may once have followed 6 directly, and that 7 through 11 was inserted afterwards. Surely that cannot be correct; 12 does not continue 6 any better than it does 11. What seems likely is that verse 12 was added from somewhere, not quite heedlessly but almost. Once we move it away, verse 11 will close the thought, and 13 can begin a new one. And when verse 12 of chapter 7 is put into chapter 5, the "therefore" is just what was needed; wrinkles in both chapters have been smoothed out. It is not a small, merely scholarly matter, for the verse, now where it belongs, is one of the most important elements in human thought.

16. (to p. 67): The King James version (here quoted) takes the liberty of translating the Greek *kai* at the beginning of Luke 6.32

not as *and* but as *for*, seeing that the thought is abrupt. Dihle (p. 113) translates the *poiete* as an indicative rather than the familiar imperative: the sense is: 31 (in a new paragraph, where an old moral proverb is surprisingly, though not yet clearly, made into a reproof:) And you live by the golden rule; 32 (now unfolding the surprise fully:) And that is not enough.

It is a brilliant interpretation; but actually the imperative (as in Matthew 7.12) can be read just as well: 31 (straightforwardly with or without a new paragraph) And live by the golden rule; 32 (here all at once the surprise of a wonderful sudden thought) And that is not enough.

17. (to p. 68): The Danby translation was published by the Oxford University Press in 1933. Those not familiar with the *Mishnah* may want a specimen of how the law is recast. "And if any of the flesh of the sacrifice of his peace offerings be eaten at all on the third day, it shall not be accepted, neither shall it be imputed unto him that offereth it: it shall be an abomination, and the soul that eateth of it shall bear his iniquity" (Leviticus 7.18). "If a man slaughtered the offering purposing to toss its blood or some of its blood outside [the Temple Court], or to burn its sacrificial portions or some of its sacrificial portions outside, or to eat its flesh or an olive's bulk of its flesh outside, or an olive's bulk of the skin of the fat tail outside, the offering becomes invalid, but punishment by Extirpation is not incurred [by them that eat thereof]. If he purposed to toss its blood or some of its blood on the morrow, or to burn its sacrificial portions or some of its sacrificial portions on the morrow, or to eat its flesh or an olive's bulk of its flesh on the morrow, or an olive's bulk of the skin of the fat tail on the morrow, the offering becomes Refuse, and punishment by Extirpation is incurred [by them that eat thereof]" ("Zebahim" 2.2: p. 469, Danby).

18. (to p. 68): "Soncino edition": The Soncino edition was translated by various hands and edited by Isidore Epstein; it was published at London in 1935; the pagination begins anew with each tractate, so some wrongturnings are to be put up with. The table of contents to the Danby *Mishnah* is useful (to the non-specialist) in locating the tractates of the *Gemara*. As a specimen I quote part of the comment on the *Mishnah* "Zebahim" passage in the preceding note: "An objection is raised: If one slaughters a burnt-offering [intending] to burn as much as an olive of the skin under the fat-tail out of bounds, it is invalid, but does not involve *kareth* [Extirpation]; after time, it is *piggul* [Refuse], and involves *kareth*. Eleazar b. Judah of Avlas said on the authority of R. Jacob, and thus also did R. Simeon b. Judah of Kefar 'Iccum say on the authority of R. Simeon: The skin of the legs of small cattle, the skin of the head of a young calf, and the skin under the fat-tail, and all cases which the Sages enumerated of the skin being the same as the flesh, which includes the skin of the pudenda: [if he intended eating or burning these] out of bounds [the sacrifice] is invalid, and does not involve *kareth*; after time it is *piggul*, and involves *kareth*. Thus [this is taught] only [of] the burnt-offering, but not [of] a sacrifice. As for R. Huna, it is well, it is right that he specifies a burnt-offering. But according to R. Hisda, why does he particularly teach 'burnt-offering': let him teach 'sacrifice'?—R. Hisda can answer you: I can explain this as referring to the fat-tail of a goat; alternatively I can answer: Read 'sacrifice.'"

Those who are unfriendly to such legalisms in religion will have to acknowledge that the Gemara is faithful to the Mishnah, and the Mishnah to Leviticus, and that similarly on more devious matters the Mishnah and the Gemara meet the challenge (of dividing and subdividing) without effort. In Christian studies the analogue is the allegorical commentary by the church fathers and doctors. On both traditions Farrar is the best guide you could want.

19. (to p. 68): "The Talmud is the product of Palestine, the land of the Bible, and of Mesopotamia, the cradle of civilisation. The beginnings of Talmudic literature date back to the time of the Babylonian Exile in the sixth pre-Christian century, before the Roman Republic had yet come into existence. When, a thousand years later, the Babylonian Talmud assumed final codified form in the year 500 after the Christian era, the Western Roman Empire had ceased to be. That millennium opens with the downfall of Babylon as a world-power; it covers the rise, decline and fall of Persia, Greece and Rome; and it witnesses the spread of Christianity and the disappearance of Paganism in Western and Near Eastern Lands" (Hertz).

20. (to p. 70): It has been argued "that Jesus' debates with the Pharisees were actually disputes recorded in the Talmud between Bet Shammai and Bet Hillel, with Jesus adopting the views of Bet Hillel" (Falk, p. 8). My own argument is that the golden rule in Judaism, even after Hillel (as we see from the Talmud), applies only among the children of Israel (Leviticus 19.18), whereas Jesus to the contrary teaches, "Love your enemies" (Matthew 5.43–44). Besides, the thesis that the New Testament really records the disputes between Hillel and Shammai is hard to accept, whereas the Jesus rule is not to be challenged similarly, for it is a matter of ethical philosophy, not of history, and can be followed without affirming that it was ever said.

21. (to p. 72): Harris Kaasa, a Lutheran student for the ministry, lodging in a room next to mine, used to ask me every now and then to turn on a light for him, but that is because he was wet from a shower and fearful of a shock. I regard both my friend and Senator Lieberman as cautious to a fault. It is the law that "in the seventh year shall be a sabbath of rest unto the land" (Leviticus 25.4; "let the field rest fallow every seventh year," mandate 134 of the 613); but Jewish farmers in Israel sometimes

bypass the law by selling their land for a year to Gentiles and then buying it back. I myself might do the same; for laws sometimes have to be bypassed; but I do not approve.

In Judaism there are "the seven rabbinical commandments," including the ablution of the hands before eating. Since Jesus did not put value on that ablution, and did not name the commandments of Moses with precision, his heart would not have been in the rabbinical seven any more than in the Noachian seven or the 613.

The Catholic church has, as a supplement to the ten commandments, certain "commandments of the church." St. Antoninus of Florence, in the fifteenth century, listed ten of them: one was to tithe; another, to attend mass every Sunday; a third, not to receive the eucharist from a priest openly living in concubinage. They are good regulations so long as only minor worth is given to them. I know a Catholic who, upon being asked which was the more important, to attend mass or to be generous towards your neighbor, gave what I regard as the wrong answer.

Craig Staudenbaur once showed me an announcement by Merton College, Oxford, offering a fellowship to a humanist. He was applying and suggested that I do so too. That was generosity beyond the golden rule. For since there was only one fellowship, he was lowering his own chance by bringing a rival into the competition. I do not recall having done the like myself.

22. (to p. 80): I would offer an instance of (possible) moderate anti-Semitism from today and also one of (possible) moderate anti-Gentilism. John Strugnell, editor-in-chief of the Dead Sea scrolls, gave an interview to an Israeli newspaper. As an aftermath he was asked to resign and did so. The reason given to the world was ill health. A minor reason alleged was alcoholism. The true reason is to be found in his statements. The interview is reproduced in the volume *Understanding the Dead Sea Scrolls*,

edited by Hershel Shanks, who afterwards discusses what Stugnell has said. (What follows here is condensed but otherwise unchanged. It is given in segments, as the interviewer leads from one thing to another.)

"I'm not an anti-Semite . . . I don't know anyone in the world who's an anti-Semite . . . Judaism is originally racist . . . it's a folk religion; it's not a higher religion . . . An Anti-Judaist, that's what I am . . . The correct answer of Jews to Christianity is to become Christian . . . I don't, when I'm working on a Qumran text, think how stupid and wrong the Jews were . . . It's a horrible religion . . . I believe that the answer for Islam, and Buddhism, and all other religions is to become Christian. Judaism disturbs me in a different sense, because, whereas the others became Christians when we worked hard on them, the Jews stuck to an anti-Christian position . . . I dislike Israel as an occupier of part of Jordan. And it's quite obvious that this was part of Jordan . . . some of my friends are Israelis. But the occupation of Jerusalem—and maybe of the whole state—is founded on a lie . . . I don't think that the maintenance of an Israeli state or a Zionist state is impossible . . . You've got four million people here, even though the Zionists based themselves on a lie. But they're here now, you're not going to move populations of four million. Not even the Nazis managed that . . . Am I opposed to Zionism? . . . It would've been nice if it hadn't existed, but it has, so it's covered by a sort of grandfather clause . . . Racial sterotypes are one of the greatest things in our humor—where would we be without Armenian jokes, Polish jokes, Jewish jokes? This may be taken to mean that I detest a whole class of people, but that's not true. . . ."

I gather that Strugnell bears rancor against Jews and Judaism partly from a missionary commitment; as a warrior of the Christian faith he takes no prisoners; if you are not converted you must be damnably stubborn. But an equal cause of his feeling is political, and here there are two critical moments. He holds that the British mandate from the United Nations in 1917, to make for the Jews a homeland in Palestine, was unjust to the Arabs living there. (*The Economist*, 20 January 2001, p. 81, sums up Britain's motives as a mixture of idealism, greed for another outpost, and respect for "what politicians such as Lloyd George took to be the mysterious power of world Jewry.") The second moment that determined Strugnell's feeling came only a generation ago. The continuing occupation of the land taken in 1967 he regards as another injustice, though all the same he does not think the Zionist state ought to be dismembered. What seems to me unsuitable in the interview is the choice of language. No one likes to be called stupid or to hear his religion described as horrible. Shanks acknowledges that Stugnell was the first to hire Israeli and other Jewish scholars to join the Catholic coterie in whose hands the scrolls lay. Among those beholden to Strugnell were Elisha Qimron, Devorah Dimant, Emanuel Tov, Joseph Baumgarten, Jonas Greenfield, Jacob Sussman, and Shemaryahu Talmon. It looks to me as if Strugnell went beyond the golden rule. But because he proved himself so disagreeable, both to Judaism as a religion and to Israel as a modern state, as well as for reasons too small to mention here, Shanks brands him an anti-Semite.

I would say that if Strugnell is an anti-Semite then Shanks is an anti-Gentile to just as great a degree. Or we could say that Strugnell is a pro-Gentile and Shanks a pro-Semite. Those who are wary of anti-Semitism in others ought to look at themselves for traces of anti-Gentilism, and similarly of course the contrary. Here (I believe) the one man is as much to blame as the other. Between any groups that recognize each other as different, minor matters loom large, and large ones are huge. In my opinion both Strugnell and Shanks have increased the sum of ethnic unfriendliness.

The restricted sense of *anti-Semite* is now the correct one. It might be put among the elements of language that H. W. Fowler calls sturdy indefensibles. There is no need for a term that would mean animosity against all the Semites. Some of us have been persuaded to hate President Hussein of Iraq, but not because of his race, for no one hated King Hussein of Jordan. The Semites as an extended nation are not disliked any more than the peoples of the Subcontinent or the Pacific rim. Hard feeling against the Jews, though, because they are competitive or successful or exclusive or for some other reason, is met with fairly often. I once had a Jewish acquaintance who dated a number of Gentile girls. He would tell them right off that he was Jewish. Then, after a few drinks, he would say, "Really, I'm a Navajo, but I say that I'm Jewish because people resent the Navajos." And the girl would say, "No, I don't think people resent the Navajos."

23. (to p. 81): I owe almost the entirety of this paragraph to Herford, *Christianity in Talmud*, but the derivation of *ben Stada* from *anastasis* is mine, against Herford, p. 345, who offers *anastatos*, which he translates as "seditious." His introduction is valuable as a comparison of Rabbinical Judaism (interpretations of the pentateuch upon the names of authorities from the past) with the teaching of Jesus (which sets aside the pentateuch whenever a seemingly better end comes to mind). "Rabbinism prescribes what a man shall *do*, and defines his service of God in precise rules, while it leaves him perfectly unfettered in regard to what he shall *believe*," whereas Christianity came to prescribe what a man should *believe*, but left him free to *do* whatever he thought right (p. 16). (It may be that Romans 9.30–31 says the same.)

In Islamic writings of the eighth through the eighteenth centuries, Jesus (sometimes called Christ and sometimes spoken of as the son of Mary) is a wise, saintly, kindly figure, and also a Muslim in telling against wine; there is of course no thought that he is the incarnation of God. Jesus of Islam counsels the golden rule (in its double-negative form), advises that a man guilty of adultery should be stoned but not by anyone similarly guilty, remarks on casting pearls before swine, offers his other cheek to be slapped, warns that a rich man can no more easily enter the kingdom of heaven than a camel can pass through the eye of a needle, and says to God, "Not as I will, but as Thou wilt" (see Khalidi).

That is, while Jesus in the Judaism of the Talmud is regarded as an enemy, in Islam before the modern period he is altogether good.

24. (to p. 94): Am I condoning terrorism? My brother's daughter, well loved by me, lost her life to the Palestine Liberation Organization. Her plane westwards from Athens had originated in Israel; it went into the sea. She was a person of quality in character and in ability, a petroleum geologist with a doctorate from Stanford. So I am by emotion greatly against terrorism. I am also against giving cause to terrorists.

Are we to make preventive war on Islam to keep it from terrorizing Israel, ourselves, and the other lands of the "Jews and crusaders"? No, a vote to invade Iraq is a vote against the sermon on the mount. The matter is not between a strong arm or a weak one; it is whether to have strength of mind. We would be provoking terrorism forevermore, shedding the blood of our heirs in time to come. We would also be shedding our blood today; those who decide on war should be made to supply their own sons and daughters as enlisted troops.

25. (to p. 109): After the United Nations partitioned Palestine into a Jewish portion and an Arab portion, Jews everywhere could think that biblical promises to them had been kept. So there came

to be a reason for double loyalty, such as many another type feels in his bones (Muslims face towards Mecca when they pray). The May 1999 "Statement of Principles for Reform Judaism, Adopted at the 1999 Pittsburgh Convention" speaks warmly, some might say too warmly, of the allegiance owed by those abroad to the homeland of Israel. The statement also admonishes the Israelis to respect the ideas of Jews in other lands.

Some African-American groups, such as the Black Muslims or the New Black Panthers, furnish interesting twofold opposition. They resent their neighborhood Jewish store owners and landlords, and from their alliance with the Arab world they resent Israel as well.

Since so much of America is Jewish by contribution and ownership, our country as a whole has a special relationship with Israel (as for other reasons we have one with the United Kingdom), and the Israel lobby in American politics is notoriously powerful (see Lind). It may be a factor in our animosity towards Iraq ("O daughter of Babylon, who art to be destroyed," Psalms 137.8). If a congressman argues for even-handedness in the Middle East, it can be his undoing, as it was with Paul McCloskey and others told of in *They Dare to Speak Out*. Not that American Jews, in this respect, differ from any other group, except in their strength. Catholics and Baptists also boycott what they disapprove of, and so do African-Americans, Cuban-Americans, and gyneco-Americans.

26. (to p. 119): Over forty years ago these words were assembled by a chaplain when a general asked for a non-denominational prayer: "Almighty God, who art the Author of liberty and the Champion of the oppressed, hear our prayer. We, the men of Special Forces, acknowledge our dependence upon Thee in the preservation of human freedom. Be with us as we seek to defend the defenseless and to free the enslaved. May we ever remember

that our nation, whose motto is In God we Trust, expects that we shall acquit ourselves with honor, that we may never bring shame among our faith, our families, or our fellow men. Grant us wisdom from Thy mind, courage from Thine heart, strength from Thine arm, and protection by Thine hand. It is for Thee that we do battle, and to Thee belongs the victor's crown. For Thine is the kingdom, and the power and glory, forever. Amen" (from the Lansing *State Journal*, 2 February 2002, p. 6D).

It is a compromise between (1) separating church and state, and (2) giving to the troops what they need to do their best. The solution is not a perfect one, but no perfect one is possible; as a solution the compromise is all right.

The pledge of allegiance to the flag ought to unite Americans and did so as I learned it in school. But then the words "under God" were added. A court of appeals has now ruled that the addition was against the guarantee of religious freedom. In protest the United States Senate has voted 99 to 0 to keep the words. Will the Supreme Court hear arguments? The general feeling appears to be that if you believe in God you ought to say so in affirming your patriotism. It is like putting a favorite ingredient into a recipe where it does not belong. "Render to Caesar the things that are Caesar's, and to God the things that are God's" (Mark 12.17).

Similarly, those who take an oath of office or give testimony are asked to say, "So help me God." There are three reasons not to do so: (1) an affirmation "under penalty of perjury" would be more democratic, (2) to say "God" needlessly may be against the commandment, and (3) it may also be against the teaching of Jesus (Matthew 5.34–7).

Further, to put your hand on the Bible as you swear means that you favor all it contains. I am not the only one who does not. Jesus set much of it aside.

For some time "prayer breakfasts" have been held by the

President. Like the motto "In God we trust" on coins, they do not damage greatly, but only somewhat, the rights of those who want to keep religion separate from government. I should favor instead a "breakfast of charity."

27. (to p. 128): Many who would like to believe come undone because they cannot, as in *The Flight of Peter Fromm* by Martin Gardner. Or a heart divided might believe in miracles but resist them, as in *Cold Heaven* by Brian Moore. Those two theological novels, equaled only by Anatole France's *Thais*, are not merely the foremost members of their kind; they stand well with prose writing of any kind.

28. (to p. 136): "Christ our passover is sacrificed" *to pascha hemon etuthe Christos* (1 Corinthians 5.7) may be the first instance of typology and the origin of that way of thinking. And the *pascha-paschein* etymology may there be implicit, though I do not believe it is. Philo associated the two words, *pascha* and *paschein*, when he explained *pascha* the "passover" as a departing from the *passions* (*Special Laws* 2.147, *Allegorical Interpretation* 3.94.7, and elsewhere). There is no typology in that interpretation, but there may be another first instance, namely an explanation from a contrary; later there would be Isidore of Seville's *lucus a non lucendo* "(it is called) a grove because it does not let the light through," or *canis a non canendo* "a dog because it does not sing." It may also be thanks to Philo that the passover came to be explained as a passing over from Egypt and even as a passing over the Red Sea.

29. (to p. 140): Another verse that might be cited is "in the ninth day of the month at even, from even unto even, shall ye celebrate your sabbath" (Leviticus 23.32), where the ordinal 9th is a problem. Can it have been an overcorrection of *8th*, seven days

after the 1st? (My professor of Gothic, C. J. S. Marstrander, went wrong similarly when he said to me, "I lost my train this morning." He was halfway thinking in Norwegian, where the word for lose is *miste*.) On the other hand the 10th (for reasons unclear) is the Day of Atonement, so the reading (Leviticus 23.32) could perhaps be 9th after all, or 10th (see *Eerdmans Dictionary of the Bible* "day").

30. (to p. 145): "They pierced my hands and my feet" (Psalms 22.16) is what the verse means in Hebrew, and what it meant in Greek or Aramaic in the time of Jesus. But the original sense may have been that beasts of prey "picked clean my hands and my feet" (Dahood, pp. xxx–xxxi). The psalm is hard to follow; it has surely been misshapen. Verses 16 and 17 read: "For dogs have compassed me: the assembly of the wicked have inclosed me: they pierced my hands and my feet. I may tell all my bones: they look and stare upon me." Is there a thread of continuity? The thought may be: "Wild dogs have surrounded me; terrible creatures enclose me. They have picked clean my hands and my feet; my bones are bare for the counting; I am a dreadful thing to see."

The issue is of moment if I am right in thinking that "they pierced my hands and my feet" brought all the rest of the 22nd psalm to the mind of those who were retelling the story of Jesus. That is: (1) the sense is likely to have once been, "they picked clean my hands and my feet"; (2) if that sense had not been lost—and replaced by the one familiar to us, "they pierced my hands and my feet"—the verse would not have seemed to foretell the crucifixion; (3) the verse would then not have brought with it, into the gospel tradition, the other verses, from the psalm, that seemed prophetic also; (4) there would have been no narratives upon the words, "My God, my God, why hast thou forsaken me? . . . All they that see me laugh me to scorn . . .

They part my garments among them, and cast lots upon my vesture."

31. (to p. 146): With Matthew 27.46–9 may be compared lines 681–9 of the *Agamemnon* of Aeschylus. The chorus say: "Who named you so rightly Helen!" with the name in the accusative, *Helenan* (the nominative being *Helena*). Then they explain *helenan* as if it were the accusative of *helenas*, a compound of *hel-* "seize" + the accusative *nan* (its nominative being *nas*) "ship." The inevitable translation, by George Thomson if not by someone earlier, is "the hell of ships," the hell of men, the hell of cities: *helenas*, *helandros*, *heleptolis*. Though grim, it is word-play, and it is fine poetry. My comment upon Matthew 27 (Mark 15) would be to the similar credit of that evangelist. Matthew 27.47–9 (Mark 15.35–36) is then to be rendered as: ". . . This man called out *Eli Jah* . . . let us see whether Elijah will come." Now the passage makes sense in all ways.

32. (to p. 151): The name Mary has sounds in common with a Hebrew word for magnify, though actually that word means rebellious against authority, as in a story about Miriam (Numbers 12.1–11). Some early man of letters, reflecting upon the word as used by Elizabeth in a lost document written in Hebrew, and taking the word in a special sense, may have been led by its similarity to "Mary" to ascribe the "magnify" passage to her. Though utterly implausible, that may have happened. For if "Abraham" can mean "father of many nations" (Genesis 17.5), where the *r* is unaccounted for, who will say there cannot possibly have been wordplay on "magnify"? What seems like-lier is that the Baptist was to be by name, as well as in the flesh, born of a second Hannah (a woman past the age of childbearing). The magnificat as spoken by Elizabeth would be an element in the antitype of the Hannah type.

33. (to p. 152): Does this verse not mean drinking wine, rather than juice, milk, or water? Methodists, Mormons, and Muslims agree that "wine is a mocker" (Proverbs 20.1), though some of them are moderates, as I take Jesus to have been (my donkey-guide in Luxor, Yosef, had no sense of wrongdoing when he used alcohol and tobacco within limits). At Cana the guests would drink at a wedding until their judgment was impaired, and Jesus furthered the custom. There is no other way to explain the verse "Every man at the beginning doth set forth good wine, and when men have well drunk, then that which is worse; but thou hast kept the good wine until now" (John 2.10).

34. (to p. 154): My quarrel with Hans Küng is twofold. (1) He doubts (p. 44) whether the nativity chapters are genuine because there is nothing like them in Mark, John, or Paul, so that "belief in Christ in no way stands or falls with the confession of the virgin birth." Here I would remark that the same argument tells against "Love your enemies" (Matthew 5.43, Luke 6.27), for those words as well are not to be found in Mark, John, or Paul. (2) Küng follows his Swiss compatriot Carl Gustav Jung in holding that "the narrative of the virgin birth is not a report of a biological fact but the interpretation of reality by means of a primal symbol." And again I find that what is said about one matter might be said about others just as well. The resurrection, the raising of Lazarus, the healing at a distance, the walking on water, the feeding of many with small provisions—can all be vaporized into primal symbols. And so can any other flesh-and-blood story from our realm of truth.

Küng is among those theologians and other faithful who believe in some of the Bible but not in all of it. That seems to me better than believing in all of it. I myself do not absolutely be-lieve in any of it as a record of happenings. To me the Bible and

Homer are equally to be relied upon. That there was a Jesus and a war at Troy does seem rather certain, but I would not subscribe to much else. The elements I regard as the likeliest to be authentic are those contrary to expectation. The sermon on the mount (or the plain) and the parable of the Good Samaritan, because they were against common opinion, are to me more credible as history—as things said or done—than any other biblical matter is. And I find them the greatest of ethical lessons whether Jesus ever said them or not. The gospel foreground and background are picturesque enhancements, possibly genuine, possibly not, and certainly urgent. The famous sermon and the foremost parable are not absolutes, though. They are only thoughts that should always be with us.

35. (to p. 154): My phrase "appalling bad taste" is from Evans, p. 180. The "Father of Latin theology," as the *Oxford Dictionary of the Christian Church* calls Tertullian, is best known from the words *credo quia absurdum est*, "I believe because it is absurd," which are quoted by Voltaire, Auerbach, and any number of others. Tertullian did not actually ever say them, but they may be gathered from *De carne Christi* 5. Was he reveling in paradox? To my mind the phrase and Tertullian may mean that earthly matters are known by reason and the senses, but unearthly matters by other means. That is, what you cannot prove but still have faith in (and would say *credo* about) is irrational (*absurdum*). I would venture that in this matter Tertullian was influenced by 1 Corintians 1.18–25.

Augustine and Jerome compared Mary's birth canal with the closed passage of the sanctuary which the Lord God should come through (Ezekiel 44.1–2), or with the shut doors that were no hindrance to an apparition of Jesus (John 20.19). The dogma is that she was a virgin before, while, and after she gave birth, *ante partum, in partu, post partum* (see Resnick). Such an examination of her body is disrespectful to the woman regarded by many as the mother of God. I would also rebuke John Chadwick (p. 229), who says in his discussion of *parthenos* that Mary "was of course taken as a wife by Joseph before giving birth, so that at this time she was no longer *parthenos* but *gune.*" (Since Chadwick allows that he has found no certain instance of *parthenos* "virgin" contrasting with *gune* "woman" in an early author, I will mention Theocritus 27.65.)

36. (to p. 159): "Ye shall not have gone over the cities of Israel, till the Son of man be come," Matthew 10.23; "For nation shall rise against nation, and kingdom against kingdom: and there shall be famines, and pestilences, and earthquakes . . . and then shall appear the sign of the Son of man in heaven: and then shall all the tribes of the earth mourn, and they shall see the Son of man coming in the clouds of heaven with power and great glory . . . be ye also ready: for in such an hour as ye think not the Son of man cometh," Matthew 24.7–30–44; "And there shall be signs in the sun, and in the moon, and in the stars; and upon the earth distress of nations, with perplexity; the sea and the waves roaring; men's hearts failing them for fear, and for looking after those things which are coming on the earth: for the powers of heaven shall be shaken. And then shall they see the Son of man coming in a cloud with power and great glory. And when these things begin to come to pass, then look up, and lift up your heads; for your redemption draweth nigh," Luke 21.25–8; "it is high time to awake out of sleep: for now is our salvation nearer than when we believed," Romans 13.11; "the time is short . . . the fashion of this world passeth away," 1 Corinthians 7.29–31.

37. (to p. 161): See the review article "The War Over the Scrolls," by Geza Vermes, which deals with such matters as the allegorical reading by Barbara Thiering (who argues that the Baptist is the Teacher of Righteousness in the scrolls, and that Jesus—divorced, remarried, and the father of four—is the Wicked Priest).

As mentioned by Pliny and confirmed by the scrolls, the Essenes were a monastic order with a spiritual retreat not far from Jerusalem. If they were widespread as well, that may have been after their habitation had been ruined by the Romans. Josephus (*War* 2.119–166) said there was a community of Essenes in every town, and described them as (1) devoted to the sun at daybreak, (2) austere but likely to enter your house uninvited, (3) convinced that women are by nature unfaithful, and (4) so scrupulous that they washed their hands after defecating (the disciples of Jesus did not wash before eating, Matthew 15.2, Mark 7.3).

38. (to p. 170): Some emendations, such as Bullen's *on kai me on* "being and not being" for *oeconomie* in *Dr. Faustus*, are welcomed by everyone. Others, such as the probably authentic "a rose by any other *word* would smell as sweet" for "name" in *Romeo and Juliet*, have to be rejected because we are used to something else. "It is easier for a camel to pass through the eye of a needle" (Matthew 19.24, Mark 10.25, Luke 18.25) ought to, but is not likely to, give up its *kamelos* "camel" for *kamilos* "rope." Similarly with "Consider the lilies of the field, how they grow; they toil not, neither do they spin: and yet I say unto you, That even Solomon in all his glory was not arrayed like one of these" (Matthew 6.28–29, Luke 12.27). We admire the thought that the lilies are more beautiful than the array of Solo-

mon, but "how they grow" is stuffage (we are not asked to behold the fowls of the air, how they fly, in Matthew 6.26), and the parallelism is low-grade (since "toil," instead of being comparable to "spin," includes it). The true reading, confirmed under ultraviolet light, is "Consider the lilies of the field; they card not, neither do they spin" (Bartlet, Skeat). It will not move those who like to stay put. Brewer's *Dictionary of Phrase* tells the story of *mumpsimus*, a word given currency in 1545 by Henry VIII. An old cleric was accustomed to say, *quod in ore mumpsimus* instead of *quod in ore sumpsimus* "which we have taken in our mouth," and, when the mistake was pointed out, allowed, "No, I like my old mumpsimus better than your new sumpsimus." That is why *agape* in the Greek text of Jude 12 has not been given up yet, and it is why "they toil not, neither do they spin" will never be given up. We are mumpsimus lovers, most of us, in most things.

39. (to p. 177): If relics have power, guilt is negotiable. Do we not ask in the Lord's prayer that our debts be forgiven to the same degree as we ourselves are forgiving? But where is the holy cross today, and where is the ark of the covenant? Should they not have been indestructible? The warriors of Mohammed allowed their foe, parched, to bivouac overlooking the sea; the knights saw the water and were frantic to drink from it. Then the Muslims set fire to the grass in between, so that the thirst would be beyond torment, and in the ruination that followed they captured the cross. As told in the book *The Crusades Through Arab Eyes* it is a story to bring cheers. Its like is the Canaanite legend of how, when Joshua was demolishing Jericho, a war party in worship of Baal fell upon the ark of the covenant and smashed the tablets of the commandments into powder (the papyri recounting this legend have not yet been found).

40. (to p. 178): It is disputed whether the Holy Ghost proceeds from the Father (John 15.26) or from the Son as well (John 16.13–15, 20.22). In Byzantine times, thousands were killed or blinded in religious wars because they did not prevail on the matter. In *Paradise Lost* 3.1–2 light is the "offspring of heav'n first born," but alternatively the light may in a mystery be the Holy Ghost proceeding from "th' Eternal, Co-Eternal Beam," that is, from the Father and the Son. In Neoplatonism there is the trinity of the One, the Word, and the Spirit; and the Spirit has the epithet "first born" *protogonos*.

41. (to p. 179): "God again": William E. Channing, the most famous among the Unitarians in our country and a spokesman for the others, did not believe in the Trinity, or in the duality of Jesus as God and man, or in the sequence from original sin to atonement, but did believe that Jesus had been sent among us for our betterment and that he performed the miracles and rose from the dead (see Channing, vol. 3, pp. 85–89, 130–131, and Howe, p. 88). The Unitarians emphasized the merit rather than the depravity of man, and were minded towards improving this world rather than fearful of the next. It was an antidote to Calvinism. They influenced the Congregationalist Church (the embodiment of New England at one time), and their attitude on social issues became a part of America. A liberal Presbyterian minister, after he had given a sermon, asked Charles W. Eliot, the President of Harvard (the stronghold of Unitarianism), whether he had liked it, and Eliot answered, "Very much; it was all straight out of Channing" (see *Charles W. Eliot*, v. 2, p. 507). In 1961 the American Unitarian Association combined with the Universalist Church of America, whose special article was that all should finally be saved.

There is a resemblance with the Baha'i, but (1) the Unitarian

Universalist belief is within the biblical tradition, while the Baha'i belief is from several other religions as well, and (2) the Unitarian Universalist places of worship are many but all within the United States, while those of the Baha'i are few (and heavenly: see Badiee) and as international as can be.

I am with the Unitarians as they disbelieve in original sin and atonement, and as they would apply their religious commitment to social issues. I am against (many of) them as I doubt (1) that a Controller has ever managed the world through miracles or in any other way, (2) that we shall live again, and (3) that the world came into being by the will of a thoughtful Creator.

42. (to p. 181): Bultmann's *Offenbarung*, containing the essay here spoken of, was reviewed by Wilder among others, and there have been books on the Bultmann thesis by I. Henderson (1952), L. Malevez (1954), G. Miegge (1956), B. H. Throckmorton, Jr. (1959), J. MacQuarrie (1960), and S. M. Ogden (1961). None of these scholars, any more than Bultmann himself, would say as I would: (1) that no verse of the Bible is really evidence of what happened on the cross or afterwards, or (2) that the magical elements (such as God in Christ) ought to be thought less important than ethics.

43. (to p. 182): I am of one mind about all the elements—whether Judaic or Christian—that join the worldly with the otherworldly. The reenactment of the passover means to some of us that God favored our people. The reenactment of the Last Supper means to others of us that our master was an aspect of God. I myself do not hold either the passover ceremony or the Christian eucharist to have been ordained in heaven. I do however hold that having a part in those rites, or in others, can be an experience of such intensity as to work a change, towards the better, in the worshiper.

44. (to p. 183): The *Dies irae* should be at hand if not by heart.

Dies irae, dies illa
solvet saeclum in favilla,
teste David cum Sibylla.

Quantus tremor est futurus,
quando judex est venturus
cuncta stricte discussurus.

Tuba mirum spargens sonum
per sepulcra regionum
coget omnes ante thronum.

Mors stupebit et natura,
cum resurget creatura
judicanti responsura.

Liber scriptus proferetur,
in quo totum continetur
unde mundus judicetur.

Judex ergo cum censebit,
quidquid latet, apparebit;
nil inultum remanebit.

Quid sum miser tunc dicturus,
quem patronum rogaturus,
dum vix justus sit securus?

Rex tremendae majestatis,
qui salvandos salvas gratis,
salve me, fons pietatis.

Recordare, Jesu pie,
quod sum causa tuae viae,
ne me perdas illa die.

Quaerens me sedisti lassus
redemisti crucem passus;
tantus labor no sit cassus.

Juste judex ultionis,
donum fac remissionis
ante diem rationis.

Ingemisco tanquam reus,
culpa rubet vultus meus;
supplicanti parce, Deus.

Qui Mariam absolvisti
et latronem exaudisti,
mihi quoque spem dedisti.

Preces meae non sunt dignae
sed tu bonus fac benigne
ne perenni cremer igne.

Inter oves locum praesta
et ab haedis me sequestra
statuens in parte dextra.

Confutatis maledictis,
flammis acribus addictis,
voce me cum benedictis.

Oro supplex et acclinis,
cor contritum quasi cinis,
gere curam mei finis.

Some years ago an essay or review in the *Times Educational Supplement* spoke against the modern admiration of Michel-

angelo's delicately muted colors. On the contrary (said the re-
viewer) *The Last Judgment* in its time had such power in its
colors that the effect was one of three dimensions; the viewer felt
that the judgment was taking place in his presence.

45. (to p. 184): The Christian idea of an afterlife assumes that
we shall be as we were. "I know that my Redeemer liveth, and
that he shall stand at the latter day upon the earth: and though
after my skin worms destroy this body, yet in my flesh shall I see
God" (Job 19.25). It was believed that David the psalmist had
foreseen the resurrection of his descendant Jesus (the prophecy:
"thou wilt not leave my soul in hell; neither will thou suffer
thine Holy One to know corruption," Psalms 16.10; the fulfillment: "his soul was not left in hell, neither his flesh did see
corruption," Acts 2.31). That is, we shall live again in the
epidermis we wore on earth. Is it not for many of us a hateful
prospect? Towards the end of "General William Booth enters
into Heaven," one of the greatest of all American poems, Vachel
Lindsay tells how Booth, the founder of the Salvation Army, is
leading his redeemed in parade at the place of judgment:

[Sweet flute music]
Jesus came from out the Courthouse door,
Stretched his hands above the passing poor.
Booth saw not, but led his queer ones there
Round and round the mighty Courthouse square.
Then in an instant all that blear review
Marched on spotless, clad in raiment new.
The lame were straightened, withered limbs uncurled,
And blind eyes opened on a new sweet world.
[Bass drum louder]
Drabs and vixens in a flash made whole!
Gone was the weasel-head, the snout, the jowl!

Sages and sibyls now, and athletes clean,
Rulers of empires, and of forests green!
. . .

It is a grand conception and I would say that what is true for our bodies will be true for our souls as well. If there is a judgment, and if God keeps the Jesus rule, we shall be made perfect.

46. (to p. 185): The wager is in Pascal's *Oeuvres*, vol. 13, pp. 141–155. Some praise this argument, but I would not. Others praise Pascal for his style, but I find that his grammar was imperfect: je suis un de ceux qui sait, "I am one of those who knows," he wrote to Fermat on 10 August 1660 (vol. 10, p. 4). He did however contribute to mathematics, as I would give almost anything to have done.

47. (to p. 193): I admire the paper because it connects two widely different matters: (1) what looks like selflessness, and (2) an unusual genetic make-up. Similarly: (1) butterflies migrate, and (2) they carry pieces of iron. Or: (1) the dinosaurs became extinct, and (2) cold causes the embryos in the eggs of reptiles all to be female.

Hamilton aimed at a general theory of "social behaviour under relatedness," and *Narrow Roads* is useful not just for his papers, but also for where he was in his thinking when he wrote them. E. O. Wilson and Richard Dawkins are prominent among those who have used Hamilton's work. Wilson was once attacked for his chapters on human evolution by a sizable coterie of colleagues at his own university (I regard the attack as fascist). He replied in the *New York Review of Books* for 11 December 1975, referring to other views of his—on slavery in ants and humans, on the dangers of international enmity, and on overpopulation— that I admire. Dawkins in *The Selfish Gene* holds that the worker bees are not altruistic, but just the opposite, and I agree. His title might mean that *any* gene is selfish (the one for brown eyes tries to dominate the one for blue eyes); or the title might designate a particular gene, one for selfishness ("the *selfish* gene" would then be an expression like "the *brown eye* gene"). I doubt whether there is a single gene for selfishness. I do think there is a factor (a gene or a set of genes) for recognizing one's own likeness. A fine obituary notice of Hamilton and his arguments appeared in *The Economist*, 18 March 2000, p. 88. For where ethical biology, or biological ethics, stands today, see Schwartz.

I have just said "stands today," but the Hamilton thesis about bees may need to be modified to take account of the naked mole rat, "the first undeniably eusocial mammal known" (*Science News* 2 December 2000).

48. (to p. 195): Judaism, Christianity, and Islam do not allow that the world will change except in the epoch of the close. To the contrary the Mormons (a sect of exemplary honesty, cleanness, and generosity) and Teilhard de Chardin (a scientist though a man of the cloth) look for eternal progression, as I do. Both the Mormons and Teilhard believe, though, that God has brought things about. I believe that things have happened and that there is no value in crediting or blaming God.

If Jesus is rightly called godlike, his goodness was from within, not from without. The Jesus rule was (so to speak) a quantum leap, or an alchemy of lead into gold, but it was natural, not supernatural. The finding of that rule was for us what the beginning of flight was to those relatives of ours that sing in the trees. What will be the next quantum leap? It may be a more considerate knowledge of each other, such as the elements of the slime molds seem to have. I cannot speak of that knowledge further, for I am no more advanced than anybody else.

How did life begin if by evolution rather than creation? What was the ultimately primitive form? The thing to look for is a process that furthers its own recurrence and allows for change. The conditions at the beginning were: the basic elements (oxygen, hydrogen, nitrogen, carbon, sulfur, iron), high temperature, and high pressure; they can be provided in a laboratory. The theory once was that complex chemicals formed one by one independently and afterwards became assembled. The overwhelmingly more likely theory is that *simple* composites went through elementary transformations and ended up as they had been, the cycle or metabolism afterwards becoming more complex in one way or another. (Credit is due to Günther Wächterhäuser for the argument and to George D. Cody with his colleagues for the experiment: *Science* 26 August 2000, pp. 1307–8 and 1337–1340; see also the New York *Times* 25 August 2000, p. A17.) Such processes may be ongoing: unknown structures and systems may be in formation today in volcanoes and the other factories of hell.

The dissolution—of life, matter, spacetime—at the other temperature extreme, where liquid helium runs uphill, may be comparably hadean. (In Dante the ultimate punishment is at absolute cold, as Satan flapping his wings in fury makes himself more immobile than ever.)

49. (to p. 198): An intriguing idea is that, since light is bent by a gravitational field, what appears to be over here is actually over there also, as the light has gone around and come back; we may even be able to look at the earth as it was in an earlier time: see *Scientific American* (April 1999) 90–97. Likewise revisionary are the demonstrations that matter can be made to exceed the speed of light. The 24 May 2002 issue of *Science* and the January 2001 issue of *Scientific American* are devoted largely to papers on cosmology.

50. (to p. 202): All the ancients regarded Homer as I do. Among moderns who do so there is Robert Calasso, whose *Marriage of Cadmus and Harmony* is of Nobel-prize quality (no, better than that). *The Song of Roland*—though comparable to Homer in strength, nobility, and wit—has these limitations in conception and form: (1) it is not even-handed like the *Iliad* (which follows the Jesus rule towards the Trojans), but in its single-minded warrior's loyalty to God resembles the Old Testament, and (2) being in stanzas on a given assonance, it cannot sustain seriousness.

I am told that the highly creative film director Derek Jarman thought only Eisenstein (the director of "Potemkin") made movies that brought Rembrandt to mind. Among movies of the more ordinary kind my favorites are "The Blues Brothers" (the most fun in any medium) and "Breaker Morant" (of Homeric character, design, and execution).

Among my teachers as an undergraduate, S. E. Sprott had the best taste in literature, except that Joyce Hemlow matched him in this respect. Sprott also devised the best examinations that I know of. Others would set questions that could be answered from *Masterplots*. Without supplying a text or otherwise making matters easy, Sprott would ask the candidate to "Discuss three or four examples of Milton's grand style." (Besides making his mark as a scholar he has written, for *The Dalhousie Review* 47 (1967) 380–2, a grave, rhymed, stanzaic, octosyllabic Miltonic poem; and his beautiful tribute to that other teacher of mine, entitled "Joyce," may be the most difficult poem in the English language:

if scholars rein their clatter off beach pebbles
the fish hawk teaching up and down the shore
will centre all that cove of yarners with pinions
upright as fingers pressed on mouths he drops

to catchpoint and the pool's lip fills and trembles
birds weave the outport into a community
where no one calls them terns what anguish she raveled
by hauling up a keel on curlew island
small ones of fluff on the wave with legs treadling
big ones frantic to swing them back against wind
the young girl threaded shanks into the dory
and pulled off shore to mend the felly's peace
with oars that lulled the water then hung still
so the globe spinner told it in her house
where the deer comes and sleeps below the hill

One result of requiring my own students to learn a good deal by heart has been that I will be strolling in an airport somewhere and a thirty-five-year-old woman, whom I do not quite recognize, with whiskey on her breath, will come over and stand close enough to brush me with her breasts, and begin reciting poetry. More gratifying happiness than that is hard to imagine.

51. (to p. 204): On visits to Oxford in the summer around thirty years ago I would attend vespers every day at St. Mary's, the university church. The celebrant was of a grand but warm demeanor; the liturgy from the Book of Common Prayer was in language at its worthiest; the setting was of old elegance. Why more were not attending I cannot imagine unless they had no sense of beauty or were afraid of being scoffed at. But other venues, such as a Greek village church, are just as fine. I have also been moved by Jewish and Muslim services, the one with a homily towards upright behavior "for God, for family, and for Judaism," the other with its utter abasement before God "the merciful, the compassionate." The Baha'i service I have attended seemed to me another way of following the Jesus rule.

Works cited

Ackerley, J. R., *My Dog Tulip* (New York 1965): p. 51

Adams, Dickinson W.: see Jefferson

Alt, Albrecht, *Essays on Old Testament History and Religion*, trans. R. A. Wilson (Oxford 1966) 113–132: 54

Anderson, R. T., in the *Anchor Bible Commentary*: 44

Badiee, Julie, *An Earthly Paradise* (Oxford 1992): 250 n.41

Bagnall, Roger S., in *Journal of Theological Studies* 51 (2000) 577–588: 8

Barker, Ernest, "Crusades," *Encyclopaedia Britannica* 11th edition: 92

Barr, James, *The Variable Spellings of the Hebrew Bible* (Oxford 1989): 50

Bartlet, J. Vernon, "Oxyrhynchus Sayings of Jesus," *Contemporary Review* 87 (1905) 124: 248 n.38

Bernard, J. H., *John*, ICC (Edinburgh 1928): 129

Black, Matthew, *An Aramaic Approach to the Gospels and Acts* 2nd edition (Oxford 1954): 139

Bloedhorn, Hanswulf, and Hüttenmeister, Gil, "The synagogue," *The Cambridge History of Judaism* 3.282: 224 n.7

Brown, Raymond E., *The Birth of the Messiah* (New York 1977): 149

Bultmann, Rudolf, *Kerygma and Myth*, trans. R. H. Fuller, S.P.C.K. (London 1955), reprinted from *Offenbarung und Heilsgeschehen* (Munich 1941): 180

Butler, E. M., *The Myth of the Magus* (Cambridge 1948): 181

Calasso, Robert, *The Marriage of Cadmus and Harmony*, trans. Tim Parks (New York 1993): 256 n.50

Cameron, Ron, *The Other Gospels* (Philadelphia 1982): 57

Chadwick, John, *Lexicographica Graeca* (Oxford 1996): 246 n.35

Channing, William E., *Works* 8th edition (Boston 1848) 3.59–103 "Unitarian Christianity," and 3.105–136 "The Evidences of Revealed Religion": 249 n.41

Charles, R. H., *The Apocrypha and Pseudepigrapha of the Old Testament* (Oxford 1913) 2.185: 16

Confucius, *The Life and Teachings of*, translated by James Legge (Philadelphia 1867); reprinted as *The Four Books* with the Chinese original facing (Shanghai 1933): 63

Cross, Frank Moore, Jr., *Ancient Library of Qumran and Modern Biblical Studies* (New York 1958): 161

Dahood, Mitchell, *Psalms III: 101–150* The Anchor Bible (Garden City 1970): 242 n.30

Danby, see *Mishnah*

Daube, David, *Studies in Biblical Law* (Cambridge 1947): 18

Dawkins, Richard, *The Selfish Gene* (New York 1976): 253 n.47

Dihle, Albrecht, *Die goldene Regel* (Göttingen 1962): 231

Dix, Gregory, *Jew and Greek* (London 1953): 168

Dow, Sterling, "The Greeks in the Bronze Age," *The Language and Background of Homer*, edited by G. S. Kirk (Cambridge 1964): 229 n.14

Driver, G. R., and Miles, John C., edd. *The Babylonian Laws* (Oxford 1952–55), 2 vv.: 61

Duckworth, George E., *Structural Pattern and Proportions in Vergil's Aeneid* (Ann Arbor 1962): 50

Dworzak, Thomas, photograph with caption to "Letter from Afghanistan," by Jon Lee Anderson, *The New Yorker* 24 December 2001: 93

Eginhardt, Einhard: see Firchow

Elert, Werner, *Eucharist and Church Fellowship in the First Four Centuries*, translated by N. E. Nagel (St. Louis 1966): 180

Eliot, Charles W. *[Works]*, ed. William Allan Neilson (New York 1926), 2 vv.: 249 n.41

Epicurus: see Lactantius

Epstein, Isidore: see *Talmud*

Evans, Ernest, *Tertullian's Treatise on the Incarnation* (London 1956): 245 n.35

Falk, Harvey, *Jesus the Pharisee* (New York 1985): 233 n.20

Farrar, Frederic W., *History of Interpretation* (New York 1886): 232 n.18

Firchow, E. S., and Zeydel, E. H., editors of *Einhard, Vita Karoli Magni: The Life of Charlemagne*, Latin text with facing translation (Coral Gables 1972) 54–55: 229 n.14

Foote, Henry Wilder: see Jefferson

Freedman, David N., "The Nine Commandments," *Bible Review* 5 (1989) 28–37: 48

Gemara: see *Talmud*

Gladwell, Malcolm, "The Physical Genius," *The New Yorker* 2 August 1999: 158

Goodenough, Erwin R., *The Jurisprudence of the Jewish Courts in Egypt* (Amsterdam 1968): 12

Gray, Francine Du Plessix, "The Child Queen," *The New Yorker* 7 August 2000: 51

Greene, Brian, *The Elegant Universe* (New York 1999): 198

Grossman, Edward, "Koestler's Jewish Problem," *Commentary* 62 (December 1976): 222 n.1

Hamilton, W. D., *Narrow Roads of Gene Land* (Houndmills and New York 1996), 2 vv.: "Hamilton's Rule," 1.11–82, reprinted from *Journal of Theoretical Biology* 7 (1964) 1–52: 193, 253 n.47

Hendel, Ronald S., chapter 13 of *Understanding the Dead Sea Scrolls*, edited by Hershel Shanks (New York 1993): 225 n.8

Hengel, Martin, *The Cross of the Son of God* (London 1986): 145

Herford, R. Travers, *Christianity in Talmud and Midrash* (Clifton 1966, reprinted from a 1903 edition): 237 n.23

Hertz, J. H., foreword to *Nezikin* (see *Talmud*): 233 n.19

Howe, Daniel Walker, *The Unitarian Conscience* (Harvard 1970): 249 n.41

Hurles, Matthew E., "European Y-Chromosomal Lineages in Polynesians," *American Journal of Human Genetics* 63 (1998) 1793–1806: 222 n.1

Hüttenmeister, see Bloedhorn.

Jacquard, Roland, *In the Name of Osama bin Laden*, trans. George Holoch (Durham 2002): 94

Jefferson, Thomas, *The Jefferson Bible*, Henry Wilder Foote, Donald S. Harrington, O. I. A. Roche (New York 1964); *Jefferson's Extracts from the Gospels*, Dickinson W. Adams, Ruth W. Lester, Eugene R. Sheridan (Princeton 1983): 212

Jeremias, Joachim, *The Eucharistic Words of Jesus*, trans. Arnold Ehrhardt (Oxford 1955): 134

Khalidi, Tarif, *The Muslim Jesus* (Harvard 2001): 238 n.23

Knopp, Konrad, *Theory and Application of Infinite Series*, trans. R. C. H. Young (New York n.d.) pp. 412–414): 205

Koestler, Arthur, *The Thirteenth Tribe* (New York 1976): 221 n.1

Küng, Hans, *Credo* (New York 1993): 244 n.34

Lactantius, *Liber de ira dei* "On the wrath of God," chapter 13, *PL* 7.121, *Ante-Nicene Fathers* 7.271; see also Minucius Felix, *Octavius* chapter 12, *PL* 3.282, *Ante-Nicene Fathers* 4.179: 188

Lind, Michael, "The Israel Lobby," *Prospect* April 2002: 239 n.25

McHugh, J. F., "The Sacrifice of the Mass at the Council of Trent," in *Sacrifice and Redemption*, ed. S. W. Sykes (Cambridge 1991): 137

Melito, "On the Pascha," ed. Othmar Perler, *Sources chrétiennes* 23 (1966): 136

Mishnah, the, trans. Herbert Danby (Oxford 1933): 68; see also *Talmud*

Moore, George Foot, *Judaism* (Harvard 1927), 3 vv.: 44

Nahmanides, that is, Ramban, *Writings & Discourses*, trans. Charles B. Chavel (New York 1978) 1.64: 72

Nielsen, Eduard, *The Ten Commandments in New Perspective*, Studies in Biblical Theology, 2nd series, 7 (Naperville 1968): 228 n.13

Neilson: see *Charles W. Eliot*

Pascal, Blaise, *Oeuvres* (Paris 1904–14), 14 vv.: 253 n.46

PG = *Patrologia Graeca*, ed. J.-P. Migne (Paris 1857–66), 161 vv.

PL = *Patrologia Latina*, ed. J.-P. Migne (Paris 1878–90), 221 vv.

Ramban, see Nahmanides

Resnick, Irven M., *Journal of Theological Studies* 39 (1988) 130–134: 246 n.35

Rigg, Horace A., *Journal of Biblical Literature* 54 (1945) 417–456: 229 n.14

Robinson, Gnana, "The Idea of Rest in the Old Testament," *Zeitschrift für die alttestamentliche Wissenschaft* 92 (1980) 32–42, supplementing his dissertation, *The Origin and Development of the Old Testament Sabbath* (Hamburg 1975): 29

Robinson, Sinclair, and Smith, Donald, *Practical Handbook of Canadian French* (Toronto 1973) 143: 226 n.10

Sandbach, F. H., *The Stoics* (London 1975): the translation of the *Hymn to Zeus* by Cleanthes is on 110–111: 15

Sanderson, Ivan T., *Animal Treasure* (New York 1937) 87: 199

Schaff, Philip, *The Creeds of Christendom* (New York 1877) 2.45: 179

Schwartz, Baruch J., "Ten Commandments," in *The Oxford Dictionary of the Jewish Religion* (New York and Oxford 1997): 229 n.13

Schwartz, James, "Oh My Darwin," *Lingua Franca* November 1999: 254 n.47

Segal, J. B., *The Hebrew Passover* (London 1963): 140

Shanks: see *Understanding*

Silver, Daniel Jeremy, "What We Said about Lebanon," *Journal of Reform Judaism* Spring 1983: 221 n.1

Singleton, Charles S., "The Poet's Number at the Center," *MLN* (Modern Language Notes) 80 (1965) 1–10: 50

Skeat, T. C., "The Lilies of the Field," *Zeitschrift für die neutestamentliche Wissenschaft* 37 (1938) 211–214; see also *Journal of Theological Studies* n.s. 13 (1962) 331: 248 n.38

Smith, Morton, "The Gentiles in Judaism," *The Cambridge History of Judaism* 3.198: 9

Specter, Michael, "The Doomsday Click," *The New Yorker* 28 May 2001: 96

Stamm, J. J., with Andrew, M. E., *The Ten Commandments in Recent Research*, Studies in Biblical Theology, 2nd series (Naperville 1967): 18

Strauss, David Friedrich, *A New Life of Jesus*, authorized trans., 2 vv. (London and Edinburgh 1965): 147

Symonds, John Addington, *A Problem in Modern Ethics* (1891) and *A Problem in Greek Ethics* (1906), both privately printed: 112

Talmud [*Mishnah* and *Gemara*], the Babylonian, trans. various hands, ed. (with an "Introductory Essay" to the tractate "Baba Mezia") by Isidore Epstein, Soncino ed. (London 1935–52), 18 vv.: 54

Thiessen, Gerd, *Social Reality and the Early Christians*, trans. Margaret Kohl (Minneapolis 1992): 67

Thomas, Mark G., "Founding Mothers of Jewish Communities, *American Journal of Human Genetics* 70 (2002) 1411–20: 222 n.1

Understanding the Dead Sea Scrolls, ed. Hershel Shanks (New York 1993): 234 n.22

Vermes, Geza, in *The New York Review of Books* 11 August 1994: 247 n.37

Weber, Eugen, *My France* (Harvard 1991): 13

Wellhausen, J., *Die Composition des Hexateuchs und der historischen Bücher des alten Testaments*, 3rd edition (Berlin 1899): 227 n.11

Whitman, Cedric H., *Homer and the Heroic Tradition* (Harvard 1958): 50

Wilder, Amos N., in *Journal of Biblical Literature* 69 (1950) 113–127: 250

Wilson, E. O., in *The New York Review of Books*: 253 n.47

Index of subjects

The contents pages are the best guide to the topics. The pages of works cited are the best guide to the authors named. The supplement that follows may be useful.

of silver 146–147; vinegar to drink 147; third day 147; "a virgin shall conceive" 153–155; prepare the way of the Lord 155–156; fulfillment invention 156; the completion of Judaism 167; see also types

sudden ideas, momentous, surprising: that the golden rule is not enough 67, 231 n.16; that rowdiness at the communal meal is why some are dying 165

supernatural: demons in the time of Jesus 16; miracles of Elijah and Jesus 126; gift of healing 157; power in the believer 158; the power of prayer 158; punishment for unworthy communion 165; a real presence 170–173; the power of relics 176–177; Merlin, Faust, Grandier 181; see also God

types with antitypes: Adam's transgression 129; "Christ our passover . . . bread of sincerity and truth" 133; passover lamb, killed at the 9th hour, 133–137; passover bread 133–137; Jonah 143; Isaac 143; Hannah, Elizabeth, Mary 148–153; antitypes invention 156; the completion of Judaism 167; see also prophecies fulfilled, words explained

words explained: Yhwh "existence" 21, 131, 196; sabbath (four senses) 24, 139; Jephthah 78, Noah 78, Ham 79, Canaan 79; Adam 131, Abraham 131, Isaac 131, Jacob 131, Israel 131, Moses 131; Hebrew psh as "pass over" 131–132; Greek pascha as paschein "passion, suffering" in Luke 22.15 and elsewhere in the gospels implicitly 136; in Philo from the contrary 241

Index of arguments

The thesis of this book and the contention of the chapters will be gathered from the first two paragraphs of the preface and from the summaries. But there are also some specific arguments that scholars may be willing to consider.

a. Jesus thought of himself as a Jew with respect to a Samaritan or a Gentile, but as a Galilean (from "Galilee of the Gentiles") with respect to a Judean I 2 (pp. 9–12)

b. The evangelist John may have implicated the Jews for political reasons I 2 (p. 12)

c. In the Song of Moses the Most High is above the Lord I 3 (p. 13)

d. The other-gods and image commandments were confounded when an addition to the one became attached to the other I 3 (pp. 17–21)

e. In several verses the sense of *sabbath* is still the day of the full moon I 4 (pp. 25–28)

f. The commandment in Deuteronomy has a fourth sense of *sabbath* I 4 (pp. 30–31)

g. The covet commandment bore upon all the others I 6 (p. 48)

h. Matthew 7.12, the golden rule, should come after 5.45 II 4 (p. 66)

i. The Jesus rule was meant to go beyond the golden rule; it is not a part of Judaism II 4 & II 5 (pp. 67–73)

j. Jesus taught his rule not only in the sermon on the mount (or the plain) but also in the parable of the Good Samaritan II 6 (pp. 74–76)

k. That foremost of the parables also teaches, as some other sayings of Jesus do, that the law is sometimes to be laid aside II 6 (pp. 76–77)

l. To turn the other cheek was an idea, like a proverb, not a directive; the Jesus rule has its limits; it is no more absolute than, to Jesus, the ten commandments were II 9 (pp. 84–90)

m. The Jesus rule of generous fairness towards everyone is against both Testaments, but would be a faultless basis for new commandments II 10 (p. 90)

n. When we speak of God we should say whether it is as manager, as judge, or as creator III introduction (p. 126)

o. All four gospels tell of a betrayal at bread in a Last Supper, fulfilling the prophecy of Psalms 41.9; in John the supper is on the day before the passover and Jesus will be the passover lamb; in Matthew, Mark, and Luke the supper is a passover meal and the body of Jesus is within the bread; but this bread of the meal (and the body) does not combine well with the bread of betrayal III 2 (pp. 129–130)

p. It is not that at first (1) the Last Supper and the crucifixion were thought to have been at the time of the passover, and that afterwards (2) Jesus became regarded in a mystery as the lamb and the bread; but that (2) was the earlier and (1) the later III 4 (pp. 132–5)

q. It was by etymological typology, summed up in Luke

22.15, that the suffering, or passion, *paschein*, came to be regarded as a passover, *pascha*   III 4 (pp. 136–9)

r. Before it was normalized, this verse, Luke 22.15, had the word "in haste" from the passover ritual   III 6 (pp. 141–2)

s. There was the thought that Psalms 22.16, "they pierced my hands and my feet," had foretold the crucifixion; afterwards the evangelists came to see that other parts of the psalm were being fulfilled piecemeal   III 7 (p. 145)

t. Psalms 22.1 is fulfilled in Matthew 27.46 savagely: Jesus calls out *Eli, Eli*; the crowd say, scoffing, "He is calling on God the Lord" *Eli Jah*, and then they complete their jest, "Let us see if Elijah will come to help him"   III 7 (pp. 145–6)

u. Paul understands why some are dying before the second coming: it is because they eat and drink unworthily at the fellowship meal (1 Corinthians 11.30); the Last Supper is being reenacted; bread is to be eaten together "in remembrance," with renewed betrayal by some, until Jesus should return; in these thoughts lies the origin of the eucharist   III 14 (pp. 162–5)

v. Neither *agapais* nor *apatais* can be right in Jude 12 and 2 Peter 2.13; neither word makes good sense and neither is grammatical; the correct reading in Jude (confirmed by Orpheus, *Lithica*) is *houtoi eisen hai en tois achatais humon spilades* "these are the spots in your agates"; the love feast should be kept, but not because it is biblical   III 15 (pp. 167–9)

w. If we think of his ethical teachings rather than of the miracles, the creed might go like this: *I believe that Jesus, who taught us to be generous even to our enemies, knew eternal truth, and that if humanity follows the Jesus rule it may live for ever*   IV 3 (p. 182)

x. God is surely not to be bargained with; so an exemplary life may not admit us to heaven; in Job the friends are rebuked for believing they understood the ways of God   iv 5 (pp. 185–7)

y. To see ourselves in others, an aspect of the Jesus rule, is to further our survival as a race; it is to become ever more godlike, if the primary quality of God is being   iv 7 (pp. 193–5)

z. Our study of the physical world diminishes the Bible stories, but not the Jesus rule   iv 8 (pp. 198–9)

also by William Whallon

Formula, Character, and Context: Studies in
Homeric, Old English, and Old Testament Poetry

Problem and Spectacle: Studies in the Oresteia

Inconsistencies: Studies in the New Testament,
the Inferno, Othello, and Beowulf

A Book of Time

The Oresteia / Apollo and Bacchus
(from Aeschylus, Sophocles, Euripides, and Homer)